Indo-U.S. Civil Nuclear Deal

Volume–3

Edited by

Rahul Bhonsle
Ved Prakash
K.R. Gupta

ATLANTIC
PUBLISHERS & DISTRIBUTORS (P) LTD

Published by

ATLANTIC

PUBLISHERS & DISTRIBUTORS (P) LTD

7/22, Ansari Road, Darya Ganj,
New Delhi-110002
Phones : +91-11-40775252, 23273880, 23275880, 23280451
Fax : +91-11-23285873
Web : www.atlanticbooks.com
E-mail : info@atlanticbooks.com

Branch Office
5, Nallathambi Street, Wallajah Road,
Chennai-600002
Phones : +91-44-64611085, 32413319
E-mail : chennai@atlanticbooks.com

ISBN 978-81-269-1276-6 (Vol. 3)
ISBN 978-81-269-0715-1 (Set)

Printed in India at Nice Printing Press, A-33/3A, Site-IV,
Industrial Area, Sahibabad, Ghaziabad, U.P.

Preface

Decisions for and on behalf of the people in a modern state are made by the government. People generally approve these once in five years when they vote in or vote out an incumbent government. When people vote back a sitting government to power in India it surprises many. So when Prime Minister Dr. Manmohan Singh took oath for the second time on 22 May in New Delhi, after the United Progressive Alliance had won a decisive majority in the Lok Sabha Elections held in April and May 2009, there was disbelief in many quarters. A victory, particularly an electoral one, has many fathers, but one of the key contributors for Dr. Manmohan Singh's re-anointment to power was successful conclusion of the 123 Agreement with the United States of America in October 2008.

While it may be true that many in India may not know or even care about the Agreement. But people know and trust Dr. Manmohan Singh and they are sure that he had risked his political future for this Agreement and therefore it was a win-win one for India and thus they must vote him back to power. That is the simple logic by which India's masses voted and gave a thumping yes to the 123 Agreement and the Indo-U.S. nuclear deal in turn. In a way the extensive debate that preceded signing of the Agreement contributed to building opinion on an issue which was far removed from general public interest but which greatly raised stakes of the government and those who stood for it ultimately gained.

Coming to the issue proper, it is natural to believe that nation states following parallel democratic ideals of liberty, freedom and rule of law will be aligned in global polity. But such is the complexity of international relations that paradox frequently becomes reality. Indo-U.S. relations over the years signify this truism. Thus, tracing the ups and downs of association between two largest democracies in the world can unravel the mysteries of global politics ranging from—powerful themes as the Cold War, balance of power to—unipolarity and emerging concepts such as unalignment professed by India today. The Indo-U.S. nuclear deal ran the gauntlet of this entire debate both in India and the United States, and the country as well as the international community was perhaps all the more rich for having underlined the themes that made the governments accede to this historical document.

Thus, signing of the 123 Agreement (Agreement for Cooperation Concerning Peaceful Uses of Nuclear Energy) on 10 October 2008 by India's then External Affairs Minister, Pranab Mukherjee and U.S. Secretary of State Condoleezza Rice will remain an epochal event despite uncertainties of the global future, permanently etching a mark on Indo-U.S. relations.

The pace of the 123 Agreement in its final stages was breathtaking. The signing followed presidential assent to the United States India Nuclear Cooperation Approval and Non-proliferation Enhancement Act on 8 October and places Indo-U.S. relations on a well defined positive trajectory. As Indian Prime Minister Dr. Manmohan Singh remarked most appropriately it is, "an honourable deal that is good for India and good for the world".

At this point it may also be appropriate to briefly survey Indo-U.S. relations which have seen many phases over the years. As the two largest democracies in the world, it was natural to expect a strong and supportive relationship. The first glow of warmth in Indo-U.S. relations came in the wake of India's war with China in 1962. The United States administration supported rebuilding of the Indian armed forces, thereby in some ways laying the foundation for victories in the 1965 and 1971 wars by the country. However, the association soon suffered vagaries of the Cold War. Despite being a non-aligned country, India was seen closely linked to the Soviet camp. Signing of Treaty of Peace, Cooperation and Friendship on 9 August 1971 as a prelude to the war in Bangladesh and the move of U.S. Seventh Fleet to the Bay of Bengal in December the same year purportedly to pressurise India were low points in Indo-U.S. relations.

The relationship deteriorated further with India's reluctance to oppose Soviet invasion of Afghanistan thereby placing U.S. and India on opposite poles of global power relations till 1989. There was limited improvement in relations thereafter until the National Democratic Alliance government under Prime Minister Atal Behari Vajpayee came to power. The Shakti nuclear test by India in 1998 was justified by Vajpayee to President Bill Clinton thus:

> I have been deeply concerned at the deteriorating security environment, specially the nuclear environment, faced by India for some years past. We have an overt nuclear weapons state on our borders, a state which committed armed aggression against India in 1962. Although our relations with that country have improved in the last decade or so, an atmosphere of distress persists mainly due to the unresolved border problem. To add to the distress, that country has materially helped another neighbour of ours to become a covert nuclear weapons state.

The U.S. was initially critical of the tests and imposed sanctions on India but gradually a broad consensus on India's significance in global polity emerged. The visit of President Bill Clinton in March 2000 to New Delhi set the tone for expanding the relationship. In 2004, Next Steps in Strategic Partnership were established and sanctions in civilian nuclear, space and high technology activities removed. However, it was President George W. Bush who transformed U.S. policy towards India to lay the foundation of what is likely to be a long and enduring relationship through the tangible instrument of the 123 Agreement.

On 18 July 2005 India's Prime Minister Mr. Manmohan Singh and U.S. President George W. Bush signed the Indo-U.S. civil nuclear deal to develop India's civilian nuclear energy program to meet its growing energy demands in a cleaner and more efficient manner. India agreed to identify and separate civilian and military nuclear facilities and programs and file an IAEA declaration regarding its civilian facilities and place these under IAEA safeguards. A separation plan was prepared in March 2006 and India agreed to place 14 of its 22 reactors under IAEA safeguards. India also agreed on unilateral moratorium on nuclear testing, promised to work with the U.S. for conclusion of a multilateral Fissile Material Cut-off Treaty, agreed to refrain from transfer of enrichment and reprocessing technologies to states that do not have them and support all non-proliferation and missile control measures.

A string of hectic legislative and political negotiations in India and the U.S. finally led to signing of the 123 Agreement three years after its initiation. For the Manmohan Singh Government, it almost led to its downfall with the Left Parties withdrawing support leading to a vote of confidence, which was finally won with relative ease.

President Barack Obama thus takes over legacy of a strong strategic foundation for the Indo-U.S. relationship which is evident from the survey carried out hithertofore. There is no doubt that there is a bipartisan support to the association as is evident from a process started by President Bill Clinton and taken to a logical conclusion by President George W. Bush through the 123 Agreement. The fruits of this Agreement are already evident with India having inked MOUs for nuclear reactors with France and Russia. Uranium supplies are being offered by Kazakhstan, and more agreements with U.S. and Canada are in the offing, thereby overcoming some of the apprehensions of skeptics of the deal.

Yet all is not well as far as inking agreements with American companies is concerned. The U.S. domestic laws are quite intricate and not as facilitating as those of other countries. The nuclear non-proliferation lobby in the United States is likely to be up in arms especially now with President Obama having declared an eventual goal of universal nuclear disarmament. This is in many ways similar to the Rajiv Gandhi, plan for, "a world free of nuclear weapons", declared at the United Nations General Assembly, New York on June 9, 1988. So, in dissonance there is congruence and we are hopeful that both India and the United States will eventually find the right balance to lead the world in universal disarmament. The driver for this could well be the new partnership that has been inked through the 123 Agreement.

It is heartening to note, however, that the Indo-U.S. nuclear deal has already started producing tangible results with the arrival of consignments of nuclear fuel from France, Russia and Kazakhstan at the Rajasthan Atomic Power Station (RAPS) site in Rawatbhata. Until the deal, such exports to India were barred by the Nuclear Suppliers Group. The nuclear fuel complex is converting 300 tons of imported raw uranium fuel, called yellow cake, into fuel bundles which will be used to restart the second RAPS power unit shut down since June 2008 due to lack of fuel. This power unit can generate 200 MW of electricity. The last nuclear import was in 2005 when the Bush administration agreed to a one-off shipment for the Tarapore reactor.

The inability to import nuclear fuel has been the main reason why India's nuclear power plants have run at around just 60 per cent of their installed capacity. The Indo-U.S. nuclear deal has given India access to nuclear fuel and latest technology to harness nuclear power as well as maintain its strategic nuclear independence.

Against this backdrop it gives us great satisfaction in bringing out the third volume of documents and papers related to the Indo-U.S. nuclear deal. The first two volumes had covered the passage of the, Henry J. Hyde United States-India Peaceful Atomic Energy Cooperation Act of 2006, by the House of Representatives in the United States on 26 July 2006, exempting India from signing the Nuclear Non-proliferation Treaty (NPT) and beginning of the political debate in India after the issue was raised by the Left Parties in the parliament. The intervening period of almost three years plus has seen both India and the U.S. almost giving up the deal and it is steadfast pursuance by George W. Bush and Manmohan Singh that has seen fructification of the 123 Agreement in its present form. Despite many controversies surrounding the Bush Presidency, this would remain a key achievement for both the leaders. For India's Prime Minister Manmohan Singh it is also an acknowledgement of his sagacity, far-sightedness, vision and resoluteness by the people of India through re-election.

The three volumes of *Indo-U.S. Civil Nuclear Deal* are thus all-inclusive covering a period of almost four years logging each and every important paper and statement in the see-saw of negotiations, conspiracy theories, pushes and pulls which marked this seminal discourse, which moved from the White House to the Indian Parliament to the International Atomic Energy Agency in Vienna to the Nuclear Suppliers Group finally returning once again to Washington.

Tracing this extensive diplomatic and nuclear legalese course has been an exciting and exhilarating experience for us and we are hoping to share the same with our readers ranging from diplomats, policymakers, analysts, academics and the lay but erudite public with growing interest in national security and development.

Rahul Bhonsle
Ved Prakash
K.R. Gupta

Contents

Indo-U.S. Nuclear Deal: Considerations and Perspectives

1

K.R. Gupta

The Indo-U.S. nuclear deal was envisaged during Indian Prime Minister Dr. Manmohan Singh's visit to the U.S. in July 2005 which led to a Joint Statement announcing a slew of bilateral measures on areas like energy, space, agriculture, commerce and science and technology. The most important development perhaps was to initiate the measure to strengthen energy security and promote the development of energy markets in India with the objective of ensuring sufficient affordable energy supplies. Stage was set to start a U.S.-India energy dialogue which led to the Civil Nuclear Cooperation Agreement between the two countries in March 2006 following the then U.S. President George W. Bush's visit to India. The framework for the Indo-U.S. Civil Nuclear Agreement was a joint statement by the Indian Prime Minister and the U.S. President under which India agreed to separate its civil and nuclear military facilities and place civil facilities under International Atomic Energy Agency (IAEA) safeguards, and in exchange, the United States agreed to work towards full civil nuclear cooperation with India. In August 2007, India and the United States reached a bilateral agreement for civil nuclear cooperation as envisioned in the Joint Statement of July 2005.

After many twists and turns of over three years during which several clauses of the deal met with severe criticism and stiff opposition from some quarters both in America and India, the two countries, finally sealed the unprecedented deal, on Oct. 10, 2008 putting an end both to controversies and to 34 years of India's nuclear isolation. India's then External Affairs Minister, Pranab Mukherjee and the United State's then Secretary of State, Condoleezza Rice signed the bilateral Civil Nuclear Cooperation Agreement—better known as 123 Agreement—so named as it directly relates to Section 123 of the United States Atomic Energy Act.

Just a day before the Agreement was signed, the House Resolution 7081 or the United States-India Nuclear Cooperation Approval and Non-Proliferation Enhancement Act became the law—thus formalizing nuclear relations between the two countries. At the time of signing, President George W. Bush said that the legislation "does not change the terms of 123 Agreement" and that the "agreement is consistent with the Atomic Energy Act." Regarding reprocessing of nuclear fuel, etc. the U.S. President Stated:

> The legislation does not change the fuel assurance commitments that the U.S. Government has made to the Government of India, as recorded in the 123 Agreement. The agreement grants India advance consent to reprocessing, which will be brought into effect upon conclusion of arrangements and procedures for a dedicated reprocessing facility under IAEA safeguards. The passage of this legislation reflects the common view of my administration and the Congress as to the value of nuclear cooperation and is in the interest of the United States and India.
>
> We all know what India stands to gain from the successful passage of the Indo-U.S. nuclear deal—the ability to import uranium fuel, nuclear reactors, their financing and empowerments, and a slew of the so-called dual use technology denied until now. But what does U.S. gain? The answer lies in contemporary international politics. The U.S. wants to befriend and strengthen India. As one unnamed official put it in 2005, the U.S. wants to "help India become a major world power in the 21st century...." We understand fully the implications, including military, of that statement.

President Bush's signing statements have special significance for India as it had some concerns about the dilution of the fuel supply assurances in the Congress. In a move that was far from acceptable to India, Howard Berman—a known critic of the deal—put on record late Tom Lantos'[1] letter stating that fuel guarantees would not hold in case India conducted a nuclear test. However, the Indian side had been assured by the Bush administration that all its concerns regarding extraneous provisions in the Congress bill would be addressed by the presidential signing statement.

Although the letter contained only unclassified information, it was kept secret under instructions from the administration for being "diplomatically sensitive". When it was disclosed, the letter caused the UPA government considerable embarrassment as it provided fresh ammunition to the opponents of the agreement, particular the Left and BJP. The former charged the government with lying to the Parliament and misleading the public while the latter sought to move a privilege motion against it. The government acted quickly, and in a bid to contain the increasing outcry against the nuclear deal, summoned all the Indian interlocutors to provide an immediate response to the contents of the letter. Putting a brave face, the government issued the following statement:

> We do not, as a matter of policy, comment on internal correspondence between different branches of another government and will be guided solely by the terms of the bilateral agreement between India and the United States, the India Specific Safeguards Agreement and the clean waiver from NSG which we hope will be forthcoming in the meeting of the NSG on September 4-5, 2008.

The U.S. Ambassador David Mulford also said in a statement to the media that the letter could not put any new conditions on the 123 Agreement. A similar view was expressed by Anil Kakodkar, Chairman of Atomic Energy Commission.

However, having faced the debilitating fuel supply cut-off for the Tarapur nuclear plant in the wake of the Pokhran explosion of 1974, and the provisions of the consequent

Nuclear Non-Proliferation Act (NNPA) of 1978 (which is now built into the Atomic Energy Act (AEA), the question of assured fuel supply for lifetime of reactors even after a nuclear test became the most important debating point in the political discussions on the deal.

In his August 13, 2007 statement, Dr. Manmohan Singh had stated as under:

> ...the March 2006 Separation Plan provided for an India-specific safeguards agreement with the IAEA, with assurances of uninterrupted supply of fuel to reactors that would be placed under IAEA safeguards together with India's right to take "corrective measures" in the event fuel supplies are interrupted. An important assurance given is the commitment of support for India's right to build up strategic reserves of nuclear fuel to meet lifetime requirements of India's reactors.... There will not be any derogation of India's right in this regard, including the right to take "corrective measures"....

The fuel assurance included in the 123 Agreement is a verbatim copy of the corresponding paragraph from the Separation Plan wherein the so-called assurances remain as vague as before, with no clear statements made on the issue by the U.S. administration as to how they are to be realised. It is in this context that the signing statements of President Bush assume great importance for India as they address its concerns about nuclear fuel supply. The 123 Agreement makes the U.S. position quite clear on the issue of maintenance of fuel supply in the event of disruption of supplies following a nuclear test by India.

The Agreement clarifies the various circumstances that could lead to disruption, which are all in the nature of market failures, and does not refer at all to disruptions following a nuclear test and the causative related national security considerations.

As regards the consistency of the proposed lifetime strategic fuel reserve with the Hyde Act provision in Section 103 (10) (a), which stipulates "any fuel reserve provided...should be commensurate with reasonable operating requirements", the administration responded thus:

> The parameters of the proposed "strategic reserve" and of India's capacity to acquire nuclear fuel for its reactors would be developed over time. Thus it is premature to conclude that the strategic reserve will develop in a manner inconsistent with the Hyde Act.

India's Sovereign Right to Test

No other issue has raised as much debate and discussion as that relating to India's sovereign right to conduct a nuclear test and the likely impact of the Indo-U.S. nuclear deal on this right. Conflicting views have come from different quarters on this issue during the past three years, i.e. since the start of discussions on the deal till its clearance in the Congress. Tom Lantos, who was Chairman of the U.S. House Committee on Foreign Affairs till February 2008, talked about nuclear fuel disruption in case India goes for a nuclear test:

> [Should] India detonate a nuclear explosive device, the U.S. has the right to cease all nuclear cooperation immediately, including supply of fuel, as well as request the return of any items transferred from the U.S., including fresh fuel. In addition, the U.S. has the right to terminate the agreement on one year's written notice. In case of termination, the commitments in Article 5.6 no longer apply.... The fuel supply assurances are not, however, meant to insulate India against the consequences of a nuclear explosive test or a violation of non-proliferation commitments.

Although the 123 Agreement does not use the word nuclear testing, detonation or explosion, yet it is couched in ambiguous language, and has a rider that the Agreement has to be implemented in conformity with the AEA, the cooperation must cease immediately in a contrary situation. The Agreement would be terminated and the U.S. would also have the right to take back equipment and material transferred under the Agreement.

The Indian government has been maintaining all along that the agreement in no way constricts India's sovereign right to test. In response to the questions raised by some nuclear scientists, Dr. Manmohan Singh said that the Agreement does not affect the requirements of India's strategic programs. Nuclear weapons are an integral part of our national security and will remain so. In July 2008 he told the Parliament that there is nothing in the Agreement that prevents us from conducting further nuclear tests if warranted by our national security concerns. The experts believe that while Dr. Singh may be correct technically in saying that India's sovereign right to test has not been taken away, its implication on the 123 Agreement will be a big restrictive factor.

Allaying fears in this regard, the Prime Minister said that an elaborate multilayered consultation process has been included with regard to any future events which may be cited as a reason to seek the cessation of cooperation or termination of the agreement, and that India's right to take "corrective measures" will be maintained even after the termination of the Agreement. The critics of the deal have drawn PM's attention towards Article 14 of the Agreement which provides for a clear right for the U.S. to terminate nuclear cooperation and to require the return of equipment and materials subject to the Agreement in all of the circumstances required under the Atomic Energy Act, including if India detonated a nuclear explosive device. Article 14 further makes it clear that cessation of cooperation and termination of the agreement that must be exercised for the right of return would be within the discretion of the U.S. government and both the actions could be taken in the unlikely case that the U.S. believed that a resolution of the problem could not be achieved through consultations.

The U.S. administration has further made it clear that the permanence of safeguards would continue even after the termination of the Agreement. Drawing attention to the relevant articles in this regard, it said:

> Article 16 of the proposed...Agreement expressly provides for the survival of essential rights and conditions on items subject to the Agreement even after termination or expiration of the Agreement, including, inter alia, with respect to the

application of safeguards (Article 10), reprocessing consent (Article 6) and peaceful use (Article 9).

The Indian side on the other hand has been emphasizing its right to take "corrective measures" even after the termination of the Agreement. The critics of the deal have pointed out that since the corrective measures cannot include the withdrawal from safeguards, it is hard to imagine what corrective measures does the government have in mind. Condoleezza Rice also reiterated the "permanence of safeguards without condition".[2]

The Indian line of thinking in this regard seems to be based on the following facts: (i) in the eventuality of India conducting a nuclear test and the U.S. going for termination of the Agreement, there will be scope for mutual dialogue to resolve the issue in consideration of the circumstances, perceived immediate security threat, etc. that warranted India's action; (ii) it would be unwise to complicate matters by insisting on India's right to explode a nuclear device, the need for which, according to some scientists may not arise in the foreseeable future; (iii) the clause regarding the permanence of safeguards even after the termination of Agreement is not going to hurt India much. The whole world, including the U.S., recognizes India's excellent record of setting credible safeguards on its nuclear program for the last thirty years. After the safeguards on the U.S.-supplied Tarapur nuclear facility expired in 1993, India voluntarily established a new agreement with the IAEA to continue the restrictions;[3] (iv) the safeguards apply only to facilities and materials manufactured by India beginning when the agreement was reached. It does not cover the fissile materials produced by India over the last several decades of nuclear activity.

Why the Nuke Deal is Crucial

Homi Bhaba was a renowned Indian nuclear scientist. He was a great advocate of civil nuclear energy. He envisioned that copious availability of nuclear energy—both fission and fusion—would serve to alleviate poverty. He knew that India was deficient in uranium but had plentiful thorium. Therefore, he formulated a three-stage nuclear energy plan: (i) heavy water natural uranium reactor at the first stage; (ii) fast breeder reactor at the second stage; and (iii) thorium-bred uranium-233 reactor at the third stage. He was hopeful that fusion energy would be tapped in India in about 50 years' time. Bhaba's plans played a major role in the development of India's atomic energy program. He repesented India in several International Atomic Energy Forums and served as President of the UN Conference on Peaceful Uses of Atomic Energy in Geneva, Switzerland. His untimely death in a plane crash in 1966 was a big blow to India's nuclear energy plans.

Those interested in India's advance in nuclear energy program are wide awake to the country's uranium shortage. M.R. Srinivasan, former chairman of Department of Atomic Energy (DAE) holds that India has only about one lac tonnes of uranium on the ground which will be sufficient to support 10,000 MW heavy water natural uranium reactors for their lifetime. There is a long-term uranium shortage if our nuclear power programme has to go beyond 10,000 MW. Srinivasan also pointed out that without at least 50,000 MW reactors producing plutonium the country cannot have a viable thorium-bred uranium-233 program.

The situation was fully known to the NDA government when it initiated the Next Steps in Strategic Partnership (NSSP) negotiation way back in 2001. It was prepared to put under safeguards two of the reactors operating at that time as well as all future reactors. Only 10 reactors were under operation at that time, and four more became operational between 2004 and 2006. The government believed that eight reactors not under safeguards would be adequate to sustain the country's strategic program. The separation plan was built around this arithmetic. The National Security Advisor, Brajesh Mishra came out in favour of 123 Agreement as he was fully aware of India's uranium crunch situation and wanted to save the future of the country's nuclear energy program.

The data published by Nuclear Power Corporation (NCP) has made it clear that all our reactors are operating at 50 per cent capacity. There was a consensus of opinion among nuclear reactor experts that they would continue to operate at that low capacity unless India signed the 123 Agreement. The situation posed a challenge to the opponents of Indo-U.S. nuclear deal.

The common criticism against the Indo-U.S. nuclear deal has been that the power generated through nuclear sources will be negligible. Government's own projection is that it won't contribute more than 3 per cent of India's energy requirements in the near future.

However, some quarters are optimistic even with these not so enthusing figures. They feel that it is wrong to assume that no private capital, no imported nuclear fuel will be available to India. They expect the DAE's thorium gamble to pay off. Some people believe that it is better to turn to the past to get an indication about the future. History shows that a country can ramp up nuclear production once it gets the right policies in place.

Everyone knows that France is the premier country in the generation of nuclear energy and has used it in industries, markets and households. It generates 70 per cent of its electricity from glow-in-the-dark fuel. Less known is the fact that this accomplishment has been made in a short span of time. In just a decade from 1989 to 1999, France was able to get 42,000 MW of nuclear-based power up and running. In a single year, 1985, the country operationalised more than 7,000 MW of nuclear power capability. In comparison, India's total nuclear power capacity today is less than 3800 MW. But there is no reason why it cannot be increased if right policies are formulated and properly implemented.

Our eastern neighbour, China is working hard to harness nuclear energy. It is estimated that between 2010 and 2015, Beijing will bring 22,300 MW of nuclear energy on stream. It plans to add another 19,400 MW during the period 2014 to 2018.

Some people believe that nuclear power is very expensive. The cost of reactors and other machinery to be imported from other countries runs into millions of dollars. A developing country like India which needs huge funds for its envisaged projects of development cannot afford to import these expensive reactors. However, some experts believe that nuclear energy is competitive with that generated by coal and gas. "In an environment similar to which exists in the West, nuclear power costs between 6.7 and 4.2 cents per kilowatt-hour and is comparable to the 10.1-3.9 cents price range for coal gas in India."[4]

India's nuclear power generation has been constrained by more than just fuel shortage. There has been a dearth of capital too. Nuclear energy is cheap over time but the initial costs are very high. There has been a want of technical know-how also. Because of the sanctions imposed on India, our engineers have had to develop expensive home-bred replacements. The nuclear deal will solve many of these problems. There will be regular fuel supply from the NSG; technology transfer from advanced countries like America and France; and installation of nuclear reactors on easy terms.

We must undo the shackles and emulate France. It is actually easier to accomplish today what France did a decade ago. During those days, reactors were small, largely in the 900 MW. Now, India's nuclear power generation capacity can be doubled with just two 1,500 MW reactors. France had to finance the reactors from its own pocket and for local consumption. Today, exporting and building reactors is a lucrative business. India may well earn huge sums by exporting nuclear technology to other countries once it establishes itself in this field.

Modern reactors are also more safe. They not only produce less waste but also come up faster than they did two decades ago. According to Anupam Srivastava, a technology expert at the University of Georgia, "New reactors take an average six years to build, have one year of trials, and link up to the grid on the eighth year."[5]

The other constraint on nuclear expansion, say some experts is a global shortage of trained engineers. Under the present system, only the government is authorised to install nuclear reactors. The private sector has not been involved in this task. Hence there is a capital constraint. The Nuclear

Power Corporation of India Ltd. (NPCIL) has cash reserves of over $2 billion. Given that infrastructure projects normally require the government to provide 20-25 per cent of the cost, this could be leveraged to as much as $12 to 15 billion which would be sufficient to pay for 10,000 MW of reactors.

The required thrust can come only through privatization. If the Atomic Energy Act is suitably amended the NPCIL will be authorised to license reactor building and operating to the private sector. It is not surprising that some major private business houses like the Tatas, Reliance, and Larsen Toubro are in talks with foreign firms about acquiring foreign technology. In course of time, the Indian companies will master the technology and get into the line themselves. In China the second generation reactors are 50 per cent local. Their next lot as per World Nuclear Association will be 75 per cent indigenous. There is no reason why such a trend cannot be set in India.

The Kazakhstan government has announced that it is willing to carry out nuclear commerce with India including supplying 'yellow cake' to the country.

Kazakhstan's ambassador to India Kairat Umarov has said that his country, slated to become the largest producer of uranium by 2010, is ready to supply uranium to India and that Kazakhstan also has the potential to take part in construction of atomic power plants.

Kazakhstan is among the four countries (others being Canada, Mongolia and Nigeria) from which India desperately seeks high-grade uranium. On September 4, 2008 the first day of NSG meeting, Kazakhstan's Permanent Representative made a speech strongly supporting India's case. This was despite the fact that Kazakhstan suffered 500 nuclear tests conducted on its territory by the USSR in the 20th century. "As for the civil nuclear cooperation between our countries, Kazakhstan is prepared to develop such interaction," said Umarov, while congratulating India for the NSG waiver.

Kazakhstan, currently the third largest producer of uranium, supported India's case at the NSG in September 2008 but, unlike Australia, has also agreed to supply uranium to India.

Umarov said that Kazatomprom, the state-owned firm which produces most of the uranium in the country, is ready with the supplies.

"Kazakhstan today is the third biggest uranium producer after Canada and Australia. It is expected that by 2010, Kazakhstan will become the largest producer of uranium with production of 15,400 tonnes annually, which will be equal to 32% of the world's total production. Kazatomprom is ready to make its supplies and has the potential to take part in the construction of atomic power stations,"[6] added the ambassador.

The government is conducting pre-feasibility studies in Nigeria, Namibia and Tajikistan to source uranium, while an amount of Rs. 1,000 crore is being spent for development of uranium mines in Andhra Pradesh to make fuel available for these reactors.[7]

UK Companies Explore $100b Market

Enthused by waiver granted by the 45-nation Nuclear Supplier Group, a British nuclear power industry's delegation came to India to explore the $100 billion market. The delegation led by UK trade and investment chief executive Andrew Cahn met Indian officials and leaders. A meeting was also held by the members of delegation with India's then Minister of State for Industry, Ashwani Kumar.

"We have discussed lots of possibilities for nuclear trade between India and UK," Kumar told reporters after the meeting. Cahn said, "The UK office of Nuclear Development Programme was being set up to ensure effective nuclear supply chain and the British industries would like to collaborate with Indian industries for the same."[8] Among others, British delegation include Richard Lambert, Director General of Confederation of British Industries and Karan Billimoria, President, UK-India Business Council.

Nuclear Power and Energy Security

The primary objective of Indo-U.S. nuclear deal is to build energy security through nuclear power. However, some people believe that the economic viability of nuclear power remains unclear till date. A detailed MIT analysis conducted in 2003 suggested that nuclear power was distinctly more expensive than the power based on coal or natural gas. But when the prices of fossil fuels increased many times those in 2003, the analysts started fearing that the world oil production would soon peak, then become stable before declining inexorably. When the prices of crude oil reached over U.S. dollar 150 a barrel in the international market, in June 2008, most of the countries stepped up their efforts to develop alternative sources of energy. With the increase in transportation costs, the corporate world also started feeling the heat of boiling oil prices. The import bill of countries like India started swelling. The Indian rupee which had gained strength against the U.S. dollar and other major foreign currencies started losing ground. Even the prices of goods of daily use shot up as the rate of inflation crossed 12 per cent. It was forecast that the oil will cross $200 per barrel, and the prices of coal and natural gas will go high in tandem, making them very expensive for power generation. However, as things turned out, the crude oil prices cooled off considerably by the end of 2008 and hovered around $50 per barrel mark, which was still a long way higher than the 2003 price of US$23 per barrel. Moreover, the oil prices are neither stable at present nor are likely to stabilize in future as they are determined by a number of factors like demand, supply level, availability of alternative sources of energy. The cartel of Organisation of Petroleum Exporting Countries (OPEC) has a major say in increasing or decreasing the supply level of oil which has a direct bearing on the price in international market. Under these circumstances, the cost of power generated through oil and other fossil fuels will remain fluctuating, making it well nigh impossible to make a lasting comparative study of economic viability of power generated through oil and nuclear power.

Nuclear power industry argues that economies of scale can substantially reduce the cost of nuclear power. The running costs of nuclear power plants are low though they have high upfront capital costs. If they are built without cost or time overruns, nuclear power could be competitive with natural gas. France, which gets three quarters of its electricity from nuclear power has shown that once production is standardized and plants are built on time, nuclear power is cheaper. The third generation power plants built in Finland were less costly than those built by the U.S. in the '70s. Fourth generation power plants which are now being made will further improve the economics of nuclear power.

Coal is by far the cheapest option for energy. However, coal-based power produces massive greenhouse gases with serious consequences like ozone layer depletion and global warming, having adverse effects on environment and ecology. The cause of environment demands that the use of fossil fuels, including coal, should be curtailed in the coming decades. Moreover, various expert committees have judged that India's extractable coal reserves may not last beyond four decades. If we do not harness nuclear energy in sufficient quantities, there will be a severe energy crisis in times to come.

In 2006, an Expert Committee on Energy estimated India's power needs at 960,000 MW by 2031-32, up from 144,000 MW today. This assumed a GDP growth rate of 9%, which is very optimistic. But if indeed India grows so fast, coal, hydel and non-conventional energy sources will meet at best 75% of India's needs in 2030, and this proportion will keep declinings as coal reserves deplete.

This leaves an energy gap of 240,000 MW in 2031-32, which is far more than India's entire installed capacity today. Nuclear energy alone can fill this gap. It is an accepted fact that India's current power generation sources will not be able to meet the demand. Unless and until nuclear energy is harnessed in a big way, the gap between demand and supply will keep on rising in future decades.

Though there is a strong case for nuclear power yet, it is possible that breakthroughs in solar or other forms of energy could make them cheaper and more easily accessible than nuclear power. History shows that technology can change in radical, unpredictable ways.

There will be many advantages if solar energy becomes the source of the future. It is available everywhere and is renewable.

It has none of the toxic, military or waste-disposal hazards of nuclear power. Recent advances in solar thermal technology show a lot of promise. Yet, nobody knows if the technology can be scaled up, work in cloudy countries, or overcome maintenance and other issues.

As things stand we face messy uncertainty today. Nuclear energy could be our only long-term saviour. But it could also be rendered irrelevant by the advance of solar or other energy sources.

In such circumstances, we need to keep all options open, aim for a mix of energy sources, and try to be at the leading edge of all technologies. An important but little discussed part of the Indo-U.S. nuclear deal is that it will enable India to participate in the international effort to develop fourth-generation (4G) nuclear power plants.

The Indo-U.S. nuclear deal offers some immediate benefits. Existing nuclear power plants are running out of fuel, and fuel imports will overcome the problem. Dual-use technologies will more easily be importable after the nuclear deal, greatly improving India's technological access. But it takes up to 10 years to build a green-field nuclear power plant, so the greatest benefits of a big nuclear push lie far out in the future.

To provide energy security India needs to be at the cutting edge of this industry in case other power sources become unviable making nuclear power absolutely essential. And to reach that stage of energy security, India needed the Indo-US nuclear deal and an end its technological isolation.

For conventional defence security, we maintain various options at considerable cost. For similar reasons, we need to push ahead with nuclear power, even if the immediate cost-benefit ratio is unclear. It is an essential energy security option for the long run.

Nuclear Power Corporation of India Ltd. has signed a memorandum of understanding with French firm Areva to set up nuclear power reactors at Jaitapur in Maharashtra. "The MoU provides for engagement of NPCIL and Areva into the discussion for preparing the contract and related detail of setting up of two to six 1,650 MW each European Pressurised Reactors (EPR) including lifetime fuel supply for these reactors," an NPCIL official said in a statement. S.K. Jain, Chairman and Managing Director of NPCIL and Anne Lauvergeon, CEO of Areva, signed the MoU. Jain said that the six nuclear reactors would be worth Rs. 60,000 crore ($12.3 billion). This is the first commercial agreement for supply of nuclear reactors after India got the waiver from the Nuclear Suppliers Group to participate in the global nuclear commerce.

NPCIL, which currently operates 17 nuclear power reactors with a 4,120 MW capacity, hopes to step up atomic power generation to 20,000 MW by 2020. Currently, EPR-type of reactors are under construction in Finland, China and France.

The French Minister for Foreign Trade, Lauvergeon, said that India has already signed a contract with Areva for importing 300 tonnes of uranium. "The government would be soon announcing more nuclear parks in other parts of the country. Some locations have already been identified. The Cabinent is looking into it," an Indian official said. "The parks", he said, "will also have a capacity of six to eight reactors."

India Gets Historic NSG Waiver

India secured a historic waiver from the Nuclear Suppliers Group (NSG) after the successful closure of the intensely contested three-day deliberations of the 45-nation group in Vienna in September 2008. The waiver will enable India to carry out nuclear commerce, ending 34 years of isolation enforced on it in the wake of the 1974 Pokhran nuclear tests. The U.S.-led proposal to lift over three decade old nuclear commerce ban against India had all the nail-biting tension of a protracted initiative that began in July 2005 to radically reorient India's nuclear status which ultimately led to victory for Washington. It is as much a vindication of India's nuclear credibility as a definitive acknowledgement of India's growing strategic relevance in the 21st century. The unprecedented decision of the nuclear cartel giving exemption to a country which has not signed the Nuclear Non-Proliferation Treaty

(NPT) and the Comprehensive Test Ban Treaty (CTBT) is a landmark step in the implementation of the Indo-U.S. nuclear deal. It is also a recognition of the fact that, for an international order, admitting India into the global nuclear fold is now deemed to be more beneficial than keeping it as a perpetual outsider.

The mood was upbeat both in the U.S. and in India after the Austrian Foreign Ministry said in a statement: "After protracted negotiations, the NSG...adopted an exemption for nuclear exports to India." The U.S. was euphoric after the NSG decision with its acting Secretary of State for Arms Control John Rood saying that the NSG waiver was a "landmark decision" and an "important moment" for strengthening the global non-proliferation regime. President Bush praised Dr. Manmohan Singh for his "strong leadership" and the success at the NSG. The Indian Prime Minister said that the waiver was a "recognition of India's impeccable non-proliferation credentials and its status as a state with advanced nuclear technology. He hailed the NSG's move to adjust its guidelines to enable full civil nuclear cooperation with India describing it as a "forward looking and momentous decision." He said in a statement that it marked the end of India's decades long isolation from the nuclear mainstream and of technology denial regime. He further stated that the opening of full civil nuclear cooperation between India and the international community will be good for the country and the world. "We look forward to establishing a mutually beneficial partnership with friendly countries in area which is important for both global energy security as well as to meet the challenge of climate change,"[9] he said.

The then Foreign Minister Pranab Mukherjee said the waiver was a culmination of a process which had started three years back. "The journey has not only been long but required several steps to be taken sequentially including intense bilateral negotiation,"[10] he said.

Opposition by Some NSG Members

The NSG typically operates by consensus. But, initially, some small NSG members voiced their reservations on India-specific waivers. Austria, Ireland, New Zealand and Switzerland expressed strong reservations over the waiver being given to India, that forced the grouping to have an unscheduled meeting after two days of deliberations failed to produce the consensus. China also raised some questions regarding specific issues. The hardline Arms Control Association (ACA)—loosely referred to as consisting of "non-proliferation ayatollahs" was critical of Bush administration allowing India to circumvent some provisions of the Hyde Act with extraordinary generosity at the NSG.[11]

Several NSG members had raised questions about rewarding India with greater opportunities to engage in international nuclear trade even while India continues to refuse to constrain its nuclear weapons programme. The ACA insisted in a lengthy analysis of the U.S. proposal. It argued that any India-specific exemption from NSG guidelines would erode the credibility of the NSG's efforts to ensure that access to peaceful nuclear trade and technology is available only to those states that meet global nuclear non-proliferation and disarmament standards. According to ACA, "One of the most notable and troublesome features is the weak and very ambiguous language. Instead of answering the question what India has done that qualifies it for a special exemption from NSG guidelines, the proposal simply recognizes India's commitments and actions that were outlined in the July 2005 joint statement."[12]

The NSG waiver came about when the U.S. government threw its weight and engaged in an intense diplomatic effort. President Bush spoke to China's President Hu Jintao and asked him to be reasonable. Washington made it clear that it had, by and large, acquiesced with India's reasoning that it should be treated as a special case nuclear power, effectively protecting it from the orthodoxy designed for non-nuclear weapons states. The breakthrough came after the U.S. President personally intervened to lobby with alies at the nuclear group to approve the trade waiver after some killer amendments cropped up.[13] Pranab Mukharjee's statement, reaffirming India's commitment to non-proliferation and disarmament goals and the reference to its voluntary moratorium on nuclear testing appears to have played a major role in placating the countries that had strong reservations about the draft. Austria issued a statement saying that it withdrew its objections after Mukherjee's statement which, it said, was decisive.[14] The Austrian foreign ministry spokesman Peter Launsky expressed a sense of relief that the waiver for India met with "international nuclear non-proliferation architecture."

China's Role at NSG

China had all along been giving the impression that it was not opposed to the waiver to India, but its opposition at the eleventh hour at the NSG meeting came as a surprise and attracted severe criticism from India. The Chinese ambassador was also spoken to by the Indian authorities and it was conveyed that Beijing's stand in the NSG "should reflect the strategic partnership between the two countries." Those who are wary of China's diplomatic antics went on to say that it first tried to build internal resistance to the deal through its friends, and when it failed, it tried to take its opposition to the international level.

China abstained at the NSG waiver talks in Vienna as Indian officials elbowed their way to a diplomatic victory though the Chinese government kept on saying that it supported India's nuclear power ambition. Even as China backtracked on its opposition to India at the NSG meeting, with Chinese foreign minister Yang Jiechi who visited India in September 2008 saying they had played a "constructive and responsible" role, India is believed to have delivered a "strong" message to China regarding its recent diplomatic objections. Answering questions, Yang essentially repeated the statement issued by the Chinese foreign ministry to coincide with the visit. He was quoted as saying that China had played a "constructive" role both earlier at the IAEA and at the NSG. The Chinese foreign minister's delegation apparently gave a detailed presentation to the Indian side, showing how they did not block a consensus at the NSG.

Earlier, the Chinese statement said it welcomed the NSG waiver but hoped this cooperation would be "conducive" to safeguarding global nuclear non-proliferation efforts. "China hopes that the decision will contribute to peaceful use of nuclear energy and international cooperation on nuclear non-proliferation," it said.

While reeling off a list of countries India was grateful to, Pranab Mukherjee purposely did not mention China. "I would like to take the opportunity to place on record Government's deep appreciation in particular for the untiring efforts of the US, France, UK and Russia throughout this process, and also the support received from the present and previous Chairs of the NSG—Germany, South Africa and Brazil," said Mukherjee.

During the debate at the NSG, China had raised a number of unspecified "concerns". As one diplomat present at the meeting said, "none of these were substantive objections and were meant to frustrate the U.S. efforts to secure the waiver. Like everybody, the Chinese also knew that delay was death for this deal".

Beijing capitulated only after George Bush called Chinese president Hu Jintao and asked him "to be reasonable" and India put some strongly-worded notes in their mailbox. After the NSG declared a consensus on the waiver for India, Chinese diplomats stressed their national position for a "balance between international non-proliferation efforts and nuclear energy."

Coming from a country with the dubious tag of "chief proliferators", few would have been taken in by the professed concern. In fact, diplomats from various countries in Vienna had few doubts that China did not want the deal to go through since they feared it would bring India closer to the deal. There was complete unanimity that China promised neutrality since it never expected the deal to go, but was forced to come out in the open because of the momentum generated by the U.S. lobbying in favour of the deal. With the NSG finally giving the waiver, China may regret the sabotage. It is sure to have set the normalization of ties with China back by a couple of years by strengthening the elements of suspicions and mistrust.

China began its efforts to block the deal soon after the IAEA safeguards agreement was cleared creating a momentum for India. Diplomats from different countries started to report that Chinese officials would quietly talk to them about "concerns" and how important it was to listen to the objections, but never really stated it on the record. The strategy was clearly to create as many obstacles to make the deal really difficult.

For the Indian establishment, the Chinese attitude has been a shock. Largely because India believed the Chinese when they indicated support to the deal, at the G8 Summit at Hokkaido in June 2008. As per Indian Government sources China had been mobilizing non-proliferation NGOs in the U.S. and Europe against the deal. That created a lot of verbal clutter on the deal, which made the decision even more of an uphill task. But when China remained the last man standing against the waiver at Vienna, it stood exposed in its opposition, days after the Chinese foreign ministry said it saw relations with India as "partners, not rivals".

Clearly, the Chinese officials' claims run contrary to the recent article in the *People's Daily*—a mouthpiece of the ruling Communist Party of China by an associate researcher at the Chinese Academy of Social Sciences, a government run think-tank—deriding the merits of the Indo-U.S. nuclear deal. He termed the safeguards agreement that India signed with the International Atomic Energy Agency (IAEA) as loose and non-binding, and talked about the apprehensions that it had raised in the international community.

Critical of the "double standards" followed by Washington on non-proliferation, the article stated, "Whether because of geostrategic considerations or driven by commercial interests, the U.S.-India nuclear agreement will have a significant impact on the international non-proliferation mechanism." It termed the initial proposal presented by the U.S. to the NSG as "vague", and complained that the deal allowed New Delhi to continue with nuclear tests "as there is no constraining link between supply of nuclear materials and India conducting a nuclear test."

This article surprised New Delhi as it believed that Beijing had considerably watered down its objection to the Indo-U.S.

deal in the run-up to the parleys at Vienna. In fact, the Chinese establishment had been making vague comments that it respected the sovereign right of every country to develop its capability for using nuclear energy for peaceful purposes but avoided any direct criticism of the deal.

However, after the article had been published, Beijing went into damage control mode, thereby indicating a split within the Establishment. The division came to the fore when its Foreign Ministry refused to endorse the article. In a bland statement its spokesperson asserted that she had not read the article. But she added that China hoped the NSG found a way to strike a balance between non-proliferation and the peaceful use of energy. It clearly implied that Beijing wanted the deal to be modified, made more palatable and was prepared to consider supporting it if the "relevant countries" provided the necessary assurances on nuclear safeguards.

Importantly, however, things are not always clear as they seem. The history of Chinese diplomacy bears testimony to the fact that its Establishment will never wash their dirty linen in the public when it comes to a crucial foreign policy issue. It seems highly implausible that the *People's Daily* would have published the article against the wishes or without the knowledge of the Chinese Government. As such, rather than indicating a real split in the Chinese leadership, the whole thing was a synchronized step to keep New Delhi guessing on Beijing's real intentions regarding its stand at Vienna.

In sum, amidst this "Chinese jugglery", New Delhi needs to highlight to the world that Beijing is far from being an "angel" when it comes to proliferation of nuclear know-how and materials. Has China forgotten that it had signed a bilateral civilian nuclear power agreement with the Reagan Administration in 1985 when it was not a signatory to the NPT?

Implications of NSG Waiver

NSG waiver for India has truly been called a historic decision as it will have wide ramifications for ending India's energy problems in general and open for it the doors of world nuclear trade in particular. The major implications of the NSG waiver are discussed below.

End of Nuclear Apartheid

The waiver is perhaps the final step in ending India's ostracism from the international nuclear club and stopping a concomitant failure to harness nuclear energy for civilian use due to sanctions imposed after Pokharan tests in 1974. India has been subjected to technology denial regime which hampered the country's research and development efforts in nuclear energy, and space industry, among others. Although India has some spectacular achievements to its name in several spheres, including Science & Technology, despite international sanctions, yet there have been several constraints in realizing the envisaged goals.

Now that the technology denial regime has been wound down, India will be immensely benefitted. It will be able to get state-of-the-art weapons and C4 ISR technology—acquiring more lethal power. Indian companies will be able to enter into cutting-edge joint R&D projects such as those in ballistic missile defence with the world's major defence contractors. Indian Space Research Organisation (ISRO) will benefit from commercially available space technologies. Due to the sanctions imposed on India, it was not allowed to purchase supercomputers for weather forecasting but will be able to do so now since the sanctions stand lifted. Needless to say that India's space faring and weather forecasting systems will get a shot in the arm. Cyclones and hurricanes frequently cause extensive damage in our Eastern Coasts of Orissa, Andhra Pradesh and Tamil Nadu. The development of proper disaster management system with the application of latest technologies, will now help us combat these natural calamities with minimum harm.

India will benefit in many other areas like medical diagnostics and inertial navigation equipment as these make use of dual-use technologies. Indian scientists will be able to travel freely and participate in international conferences for which they were hitherto routinely denied visas.

Meeting India's Energy Needs

India is a developing country with millions of people living below the poverty line. India's GDP has been growing at a rate of about eight per cent annually for the last five years except the previous financial year, i.e. 2008-09 when it grew just above 6 per cent due to some adverse effects of global economic meltdown. However, India's economy has shown a lot of resilience even in these difficult conditions, on the strength of local demand and supply resources. Goldman Sachs' report has predicted that India's economy will be the world's largest economy after China's by the year 2040. However, for this is to happen, India's energy supplies must increase at an average rate of six per cent per annum. The country's demand for electricity is likely to grow ten-fold from the present 130 giga watts (GW) to 1,300 GW by 2050.

India has very limited oil and natural gas reserves and imports about 70 per cent of its crude oil needs. With the prices of crude oil skyrocketing in the international market during 2008, India's import bill rose sharply. Though the crude oil price cooled off around US$40 per barrel towards the end of 2008 and the start of 2009, it again rose to over US$60 in June 2009. It is quite clear that the uncertainly about availability and price band of oil is likely to loom large in times to come.

The oil marketing companies have been worst affected with their under recoveries constantly remaining at a high level. The aviation industry has also been adversely impacted with rising fuel prices. Many aviation companies in India such as Jet and Kingfisher had to lay off a large number of employees as a cost-cutting move. The increasing cost of transportation led to higher prices of products and services in general in the first half of 2008. In India, though the inflation rate came below 1 per cent in April 2009, the prices of many commodities did not come down due to high transportation costs.

Though India has sizeable reserves of coal, it is of low quality. The excessive reliance on coal and oil to meet our energy needs has adverse environmental effects.

The full potential of India's hydel power has yet not been exploited, but there are several constraints and fallouts in fully realizing it. Building of dams necessitates uprooting of a large number of families. Acquirement of large tracts of agriculture land is steeped in controversies. The example of Sardar Sarovar dam on river Narmada in Gujarat may be recalled in this regard. Besides, rehabilitation of project-affected families is never an easy affair. Dissatisfaction and dissonance among the locals leads to law and order problem. The situation is often exploited by terrorists and other dissident groups to press their own demands multiplying the problems of administrative machinery and the government. In the present situation of food insecurity and higher food grain prices due to mismatch between demand and supply, encroaching upon farmland for any purpose—even development projects—is not desirable. Further, such projects destroy large number of natural habitats and cause severe damage to the ecology of the area, the ill consequences of which have to be borne by humanity at large in the shape of irregular rain patterns, recurring droughts, hurricanes, floods, etc. Non-conventional sources of energy such as solar power, wind energy and biofuel are also being exploited but cost-effective technologies for these are yet to be developed on a scale that would make a worthwhile contribution to our energy security.

At 3.50 GW (equivalent to 3,500 MW) per annum, nuclear energy contributes only three per cent to India's energy basket. The country aimed at creating nuclear power capacity of 10,000 MW way back in 2000. But this could not be achieved as India has neither modern nuclear technology nor enough uranium fuel to increase its capacity for generating sufficient nuclear power. Modern nuclear reactors in countries like France average 1,000 MW of power while Indian reactors average less than 250 MW. India has only one reactor with more than 500 MW capacity, i.e. at Tarapore, Maharashtra. With indigenous research which has been going on for a while now, it is expected to be enhanced to a maximum of 700 MW. In case the thorium cycle is mastered successfully over the next decade or so, India could increase its nuclear power capacity from 275 to 300 GW by 2050. But this would require external supplies of nuclear fuel.

The foregoing facts clearly establish that India needs both nuclear fuel supplies as well as latest nuclear reactor technology to enhance its capacity appreciably to generate enough electric power and reduce dependence on fossil fuels. India's endeavour should be to eventually enhance the share of nuclear power in its energy basket to more than 25 to 30 per cent like France and Japan and several other countries which have harnessed nuclear energy for peaceful purposes to meet their rising energy demand. The Indo-U.S. nuclear deal will go a long way in solving India's energy problems.

Nuclear Trade

The NSG waiver is a truly global opportunity. As India opens its doors for nuclear trade, it will generate worldwide business worth $40 million, allow Indian companies to supply components to foreign nuclear plant makers, offer power generation opportunities to Indian firms and increase the nuclear power level in the country to 52,000 MW by 2020. "India will set up 24 imported civilian nuclear light-water reactors along its coasts in the next 11 to 15 years," said S.K. Jain, Chairman and Managing Director of Nuclear Power Corporation of India Ltd. The corporation manages all the civilian nuclear plants in India.

Apart from countries like the US, France and Russia, more vendors will now be knocking at India's door for a share in Rs. 2.4 lakh crore project. In fact, the French nuclear major, Areva, has already set up an office in Mumbai, waiting to begin formal business discussions with the NPCIL.

Disclosing that the plan to import reactors to enhance India's nuclear power programme formed a part of the 11th Five-Year Plan (2007-12). The NPCIL chief said, "We will begin the modalities of financing the acquisition now that we have the NSG clearance."

With regard to the imported reactors, Jain said that every chosen region of the country will get reactors from one particular country only. For example, at Jaitapur in

Maharashtra's Ratnagiri district all the reactors will come from France.

Jain, one of the top nuclear officials in the country, added that the setting up of imported reactors will give a chance to Indian companies to collaborate with foreign companies. "Western technology will be married to the competitiveness of Indian industry," he said. Since the NSG approval also permits export of nuclear components from India, Jain said the U.S. manufacturers may source components from India. "Now armed with the NSG approval, India will compete with other nuclear powers to collaborate with these nations to set up their atomic power plants," Jain said.

According to some NPCIL officials, it is possible that the organisation may form a separate wing for international collaboration. "We now have a huge business opportunity and will now become truly global nuclear player," an official remarked.

Secretary-general of the Indo-American Chambers of Commerce R.K. Chopra also sees good opportunities for Indian firms. According to him, "A number of Indian companies could become a manufacturing hub for making nuclear-related parts and export them to the U.S. and other countries. India can also team up with the bigger countries and export components to smaller nations."

With India winning the backing of the NSG to trade in atomic fuel and technology in the global market, companies both at home and abroad are already eyeing a slice of the nuclear pie. One of the beneficiaries will be state-owned utility Bharat Heavy Electricals Ltd. (BHEL), the country's largest power equipment maker, which is poised to enter the nuclear reactor components business. The state-run National Thermal Power Corporation (NTPC) is also set to make its entry into nuclear power generation. Unlike private players, which will have to wait for the government to permit participation, the NTPC can power ahead. Private sector is equally buoyed by the opportunity. Rolta India which is one of the front runners in capacity-building for nuclear reactors, hopes to bag substantial engineering and design orders.

The public sector Nuclear Power Corporation of India Ltd. also plans to set up eight reactors to generate 8,000 MW of power with an investment of Rs. 50,000-60,000 crore. This will translate into a lot of business for global firms as NPCIL is planning to start deliberations with various international firms to buy over $14 billion worth of equipment for its new plants. Banks and equipment manufacturers abroad will be delighted to make funds available to India. In return, India will pay back with exports of goods and services exactly as China has been doing for the past 25 years.

According to a CII official, NTPC, Jindal, L&T, Tata Power and Reliance Power are among the key companies that would have huge business opportunities now. "Other companies, which have traditionally not been in this field are likely to foray into the area as well, owing to the magnitude of the business potential," he said, expressing confidence that since the U.S. Government has got the deal approved in the Congress, India is set to modify its Atomic Energy Act of 1962 to allow private sector participation in nuclear power generation in the country.

As the NSG waiver opens the gates for nuclear trade with India, the nuclear power generation scenario in the country will change completely in the next 15-20 years, with both foreign money and technology coming to India. The envisaged scale of nuclear power in India is enumerated below:

(i) At present, India has 14 nuclear reactors. Now, India plans to set up 24 imported light-water reactors in the next 11 to 15 years. India also plans to have 12 indigenous plants consisting of pressurized heavy-water reactors.

(ii) All the imported reactors will generate 1000 MW each. The indigenous reactors will produce around 10,000 MW. By the year 2020, nuclear power generation in India will go up to 52,000 MW from the present 4,120 MW.

(iii) India may import 18 to 20 reactors—each priced between Rs. 4,500 to Rs. 5,500 crore—from the U.S. during the next 20 years.

(iv) The main players at present are the U.S., France and Russia. Canada, Japan, UK and Germany will also step in later. More than 50 other countries, including Indonesia, Vietnam, Turkey, Saudi Arabia and Malaysia, have also shown interest.

(v) A number of coastal areas in the country have been surveyed for establishing a nuclear port consisting of imported reactors. Two locations have been shortlisted for installing light water reactors manufactured by the American General Electric and Westinghouse companies.

(vi) Now, Indian manufacturers can supply spares and components to producers of nuclear power plants. Companies like the NTPC, Jindal, L&T, Tata Power and Reliance Power may have huge business opportunities in the future.

Import of Reactors

The plan to import reactors to enhance India's clear power programs forms part of the 11th Five-Year Plan (2007-12). India will set up 24 imported civilian nuclear light water reactors along its coasts in the next 11 to 15 years. Apart from countries like the U.S., France and Russia, more vendors will now be attracted towards India to get fair share of business opportunities of setting up nuclear projects.

The global nuclear power industry grew very slowly for decades after the accidents at Three Miles Island and Chernobyl. But today's high oil and gas prices have persuaded every country once again to build massive nuclear power stations. Since this huge demand for equipment cannot be met by existing suppliers, massive new capacities are needed, part of which would have to be located in countries with low costs and high engineering skills—like India and China. Global major equipment suppliers like General Electric and Westinghouse will also need new production hubs to meet the increasing demand. They will sure find India a good production base to meet both Indian and world demand.

To begin with, the Indian companies may have technical and equity tie-ups with MNCs. This will facilitate the first stage involving transfer of know-how and indigenisation of components. But as they develop, Indian companies will improve on imported designs and become world class themselves. They will then supply not just in India but the whole world as they have done in many other fields.

This will be more than an economic achievement and will address some key security and foreign policy issues. Many in India are worried as to what will happen if future events force India to conduct a nuclear test. They apprehend that there will be fresh sanctions in such an eventuality. But those who are optimistic about India's future as nuclear exporter believe that even the sanctions will not be much effective once the world's big multinationals start producing nuclear power equipment in India. In fact, once India becomes a major equipment exporter, it will be among those that take decisions on sanctions and not remain at the receiving end of others' decisions.

Atomic Law May Be Changed

The Indian Government has announced its intention to amend the Atomic Energy Act of 1962—a necessary step for making use of NSG waiver.

The amendment could throw open the atomic energy sector to private investment in equipment manufacturing, electricity production and overall nuclear trade and commerce. At present, the entire gamut of activities connected with nuclear energy, beginning from uranium and thorium mining, is the government's monopoly and only a government company (in which the Centre has 51% or more paid-up share) can set up nuclear plants and generate power.

In 1948, the first India Atomic Energy Act was put in place when the Department of Atomic Energy (DAE) was established. It was replaced by the Atomic Energy Act in 1962. Later, the radiation protection rules were framed and assigned to the directorate of radiation protection. In 1983, regulation and safety functions were assigned to the Atomic Energy Regulation Board. The 1962 Act empowers the Centre to fix rates and regulate the supply of electricity from atomic power stations as it would prevail in case of any inconsistency with the Indian

Electricity Act in this regard. The Act also prohibits grant of patents for inventions relating to nuclear energy.

N-deal Could Help Pharma Innovations

The end of nuclear apartheld at Vienna meeting of the Nuclear Suppliers Group (NSG) and the conclusion of the controversial nuclear deal with the U.S. could spell a new era for India's biotechnology and pharmaceutical companies.

The deal is expected to open up access to critical genetic products and biomaterials, besides the latest technology to deal with them. This could help Indian laboratories boost research and companies discover new drugs, develop vaccines or create lucrative patents. Both trade and transfer agreements could result from the Vienna consensus.

The High Technology Cooperation Group (HTCG) had identified biotechnology among priority areas of focus for promoting and facilitating bilateral commerce in advanced technology items between India and the U.S.A. "Both the governments agreed to support advanced technology transfers that would stimulate capacity building in life sciences," said a top government official.

The HTCG was formed in 2002 to provide a standing framework to facilitate and promote high-technology trade between India and the U.S. and instill confidence for trade in sensitive items long kept out of India's hands because of perceived military sensitivities in the U.S.

At the last meeting of the group in February 2009, both countries agreed to engage in harmonisation of regulatory systems in medical devices, pharmaceuticals and biotechnology with the objective of improving market access. "It is a great step towards making our country self-reliant in matters of energy," Kiran Mazumdar Shaw, Chairman and Managing Director of Biocon said. Shaw, however, refused to comment on the more specific areas of gain, for the biotechnology industry in particular. Biotechnology is a highly regulated industry in both the U.S. and India, and red tape and bureaucratic hurdles linked to security and safety make the industry difficult to predict.

The chief executive officer of a leading biotech company said access to critical genetic products would spur growth in India's biotech industry. "The same genetic product is used for making some vaccines as well as anthrax. A well defined dual use technology trade protocol would help import of such products by India's bio-medical companies," he said referring to items whose trade was restricted because of fears that civilian material could be diverted for military use. Drug discovery research is also expected to get a fillip as export restrictions on dual-use machinery get eased.

India-France Sign Civil Nuclear Deal

Following the waiver granted by the Nuclear Suppliers Group (NSG), France became the first country to sign a civil nuclear energy pact with India. This pathbreaking development brings down the wall keeping India away from the nuclear technology and may act as a moot point for marking a new era of nuclear trade.

The agreement signed by Anil Kakodkar, Secretary, Department of Atomic Energy and French Foreign Minister Bernard Kouchner at the Elysee Palace marked the unshackling of India from denial regime which started after the first Pokhran test in 1974.

An official statement said: "This agreement will form the basis of wide-ranging bilateral cooperation from basic and applied research to full civil nuclear cooperation including reactors, nuclear fuel supply, nuclear safety, radiation and environmental/protection and nuclear fuel cycle management." The main effects of this agreement are outlined below:

India can now buy reactors from Areva, a French company which is considered world leader in nuclear equipment and technology.

It opens the door for India to sign similar agreements with other countries.

India can now engage in research and development in civilian nuclear sector.

India can, using its own technology and under IAEA safeguards, reprocess used nuclear fuel imported from France.

The agreement with France does not allow for transfer of reprocessing technology to India, but Kakodkar said it was only the beginning of a process of full scale cooperation and we have to be practical. "India's electricity requirements are large and we need to enhance on energy generation. Nuclear technology which is the cleanest source of energy can be a crucial addition and this agreement helps us with that," Kakodkar said.

Just after the agreement Prime Minister Manmohan Singh said, "Today we have added a new dimension to our strategic partnership by signing an intergovernmental agreement on civil nuclear cooperation. France is the first country with whom we have entered into such an agreement after the lifting of international restrictions on civil nuclear cooperation with India by the NSG. I conveyed to President Sarkozy our gratitude for France's consistent support to our nuclear initiatives." The conclusion of the agreement with France should help the French nuclear industry, given India's interest in Pressurised Water Reactors. France which meets 78 per cent of its energy needs through nuclear energy has made huge strategies in PWR technology. India is also looking at European Pressurised Reactors being built as part of a German-French collaboration.

India will not be required to amend its Atomic Energy Act to engage in nuclear commerce. However, it may be a while before a whole lot of details—from licensing to techno-economic feasibility, localization and configuration of reactors which will suit India most—are worked out.

The conclusion of the agreement with France should not be of disadvantage to American companies though there were some apprehensions in this regard.

Australia's Rigid Stand on Supply of Uranium of India

The Australian government stated that it would be difficult to supply uranium to India as New Delhi has not signed the nuclear Non-Proliferation Treaty (NPT). The Australian Foreign Minister Stephen Smith said that they have a long standing policy to sell uranium only to the countries which are parties to the NPT. Such a stand has come as a disappointment for India because Australia is world's richest nation in uranium resources, while Kazathstan, South Africa and Russia—which are willing to supply nuclear fuel to India—are already exhausting their supplies in exporting to Japan, U.S. and Western Europe. The U.S. and China, having both primary and secondary supplies, need fuel in large quantities for their own nuclear energy programs. Moreover, due to strategic interests, China is more likely to help Pakistan to harness nuclear energy than to India. This leaves Australia as the only long-term source of uranium. Australia's rigid stand on the supply of uranium to India is puzzling to say the least. The previous Australian government under John Howard was exporting uranium to India under United States' unseen pressure, but Prime Minister Kevin Rudd put a ban after coming to power in November 2008. Whereas John Howard insisted on a guarantee from India that all its uranium purchases will be used only for its civilian nuclear reactors and will not go towards its military nuclear program, Kavin Rudd stated that being a member of NPT was a necessary precondition for supply of uranium.

India's Foreign Secretary Shyam Saran was sent to Australia as Prime Minister Manmohan Singh's special envoy. Though his visit was accepted by Australia as an important recognition of India's engagement with Australia, Trade Minister Simon Crean maintained that Mr. Saran did not come to argue the case that Australia should supply uranium to India. The purpose of his visit was to give a deeper understanding of the issues behind the agreement that India was seeking to achieve with the U.S. in terms of civil nuclear use. Mr Crean said that Australia had taken "very detailed note of what the envoy had to say...and understands the importance of the agreement both to India and the U.S." However, the Indian authorities feel that these are empty words, and if Australia refuses to supply uranium to India, it is quite clear that it has not understood the importance of harnessing nuclear energy to lift millions out of poverty through growth brought by energy security, and the need to use clean fuel to save the world from the catastrophic effects of environmental pollution which is associated with rampant use of fossil fuels like coal and petroleum products.

Australia's previous government had assured India that it would supply uranium provided it was cleared by the International Atomic Energy Agency (IAEA) and the Nuclear Suppliers' Group (NSG). The Australian government's revised approach which was explained to Mr. Saran has obviously been driven by political reasons. Kevin Rudd has won elections on strong policy commitments including that he would not allow the export of uranium to nation states which are not members of NPT. The experts feel that such a rigid stand on an issue which has been discussed and debated in detail at international forums and decided by the comity of nations, is not justified. Clearly, Kevin Rudd and his Labor Party are trying to secure vote bank and get political mileage at the cost of international cooperation on energy security and clean environment.

Australia's Labor Party is excessively apprehensive in believing that the efforts to develop safeguards in ensuring that the uranium is not used for military purposes are impossible. In this regard, it can be argued that the separation of its civilian and weapon facilities under the separation plan, is an important commitment made by India, and is an integral part of Indo-U.S. nuclear deal. Under this plan, 14 of India's nuclear reactors are offered for safeguards while eight will remain unsafeguarded. Moreover, the Indo-U.S. nuclear deal is not about India's nuclear weapons program, it is about civil nuclear energy cooperation. It aims at advancing India's energy security through full civilian nuclear energy cooperation. It is quite legitimate for other nations to expect that such cooperation does not provide any advantage to India's strategic program. Hence, India agreed to the separation plan. It must, however, be clearly understood that India needs substantial fissile material to ensure that it can go through with a workable plan on separating its civilian and weapon facilities while safeguarding the independence of its nuclear deterrents.

Australia feels that there is some ambiguity on whether the 123 Agreement with the U.S. allows India to carry out any future nuclear tests without Washington cancelling the deal. In 1995, Australia suspended uranium exports to France after the latter conducted nuclear tests, claiming that any country that defies the spirit of Comprehensive Test Ban Treaty (CTBT) by pursuing nuclear testing shall be deprived of uranium.

The 123 Agreement contains the rider that it has to be implemented in conformity with America's Atomic Energy Act, and that cooperation must cease immediately in a contrary situation. The India government feels that the Agreement does not constrict India's right to test a nuclear device. The U.S. fully realises that nuclear weapons are an integral part of India's national security, given the fact that it has hostile Pakistan along its West and none-too-friendly China on its East—both having a large number of nuclear warheads in their possession. In case India conducts a nuclear test, the U.S. would consider the circumstances, perceived immediate security threat, etc. that warranted such action.

The experts feel that it is not important to discuss whether 123 Agreement restricts India's right to go for a nuclear test, because such a situation may not arise for several years to come. Why should Australia make such a huge issue of an eventuality which is not likely to occur in the foreseeable future? If time is an indicator, India exploded nuclear devices in 1998, after a period of about a quarter century from its first explosion in 1974. More than a decade has passed since the last explosion, but India has neither a plan nor intention to conduct a nuclear test. Why should Australia ignore these facts?

India is not a signatory to the NPT but it has an impeccable non-proliferation record, and the whole world knows it. India has been extremely conscious of its responsibilities about the control of Weapons of Mass Destruction (WMD) technologies and their delivery systems. What follow are very important components of India's approach to global non-perforation and international security, particularly as it has evolved since India's emergence as a nuclear weapons state in May 1998:

- Even as a nuclear weapons state (NWS), India remains committed to the goal of complete elimination of nuclear weapons on a non-discriminatory basis.

- A new global consensus on non-proliferation is called for because some NPT members both NWS and non-NWS have not only not complied with the provisions of this treaty but have also violated them flagrantly. Obviously, there is a need to go beyond the NPT. For instance, India has agreed in the Indo-U.S. joint statement of 18 July 2005 that it would not transfer reprocessing and enrichment technologies and would support international efforts to limit their spread. India has also adopted a very comprehensive WMD Export Control Act and harmonized its export control lists with those incorporated in the NSG and Missile Technology Control Regime (MTCR) guidelines. This has enabled India to fulfill the obligations prescribed in the United Nations Security Council (UNSC) Resolution No. 1540.
- The states must adhere to the commitments they made under international treaties because our own security interests have suffered due to clandestine nuclear weapons program in our neighbourhood aided and abetted by some of the NPT signatory countries themselves.

Mr. Saran, during his visit to Australia, highlighted the Indian Government's view about India's role in the nuclear power and pointed out that despite not being a member of the NPT, India has never indulged in the proliferation of nuclear expertise or materials to other countries. But there was no response from Australia except stating that they have taken note of the same. It is sad that Australia continues to ignore India's clean record and keeps on harping on the tune of NPT membership. One might ask: What is Australia doing about Iran which is a signatory to NPT but is openly defying its norms and pursuing nuclear weapons program? What about North Korea which has gone ahead with nuclear testing despite warnings from the U.S. and other countries? Nuclear proliferation of China and Pakistan is known to everyone. What does Australia plan to do to check them? India bore the brunt of nuclear and missile proliferation in the Asian region over the last decade. According to strategic affairs analyst K. Subramanyam, "The NPT regime was damaged beyond repair when the China-Pakistan combine carried out proliferation and the European countries failed the check the black market linkages between their companies and Pakistan and China...no other country was placed in the situation India faced, of a proliferating China on one side and proliferating Pakistan on the other, both in an alliance with each other." Why has Australia been a silent spectator of these developments all along? Evidently, it has no answer to these questions. As things stand, Australia has failed to make a distinction between a responsible and a rogue state. Its contention that the U.S. nuclear agreement with India has contributed to the weakening of nuclear non-proliferation, holds no water. As a matter of fact, it is some countries which are signatories to NPT that are weakening non-proliferation, and not the countries like India which have behaved highly responsibly and upheld the spirit of non-proliferation despite not being members of the NPT. Australia is also ignoring another factor that the Indo-U.S. nuclear deal has brought India under some control, which better serves the cause of non-proliferations rather than isolating the country to follow its free will.

Australia has also said that providing nuclear fuel to India may upset regional stability. Such an apprehension is totally unfounded. "By transferring nuclear warhead and ballistic missile technology and blessing North Korea's ballistic missile transfers to Pakistan, China has irrevocably altered the geostrategic equation in Southern Asia, to India's disadvantage. Quite clearly, there was a sinister purpose behind the carefully calibrated move to reduce India to Pakistan's size in geostrategic terms. A more unfriendly act cannot be conceived...."[13] While these developments are a matter of concern for India, Australia continues to show apathy and rigidity towards India. Two countries which have risen not only in the Asian region but also as global powers during the last two decades or so are China and India. Even in the trying conditions of financial turmoil worldwide, the economics of these two countries have shown a steady though less than recent years' growth. With Japan already a developed country, China and India also coming up as strong nations in Australasia, Australia has already lost much of its importance. Obviously, it is not worried about regional balance but its own declining status among the comity of nations. It has lost its supremacy in Cricket to India. The burgeoning success of India Premium League (IPL) Twenty20 matches has overshadowed Australia's domestic leaque like Sheffield Shield. In professional and higher education too India has outshone many countries including Australia. Poor economics and rising unemployment have frustrated some sections of Australia so much that they are indulging in racial abuse and attacking Indians, particularly students, at public places. These incidents show that Australia in general and some of its people in particular have been unable to accept today's reality that India is a burgeoning Asian power and has more say than Australia.

As a responsible nation, Australia must wake up to above realities and reconsider its decision of refusing to sell nuclear fuel to India. It must appreciate that both India and Australia are great democracies, vis-à-vis communist China, different political systems in most of South-East Asia, and an unstable and terrorist-ridden Pakistan. Helping India would strengthen the cause of democratic ideals.

The economists have predicted that the India's economy will become the third largest economy in the world by 2025. Australia has greatly benefited from the increasing growth of Indian economy. By their own estimate Australia's trading with India over the last 5 years has grown faster as compared to any other top market. India has already suspassed UK as Australia's 6th largest market for merchandise export. Australia is India's 10th largest trading partner. Bilateral trade between these nations has reached $12 billion. Australia exports a number of goods to India including coal, copper, ores, gold, wheat and wool. Many Australian companies have made big investment in India in manufacturing, telecommunication and mineral processing sectors. If Australia remains adamant in its stance regarding uranium supply to India, the bilateral trade will be adversely impacted, a development neither country would relish.

Controversy Surrounding the Hyde Act

Some quarters in India, particularly those who are against the Indo-U.S. nuclear deal, feel that some clauses in the Hyde Act, which was signed into law by the then President George W. Bush, will have a negative impact on India's strategic program as well as foreign policy. Section 109 of Hyde Act envisages India to jointly participate with the U.S. in a program involving the U.S. National Nuclear Security Administration to further nuclear non-proliferation goals. According to Indian nuclear scientists and experts, this goes much beyond the IAEA norms and has been unilaterally introduced without the knowledge of Indian Government. The U.S. President is required to annually report to the Congress whether India is fully and actively participating in U.S. as well as international efforts to dissuade, isolate and if necessary sanction, and contain Iran in its pursuit of indigenous efforts to develop nuclear capabilities. These as well as some other stipulations in the Hyde Act, pertaining to Proliferation Security Initiative (PSI), the Wassenaar Arrangement, etc. are totally outside the scope of the 18th July Agreement, and are an intrusion into India's independent decision-making and policy matters.

Prime Minister Manmohan Singh has allayed these fears by saying that "pending the elimination of all nuclear weapons and universal non-discriminatory nuclear disarmament, nuclear weapons are an integral part of our national security and will remain so. Our freedom of action with regard to our strategic programs remains unrestricted. The nuclear agreement will not be allowed to be used as a backdoor method of introducing NPT type restrictions on India." George W. Bush also recognised India's need to follow its strategic program within the limits of the agreement, and he recommended removing certain amendments added to both the House version and the Senate version of Hyde Act, which he thought would be deemed deal killers by India. In response to the language used in the Act by Congress to define U.S. policy towards India, Bush stated:

"Given the Constitution's commitment to the authority of the presidency to conduct the nation's foreign affairs, the executive branch shall construe such policy statements as advisory." As such, there is nothing that can be forced upon India, against its will or which is detrimental to its national security and defence preparation.

Impact on Our Foreign Policy

Our policy towards Iran had already undergone a sea change even before the Indo-U.S. nuclear deal came into existence. Our vote against Iran at IAEA was the litmus test. While India, for obvious reasons, would not welcome a new entrant in the nuclear club, this factor alone should not have swung our vote. Iran has not violated the NPT in any major way while Pakistan, China and North Korea have clandestinely and openly violated major provisions of NPT. Action taken by IAEA against Pakistan could not come to fruition due to Pakistan's intransigent stand that A.Q. Khan, the chief in charge of the Pakistan's nuclear program, would not be made available for questioning by IAEA. Pakistan has been allowed to go scot-free and unpunished due to backing by U.S. and the inability of IAEA to proceed against Pakistan.

Pakistan's doctrine of 'first use of nuclear weapons', as against ours of 'no-first use', and Pakistan's repeated threats to use nuclear weapons against India are a major cause of concern for India.

Pakistan's attitude is in stark contrast to Iran's putative intention. Some foreign policy experts believe that by our vote at IAEA we have gravely damaged our burgeoning and mutually beneficial economic matrix of deals, especially in the hydrocarbons sector, in which India remains, and will remain for the near future, a big importer. The fact that India did not energetically and implacably oppose clandestine selling of nuclear equipment by Pakistan has weakened India's position and diminished its stature within the global nuclear community, especially IAEA. This has put India in a situation where we are not even seen as a country capable of defending its strategic allies. We are already being dubbed as a U.S. stooge. All this does not square up well in our long term quest for membership of the UN Security Council.

Since 1947, our foreign policy has been defined and enunciated into a form and with such contents that it has enjoyed multi-partisan support everywhere. The nuclear component of our foreign policy has evolved from the need for autonomy in our defense and security framework. That was the reason behind Pt. Nehru's endorsement of the nuclear policy formulated by late Dr. Homi J. Bhabha.

We have also worked very hard for peaceful development of nuclear energy. We were able to withstand the political after-effects generated by 1973 and 1998 explosions. Even though 1998 explosions should have been made before the conclusion of CTBT, as done by France & China, our stature actually grew and the great powers that condemned us for our nuclear tests came back unconditionally, not only to normalize their relations but also to enter into strategic dialogue with us. This was helped, undoubtedly, by the opening up of our economy in 1991 leading to vigorous economic growth during the last decade or so.

Energy securi y is an important factor for India's fast socio-economic development. But in the present age of globalisation, multilateral cooperation holds the key to imports, exports, flow of foreign capital into the country, and technology transfer, among others. India has all along followed policy of non-alignment. The Indo-U.S. nuclear deal may be seen by some countries as India's tilt towards the U.S. and its cronies. Russia has been India's biggest supporter and helper in international affairs and vetoed twice in the UN, against the proposal of holding a plebiscite in Kashmir, to help India's cause. It has stated that it has no problems with India going for a nuclear deal with the U.S. But it is our duty to engage in stronger relations with Russia, nurturing our old friendship, through visits of diplomats and delegations, assuring that the independence of our relations with other countries, including Russia shall in no way be affected by Indo-U.S. nuclear deal. In the Asian region too, our commitments with other countries need to be fulfilled. Our Look East policy needs to be pursued vigorously to maintain our affinity with South-East Asia. At the same time our engagements with other countries and statements at international forums should not harm our relations with the Western world. Indo-U.S. nuclear deal has given us a higher status in the comity of nations. Our foreign policy should supplement this status.

President Obama Backs Indo-U.S. Nuclear Deal

Barack Obama has been speaking in favour of the Indo-U.S. nuclear deal ever since he was campaigning as Democratic presidential candidate. He voted in its favour because he believed "India is a strong democracy and a natural strategic partner for the U.S. in the 21st century." This indicates that if the deal had not matured during President Bush's tenure, it would have been considered favourably by America's new President Obama.

The Obama administration has asserted that it is committed to implement the Indo-U.S. civil nuclear deal, a landmark foreign policy achievement by the previous Bush government. The U.S. Department of Energy issued a statement following the conclusion of a three-day meeting of the 'US-India Civil Nuclear Energy Working Group' in April 2009 saying that it looked forward to India to bring its IAEA Safeguards Agreement into force, filing its declaration of facilities pursuant to the Agreement, publicly announcing reactor park sites for U.S. companies and enacting global standards of liability protection. The Indian side was represented by Ravi Grover, Director of India's Strategic and Planning Group in the Department of Atomic Energy. Discussions focused on deepening mutual understanding of each country's nuclear energy development plans, including light water reactors, near-term reactor deployment, licensing, management of nuclear waste, research and development programs, among other things.

In its public assurance to India that there will be no turning back on the deal, the Obama administration said that it will fulfil the commitments under the historic Agreement. America's Deputy Secretary of State James Steinberg said, "Both the United States and India have the responsibility to help to craft a strengthened NPT regime to foster safe, affordable nuclear power to help the globe's energy and environment needs, while assuring against the spread of nuclear weapons." Steinberg went to say that India, despite not being a signatory to the NPT, is "in the position to look at the kinds of commitments it can make to be part of an international approach." It is heartening to note that both the signatories to the deal are enthusiastic about moving forward to realise the objectives of energy security, clean environment and a proliferation-free world order.

Conclusion

Indo-U.S. nuclear deal has been the subject of much debate and discussion not just in India but internationally as well. The issue which is extremely complex—involving national and international polity, nuclear non-proliferation, diplomacy, and technicalities of the nuclear fuel cycle—has created opinion divides all over the world. In India, the showdown between the Left Parties which were a part of the United Progressive Alliance (UPA) Government in its previous term, turned into an impasse over the deal. The Left which, for all intents and purposes, wanted the deal to be discarded, withdrew support leaving the government to face a confidence vote on the floor of the house. As things turned out, the government was able to prove its majority on the back of support by some regional parties and key abstensions from the opposition camp.

During the campaign for 15th Lok Sabha elections, Indo-U.S. nuclear deal was highlighted as one of the biggest achievements of the government. Public at large also accepted it as such and conferred on the UPA an overwhelming majority. The Left is no longer in alliance with Manmohan Singh's government in his second tenure as India's Prime Minister. The deal and its follow-up will thankfully have a smooth passage. The majority government is a luxury in the present times of precarious alliances. It is an opportunity for the government to move ahead with commitments, deadlines and take initiatives to materialize benefits of the deal for the country and its people as early as possible.

For dissonants of the Indo-U.S. nuclear deal it should suffice to say that instead of engaging in fruitless disagreements, India should stand united and focus on how we best stand to gain from the deal. It is in the nation's collective interest to recognize that key aspects of the deal are beneficial to India's economic growth and its positioning among the comity of nations. As for some conditions that go with the deal, we must remember that nothing comes free in this world. If we wish to leverage on the deal with the U.S. to gain energy security and ascendancy in international circles, then there is a price for it. As much as the Indo-U.S. civil nuclear agreement is a breakthrough, it is also a friendship that is based on values and ties. It is an agreement that cements an effort that these two nations have been making for some time to bring together the world's largest democracy with the world's oldest continuous democracy. Its benefits may go much beyond energy security and clean environment and not first for India and the U.S. but for many other nations as well.

NOTES

1. He was Chairman of the U.S. House Committee on Foreign Affairs.
2. Condoleezza Rice to the Senate Foreign Relation Committee, April 5, 2006.
3. Esther Pan and Jayshree Bajoria, "The U.S.—India Nuclear Deal", CFR.org.
4. *Hindustan Times*, July 10, 2008.
5. Quoted in *Hindustan Times*, July 10, 2008.
6. Quoted in *The Times of India*.
7. *Hindustan Times*, December 21, 2008.
8. Quoted in *The Times of India*, September 9, 2008.
9. http://www.expressindia.com
10. *Hindustan Times*, September 7, 2008.
11. Chidanand Rajghatta, "Some NSG members bristle at 'clean' waiver", *The Times of India*.
12. *Ibid.*
13. Gurmeet Kanwal, "A Currency of Power", *The Times of India*, June 3, 2009.

Indo-US Civil Nuclear Deal

2

Col Ved Prakash

INTRODUCTORY

The Indo-U.S. Civilian Nuclear Deal is a landmark in the Indian foreign policy domain, which can be compared with the Indo-USSR Defence Accord of 1971, concluded a few months before the India-Pakistan War of that year. Perhaps more appropriately, it can be bracketed with the Nixon visit to China that resulted in the establishment of the U.S.-China diplomatic relations. It can be truly said that the July 2005 accord was a significant development from the point of view of international diplomacy, international politics and energy augmentation for India. In a manner of speaking, for the anti-proliferation ayatollahs of America, it was a tactonic shift in the U.S. policy of keeping those nations which had not signed the NPT at an arms length. They were the pariah nations. With this accord, Washington had executed a U-turn in its dealing with the nuclear India.

To put the issue in perspective, the journey of this accord really started with the 12-round Jaswant-Talbot talks during the Vajpayee-led NDA Government (1998-2004). The thread, rather, the gauntlet, was picked by the Manmohan Singh-led UPA Government. The "basic framework" was contained in the Manmohan-Bush Joint Statement of 18 July 2005, issued at Washington. The next step was the 2 March 2006 agreement signed by the two principals at New Delhi, that gave final shape to separation plans for India's nuclear reactors and facilities.

It should be of interest to identify the gains India hopes to make through this path-breaking agreement, and simultaneously, note the obstacles stacked against it in the way.

Advantage India

The positives expected to accrue to India are detailed below at some length:

- The accord marks the end of the technology-denial regimes which have restricted India over three decades—starting with the 1974 nuclear tests, and exacerbated by the 1998 Pokhran II tests. It indicates a new chapter for India—of engagement as equal partners in civil nuclear energy cooperation with other countries. It will help India to expand its high technology trade with technologically advanced countries.
- This initiative, the nuclear deal, is an acknowledgement of the scientific and technological achievements of our scientists. Their tireless efforts in the face of adverse conditions laid the basis for this accord, indicative of the recognition accorded to India as a state with advanced technology. The erstwhile embargo came in the way of our scientists exchanging scientific ideas and technical know-how and contributing to the global efforts to deal with the world-wide challenges of energy security and climate change.
- The deal will make a historic contribution to our nation-building effort, in respect of energy, sustainable development, technology and other aspects. It is a known fact that the availability of clean, affordable and sustainable sources of energy is a critical input if India is to maintain a healthy economic growth and abolish poverty. Crude oil, India's main energy source, is not an inexhaustible treasure and rise in its global prices puts a strain on our economy and on the daily lives of the people. Hence, the need and urgency to develop the energy sources which are clean and do not

contribute to global warming. India has and will continue to develop renewable sources of energy like biofuels, solar and wind energy as well as other sources like hydel power. Nuclear energy offers an economically and environmentally viable alternative. With the international cooperation available under this accord, India will be able to bring additional generating capacity through nuclear power into its energy mix. The accord will also help India's indigenous nuclear programme to grow rapidly. Presently, India has some 4000 megawatts (MW) of installed capacity in nuclear power. Even the existing plants operating far below their optimum level due to a shortage of uranium. The opening of international nuclear trade and commerce will afford India new opportunities to expand its nuclear power capacity.

- How is this desideratum come about? Presently, India's power generation capacity is about 1,45,000 MW. If it wishes to sustain an annual GDP growth of 9 per cent, then by 2030, its projected energy deficit would be 1,50,000 MW. Looking further into the future, by 2050, the deficit would amount to 4,12,000 MW. In working out these figures, thermal power, coal, petrol, and diesel, hydel power, and non-conventional energy sources like solar, wind, etc. have been taken into account. Even after their fullest exploitation, the projected deficit would remain. Nuclear power is the only effective way to bridge this gawning gap. As per some studies, it takes eight years to produce 40,000 MW of energy. Accordingly, by 2030, in 22 years starting 2008, India will be able to reduce the deficit to only 50,000 MW as against the deficit of 1,50,000 MW. Therefore, India will be reduce the energy deficit in 2050 from 4,12,000 MW to only 7,000 MW. Thus, the accord will reduce India's dependence on fossil fuel, thereby lowering the oil import bill.
- With the U.S. President's resolve to open U.S. market for India's exports, the FICCI chief, S.K. Poddar,

hopes the Indo-U.S. trade will double to reach the target US$40 billion in three years.

- Once approved by the U.S. Congress, the accord would recognise India as a nuclear military power and herald a major expansion in ties between the two democracies—one largest and the other most powerful, the sole super power after decades of strained relations.
- After signing of the 2 March 2006 statement, President Bush said: "Things Change, Times Change." Prime Minister Singh said, "We have made history."
- The President told the joint press conference: "Americans would benefit because increased use of nuclear power in India would reduce global demand for oil. With 1.1 billion people and one of the world's fastest growing economies, India is consuming a large share of global energy supplies a key force behind rising oil prices. Both India and America have faced terrorist attacks on their soil. We are sharing information to protect each other. We are also cooperating on the military front."
- The Prime Minister said: "The finalisation of identification of civilian facilities would begin soon. Areas covered by us are central to India's national development. They include energy, agriculture, science and technology, trade, investment and high technology, health and environment. Both countries have agreed to root out terrorism, of which India is a major victim."
- India gained the right of participation in the International Thermonuclear Experimental Reactor (ITER) Consortium, an international enterprise aimed at building a reactor that can use nuclear fusion as a source of energy.
- Even before March 2006 accord, the U.S. removed India's safeguarded reactors from the U.S. Department of Commerce Entities List.

- The accord would end India's status as a nuclear renegade and clear the way for U.S. companies to sell civilian nuclear equipment to India. In return, India would declare 14 of 22 reactors part of its civilian programme, and place them under international monitoring/inspections by the IAEA.
- IAEA Director-General Mohamed El Baradei called the deal "a step forward towards universalisation of the international safeguards regime."
- Fast breeder reactor (FBR) programme will not be subject to outside inspection. U.S. may expand the number of H1B visas for Indian scientists, engineers and physicists.

Negatives and Criticism

The critics, both inside India and the U.S. had serious worries about the implications of the accord, particularly after the March 2006 agreement on the question of separating the Indian nuclear reactors/facilities into the "military" and "civilian". Ironically, the U.S. and Indian critics are condemning the accord for dramatically opposite reason; if the former feel the U.S. has given too much, the latter over the Indians have sold their family silver rather cheap.

- Rep Edward Markey said: "It made a mockery of the cornerstone of the NPT system, which India never signed. With one simple move, the President has blown a hole in the nuclear rules the entire world has been playing by over the nearly four decades. It empowers the hawks in every rogue nation to put their nuclear weapons plans on steroids."
- Some U.S. lawmakers and many arms-control experts opined the deal would undercut the global system designed to halt the spread of nuclear arms, making it harder to rein in suspected Iranian and North Korean nuclear weapons programmes.
- The critics averred that accord excluded important parts of India's nuclear programme from safeguards. Eight reactors would not be covered by the safeguards

and could remain source of plutonium for weapons. The facilities include several civilian power plants and a fast breeder reactor that will produce large amount of plutonium.

- Greater worry for the sceptics is that the safeguards also wouldn't cover existing spent reactor fuel, which contains enough plutonium for more than 1,000 weapons, and a facility for enriching uranium, that also can be used for making nuclear weapons.
- Daryl Kimbal, Executive Director of the Arms Control Association and a staunch critic of the deal, fears "the deal would allow India to significantly increase its nuclear weapons arsenal. This is a non-proliferation nothing-burger, and Congress will see it as that if they look carefully."
- An Indian critic says that the accord will help India realize growth targets for power generation so critical to sustaining its current high rate of economic growth, there is clear evidence to suggest that the agreement will limit India's strategic posture to that of a second rate power. "The U.S. has played its card very well in getting India to sign on the dotted line. Its ruse to project the deal as a near sell-out of its own Non-Proliferation interests that will be difficult for it to push through Congress succeeded in luring India to halt the advance of its strategic nuclear posture from force in Being to Credible Nuclear Deterrence. In other words, India's posture will now for ever remain a Force in Being." The two most debilitating parts of the accord, that represent a sell-out of India's strategic nuclear posture are its consent to:
    (a) Maintain all safeguards in perpetuity.
    (b) Maintain its current moratorium on nuclear-weapon tests.
- Peace and anti-nuclear groups like Council for Liveable World are weighing in, urging supporters to lobby lawmakers to vote down the agreement.

- Nuclear testing is one of the two issues on which the U.S. has been trying to push India, the other being a treaty to loan the production of fissile material, the fuel that goes into the nuclear weapons. In mid-May 2006, the U.S. introduced a FMCT (Fissile Material Cut-off Treaty) at the UN Conference on Disarmament (CD) in Geneva. China is presently opposed to the FMCT, as it sees it as a U.S. ploy to freeze nuclear competition among the major states at the present level. In the past, India was lukewarm toward the FMCT, which it perceives as a measure to limit the size of its nuclear arsenal. But in the July 2005 accord, New Delhi had to make a concession on the issue. By committing itself to "work with" Washington, New Delhi signalled that it stands by the U.S., not with China.
- Terming the deal as a "formula for destroying American non-proliferation goals", 37 Nobel laureates urged the U.S. Congress not to approve the deal "in its current form". They wrote this in a letter, in June 2006, which was supported by the Federation of American Scientists (FAS).

India made it clear on 23 June 2006 that the landmark nuclear deal with the U.S. should be based on the original commitments, made by the two sides, side stepping new moves to link the pact to its stand on Iran's on Iran's atomic programme. India's comments came after a leading U.S. law-makers, Representative Tom Lantos (D) warned that the deal could be jeopardised if India sided with non-aligned states in backing Iran's atomic ambitions.

India's traditional ties with Iran have haunted the controversial pact since the President and Prime Minister signed it in July 2005. India's decision to vote against its old friend Iran, a major source of its soaring energy needs, at the IAEA meetings in September 2005 and February 2006 drew strong criticism at home. As a result, India has been cagey of making any clear commitments against Iran.

The Path to Fruition: Long and Tortuous

The signing of July 2005 and March 2006 were only the initial steps. The President would have to approach the Congress for approval of this agreement. The Indian side will have to conclude an India-specific agreement with the IAEA. Then the U.S. will have to get the nod from the 45-member Nuclear Suppliers Group (NSG) at Vienna. Finishing was to be the passage of India-US 123 Agreement—allowing nuclear commerce between the two countries—by the U.S. Congress.

It is worth noting that the separation of India's 22 nuclear reactors would be undertaken in a phased manner and completed by 2014.

A bill intended to implement the deal was introduced in Congress on 16 March 2006, but Under Secretary of State Nicholas Burns did acknowledge that many lawmakers "need to have further discussion and further testimony" before they would be ready to vote.

With the exception of China, other major global powers such as the UK, France, Germany and Russia willingly supported the deal, not only because it affords an important position to India in the comity of nations but also because it allows them to sell nuclear fuel, reactors and equipment to India. China, expectedly, made its displeasure with the pact clear by asking India to sign the NPT and dismantle its nuclear weapons. The official Xinhua news agency of China commented that the US-India nuclear accord "will set a bad example for other countries."

China's attitude is in keeping with Beijing's long-standing policy of hobbling India's progress towards attaining a major power status. It is bent upon limiting India's capacity for power projection. As this deal is recognition of India's rising global profile, China was doing its best to scuttle it. China persisted with its duplicitous conduct till the very last.

On 14 June 2006, the two sides had third round of talks to narrow down differences on drafting the so-called 123 Agreement. On the question of the nuclear testing by India, which could lead to an American assertion of their right to cease nuclear cooperation, there were serious differences. The two sides are continuing to explore mutually acceptable formulation. India made it clear that it could not go beyond its commitment to a voluntary moratorium on nuclear testing and accept a self-denying ordnance.

Given the amount of legal work and sensitive political issues involved, the U.S. negotiations of the 123 Agreement with other countries have often taken years.

The U.S.-Japan agreement on nuclear cooperation took nearly five years, and a similar between Washington and Euratom, the West European organisation for regional nuclear energy cooperation, took more than a decade to complete. But India and the US are hopeful that the current agreement will not take anywhere that long.

The precedent, it was believed, would make it relatively easy for the two sides to agree on the procedures for verifying the physical security of the nuclear materials obtained under the agreement. An analyst opined in June 2006: "A couple of more rounds of talks in the coming weeks are expected to produce the final agreement. By that time, the U.S. Congress would have, in all likelihood, approved a legislation to allow the U.S. Government to embark on nuclear energy cooperation with India." Not only was that an overly optimistic proposition, as the actual events were to show subsequently, there were some other related issues also that were to muddy the waters in the coming days. One was the likelihood of the Congress insisting on changing the existing U.S. laws on non-proliferation in favour of India only the condition that it would have the right to vote upon the bilateral nuclear cooperation agreement—something India was not agreeable to. In the light of this, some analysts even thought that "the two sides would want to make sure that the agreement is to the liking of the U.S. Congress and that it takes into account the unique position of India as a country in possession of nuclear weapons but is not a signatory to the NPT". But the things were not as simple as this averment would depict. How complicated the entire skin of issues—and badly tangled at that—would be seen in the last part of this introduction.

How tangled the skein was should be obvious from a perusal of things and events about mid-2006. An analyst wrote on 25 May 2006 under the caption, "India, US fight to save the nuke deal": "The civilian nuclear cooperation agreement is still alive. After weeks of getting battered by the critics of the deal inside the US Congress and elsewhere, the Bush administration and Indian Government are hitting back with a set of actions that they hope will lead to the deal's passage this summer."

India's Foreign Secretary Shyam Saran and US Under Secretary of State Nicholas Burns, the pointmen of their respective countries on the nuke deal met in London on 25 May 2006 to update each other on the steps their countries have taken so far and to coordinate tactics to ensure the smooth passage of the deal.

Burns asked Saran where India was with respect to its safeguards agreement with the IAEA. He also talked about the new US push for a global FMCT. On his part, Saran asked Burns to update him on what the Bush administration was doing with Congress to get the US laws changed to accommodate the nuke deal.

In the US Congress, even the supporters had expressed frustration that the India-IAEA agreement talks were going slower than expected. For instance, Senator Lamar Alexander, while supportive of the deal, had noted during his recent visit to New Delhi that Congress could have acted faster if India's talks with the IAEA were speeded up and Congress had an idea about the broad contours of the India-IAEA safeguards agreement. Even worse, the U.S. arms control hawks pointed to this alleged delay as evidence of Indian perfidy.

On its part, India rejected such biased arguments out of hand, claiming that safeguards agreements were proceeding as planned. It was pointed out that the nuclear pact had reciprocal steps at its core, and India was unlikely to take unilateral steps just to appease critics who are mostly opposed to the deal anyway.

A former Indian official pointedly told the Asia Times Online that the US Congress had passed a nuclear cooperation agreement with China even though Beijing had rejected a US request for minimal IAEA safeguards on US-supplied nuclear material: "It is incredible that the [non-proliferation] critics were silent when China was able to obtain congressional clearance to purchase American nuclear technology without any safeguards, but they cast aspersions on India despite its sovereign commitment to negotiate an ironclad fire wall and safeguards system with the IAEA."

Whatever India's strong reaction to the cussedness of those critics, India's compulsions and difficulties at home in respect of the nuclear pact with the U.S. are well-known. The UPA Government is hamstrung on the issue due to stiff opposition to the pact of the main opposition party, the BJP, and of its Chief—largest—supporter, the CPM-led Left Front. The Left kept threatening the UPA of withdrawing its support from the Government if it proceeded to hold formal talks with the IAEA, even though the draft agreement on the safeguards had been in the works for months on end.

One reason for this Saran-Burns meeting was the plenary of the 46-member NSG at Rio de Janeiro, beginning 29 May 2006. The NSG was required to clear an India exception before its 46-member nations could commence civilian nuclear trade with New Delhi.

The NSG operates on consensus basis, under which a single—minor—nation could block the clearance. India had launched a charm offensive, with two ministers going to Brazil and South Africa, and officials convincing other nations. Some major powers—China, Japan and the Scandanavians—were known to be against the deal. Even if a single nation could block the deal, while other opponents stayed behind. But few countries want to bear the burden of the hostility of a rising global power, such as India, observers note.

China is not showing its hand, though it is believed to have assured India not to oppose the deal. Its duplicitous role would be out in the open at the crunch time when the NSG passed India-specific clearance.

It is known that both India and U.S. were keen to have the NSG clear the nuclear deal during the session at Rio, beginning

29 May 2006. But as it turned out, smaller nations blocked any positive outcome, sending the matter to the next session.

12-13 June 2008 formal talks on the bilateral nuclear agreement—the so-called 123 Agreement—are believed to have focussed on the following:

- The differences on issues like nuclear tests in future by India and an assurance by the U.S. on sustained atomic fuel supply.
- It was learnt that the document contained an assurance on fuel supply that allowed India to stockpile fuel for the lifetime of every reactor.

It is interesting to note that despite the ongoing negotiations on the Indo-U.S. nuclear deal, NSA M.K. Narayanan on 22 June 2006 met Chairman of the International Weapons of Mass Destruction Commission Hans Blix to continue engaging in disarmament talks.

There was optimism in the air on 17 June 2006 when a top U.S. Senator, Richard Lugar, Chairman of the Senate Foreign Relations Committee, declared at the Naval War College in Newport: "It is critical that the US Congress comes to conclusions about President Bush's proposal on civilian nuclear agreement with India." He warned the Congress against rejecting or delaying the deal at the risk of losing a "critical opportunity" of expanding beyond America's Cold War structures to include dynamic nations like India.

After the NSG failed to come to an India-specific agreement in 29 May-2 June 2006 meeting, there were renewed bid to ensure that the agreement is finalized by the 109th Congress by the end of 2006. But as the things turned out, it was only the 110th Congress which approved the nuclear deal before the end of the 2008.

The Last Lap: The 123 Agreement is Approved by the U.S. Congress

After a long and tortuous journey, the first two milestones were reached:

1. The India-specific Safeguards Agreement with the IAEA was approved unanimously by the IAEA Board of Governors on 1 August 2008. Mr. Pranab Mukherjee told the Parliament on 20 October 2008: "As approved, the Safeguards Agreement reflects the key understandings upon which our civil nuclear initiative is based and enables their implementation. We will bring the agreement into force and offer facilities for safeguards in a phased manner in accordance with the provisions of the Safeguards Agreement and in keeping with our Separation Plan.
2. On 6 September 2008, the NSG adopted a decision by consensus which enables its members to engage in a full civil nuclear cooperation with India. This decision opens the door for India to resume civil nuclear cooperation with international community to meet its energy and development requirements. The significance of these two key developments was pithily put by Mukherjee in the Parliament on 20 October 2008: "As I had mentioned in my statement in this House (Lok Sabha) last July (2008), the IAEA approval and the NSG decision provide us the passport which allows us to engage in civil nuclear cooperation with our international partners. We are now in the process of getting visas by engaging with our international partners to negotiate and finalise bilateral cooperation agreements."

Two points need to be made in relation to these two agreements. First is about NSG 'bowing' before India. It needs to be mentioned that the NSG (then called London Suppliers Group—LSG) came into bring after India's 1974 Peaceful Nuclear Explosion (PNE) to block nuclear trade with India because of its "bad boy" act. Because, under the 1968 NPT, only five big boys could stage a big bang. India had not signed the NPT and still had the gall to stage a bang, PNE, in 1974. Hence, the birth of the LSG. But it failed to chastise India. Not only it refused to sign the NPT, it further staged an act of defiance by more bangs in 1998. The NSG further tightened the screw on India. But a decade later, ironically, the same NSG decides unanimously to allow India to engage in nuclear trade with its members! It, in a manner of speaking, was recognizing India as a major emerging power in the world arena—consequent to the lead given by the U.S. according this status to India through the U.S.-India nuclear deal.

Now a word on the duplicitous conduct of China on the NSG agreeing to nuclear trade with India by its members. China had publicly declared that it would not come in the way of NSG consensus on the issue. More than that, the Chinese Foreign Minister had told his Indian counterpart some months before the issue was to come up before the NSG that China would support the move. What was the reality? In the run up to the day of decision, China kept hiding behind some known no-sayers, without saying a word! And who were these nay sayers? These were small, 'insignificant' countries—essentially Scandanavians, and some others like Ireland, New Zealand, Japan, etc. When every one of these nay sayers fell in line, essentially because of frenetic diplomacy unleashed by India, then China had no option but to come out in its true anti-India colours. It was last ditch India had to cross. Prime Minister wanted to call up Chinese Prime Minister and President. Neither was "available" to take the call from Indian Premier for more than 24 hours! Finally, it had to be a call from President Bush which did the job. They fell in line like a contrite mischievous boys! The details were given in the press. India should remember this incident when the Chinese keep repeating "friendship" mantra while talking about India. This duplicity revived age-old hostility China has nurtured against India!

Situation after the 6 September 2008 NSG Decision

After the July 2005 and March 2006 agreements between India and U.S., the next most important milestone in the journey was Safeguards Agreement with the IAEA, without which nothing could move by way of nuclear trade. When it was reached on 1 August 2008, the NSG made its decision on 6 September 2008. With the latter decision, the door was open for any country to conclude bilateral pact with India regarding the nuclear trade—but so was not the case with the U.S., whose

Congress was to pass a law to allow nuclear trade between India and the U.S. Its name was Hyde Law, and this domestic law contained some provisions, which some analysts thought, had adverse implications for Indo-U.S. nuclear deal. The final milestone in this long-drawn affair was the Agreement for Cooperation between the Government of India and the Government of the United States concerning Peaceful Uses of Nuclear Energy (also, popularly known as the 123 Agreement) singed in Washington by Pranab Mukherjee and Condoleezza Rice on behalf of their respective countries on 10 October 2008.

As there was strong opposition to the nuclear deal within the U.S., so was the case in India. For nearly two years, the CPM-led Left Front had held the Congress-led UPA Government to ransom—not permitting it to move on the issue. CPM was important on this question, because it was supporting the UPA Government. It had held a gun to the government: "If you go ahead with the deal, we will withdraw support!" That would have reduced the government to a minority in the Parliament. In a democratic polity, a minority government could not have concluded such an all-important agreement with a foreign nation. The government found a way out. It enlisted the support of the Mulayam Singh-led Samajwadi Party (SP) and dared the Left to do what it wants to! After the Left did so, the government decided to have the issue debated in the Parliament. 22 July 2008 was the day fixed for the issue. The government won the motion on a tender majority but not before some dramatic moments during the day-long vote! That was when the BJP MPs flaunted wads of currency notes (worth a couple of lakhs) which they claimed were offered to them to vote for the motion. Though nothing came out of this high drama, some analysts thought it was the low tactics enacted by some politicians! Be that as it may, events moved swiftly on the question of nuclear deal after this debate in Parliament:

1. The IAEA plenary approved the India-specific Safeguards Agreement on 1 August 2008.
2. The NSG adopted a decision permitting its members to engage in nuclear trade with India.

3. 123 Agreement was signed on 10 October 2008 between India and U.S.

Now to an important practical aspect of the nuclear deal on 30 September 2008, India signed an Agreement for Cooperation in Civil Nuclear Energy with France during the PM's visit to France. A similar agreement was signed with Russia during the visit of its President to India in December 2008. The UK too is on board in this connection.

Interesting Tactics by Various Actors

The situation was certainly not re-assuring till the Parliament gave vote of confidence to the ruling UPA on 22 July 2008. The situation can be described in the following words:

> So many blessings to seek, so little time. The Indo-U.S. deal has to be approved not only by the legislative leg of the Washington power tripod it must also clear hurdles in 45 capitals (of NSG nations) in Europe, Asia and the Americas. Additionally India must work out a safeguards agreement with the IAEA, the nuclear matchdog of the world, for its civilian nuclear reactors. The multiple tracks have to move swiftly, smoothly and simultaneously so that the lack of progress in one does not block the other.

In a word, the whole world had to nod, adjust its glasses, and learn to look at India differently before benefits could accrue to it from this landmark agreement. But each power centre wanted the other to make the first declaratory move: The NSG wanted the U.S. Congress to approve the deal before committing itself; the U.S. Congress demands India's safeguards agreement with the IAEA, and the IAEA wants the layout and designs to craft an India-unique inspection agreement. So, there are games within games, being played out by various actors and entities.

"It is a circle like everything else in politics", said Hans Lundberg, Sweden's ambassador to the IAEA in Vienna, with a hint of delight.

Sweden is an Important Member of the NSG

It should be of interest to delineate the timeline being deferred time and again. May be, these datelines were set in an overly optimistic frame of mind. In a manner of speaking, it was case of ground realities overwhelming the optimism! At the late 2005 meeting, the U.S. had asked the NSG—the group controls all nuclear trade—to give India an "exemption", and there was a general expectation of decision by May 2006. Some analysts thought that through such an expectation, the U.S. seemed to be taking the NSG for granted. It was obviously a case of optimism running amok! But the March 2006 meeting in Vienna showed the NSG needed more time. The group's decisions are made by consensus, a state not easy to achieve with so many actors. U.S. Ambassador to the IAEA, George Shulte, who attended most of the confidential consultations, said the (March) meeting was "an important step forward" in putting the deal in a broader strategic context. "We would like to have a decision sooner rather than later", he said while stressing that there was no deadline. If May 2006 deadline was too much to wish for, the U.S. must have fervently, if secretly—'subconsciously' is, perhaps, a better term—hoped for decision in November 2006 session of the NSG. But even here, there was one looming, precipitated by the U.S. legislative calendar, mid-term Congressional elections in November and a possible winning or loss of a republican majority. The politics of convincing the NSG will be hard but not impossible. But in the event, the NSG did not grant "exemption" to India even in its November 2006 plenary.

It was generally understood after the two countries signed the March 2006 Separation Plan that it was for New Delhi to obtain the India-specific Safeguards Agreement from the IAEA and the U.S. was to obtain exemption for India from the NSG. It seems by mid-2006, the U.S. found the task too onerous to be achieved single-handedly by Washington. So, a U.S. diplomat thought selling the deal to the NSG was an Indo-U.S. "joint venture" and both "have to take serious 'retail diplomacy'". It was no wonder that India launched a diplomatic drive. If Minister of State Anand Sharma dashed to South Africa and Brazil and several MEA officials fanned out to different NSG-country capitals. Ronen Sen, India's Ambassador to the U.S., was traveling non-stop trying to cover all 50 states to energise opinion in favour of the agreement. The two top men in their respective fields were already vigourously on their jobs. Anil Kakodkar, Chairman, Atomic Energy Commission of India, had rushed to Vienna on 16 April 2006 to begin talks on the safeguards agreement with Director General of IAEA, Mohamed ElBaradei. Foreign Secretary Shyam Saran, by then officially the frequently-flying FS, had launched a round of curry diplomacy when he hosted NSG ambassadors soon after his Washington trip in April 2006.

If at one time, Washington and New Delhi hoped to get the deal approved before the term of the 109th Congress ended in 2006, it looked difficult if the U.S. legislative calendar would find it possible to accommodate discussion/approval of the 123 Agreement signed by the U.S. and India on 10 October 2008. These fears were born out of the fact that not only the U.S. lawmakers were engaged in two-year long frenetic electioneering, but also because, to top it all, the all-important voting was due on 4 November 2008. Over this all, there is a provision in the U.S. law that a bill must sit in the Congress for 30 days before it can be taken up for discussions in either House. In the event, the two Houses granted a waver to this stipulation, and the 123 Agreement was signed on 10 October 2008. The Indo-U.S. nuclear deal was passed by the Congress before the end of 2008.

It was not that entities like the IAEA and NSG were playing games as to who should make the first, even the two principals were engaged in various plays aimed at outplaying each other! One example should suffice. When the 123 Agreement was ready for signature, US Secretary of State Rice rushed to New Delhi to affix her signatures to it, with her Indian counterpart. There was a reason behind her rushing post-haste to India. She did not want India to know what all President Bush will say in his statement to the Congress while forwarding the 123 Agreement for its consideration. India was keen to see what wording the President uses regarding the application of the Hyde Law provisions about nuclear tests by India in future. India's contention was that the Hyde Law was a U.S. domestic legislation which cannot be applicable to an international/inter-nation agreements signed by the U.S. with any other nation. So, Rice returned without signing the 123 Agreement. Later when Bush sent the 123 Agreement to the Congress with a forwarding letter, the language used by Washington in the letter was found acceptable by India. So Mukherjee travelled to Washington and affixed his signatures to the document, with his counterpart.

India is Satisfied

All said and done, India is happy with the end product. Its reasoning is summed up hereafter:

- These agreements represent a careful balance of rights and agreements. The agreements India signed with France, U.S. and Russia provide for cooperation in various aspects of nuclear fuel cycle. They include the fuel supply assurances which are the basis of India's civil nuclear initiative as well as its right to build its strategic fuel reserves, to ensure the uninterrupted operation of its civil nuclear reactors under IAEA safeguards. These agreements and the India-specific Safeguards Agreement also provide for India to take corrective measures if necessary. These are interlocking provisions which fully protect India's rights.
- These agreements also ensure India's right to reprocess the nuclear material that it obtains from its international partners. India will be setting up a new national reprocessing facility and taking other steps necessary to operationalise these agreements and realise the full potential of the civil nuclear initiative.
- India regards these decisions/agreements as a vindication and recognition of its impeccable non-proliferation credentials. When the enabling bilateral cooperation agreements are brought into force they will provide the legal framework to negotiate and finalise commercial arrangements to source nuclear fuel for India's strategic fuel reserve as well as other nuclear equipment and technologies covering the nuclear fuel cycle.

- In achieving this result India has ensured that these agreements only relate to cooperation in civil nuclear energy and that its strategic programme and indigenous research are not affected. India's three stage indigenous nuclear programme will continue as envisaged by Dr. Homi Bhabha. Our bilateral agreements with countries like France and U.S. and Safeguards Agreement include specific provisions which ensure that there will be no hindrance to India's strategic programme even as it engages in international cooperation in civil nuclear energy.
- With these agreements, India will have new opportunities to expand its nuclear power capacity greatly, effectively bridging the energy deficit by 2030 AD, as explained above.

Critics are not Convinced

India's right to future nuclear tests has been a contested issue from the word go. A leaked American draft, seeking to make India agree to a complete loan on nuclear tests as part of the civilian nuclear deal, had embarrassed many government officials in April 2006 even as the MEA quickly rejected it saying the provision had no place in the proposed bilateral agreement. The 22-page draft (123) Agreement sent by the U.S. to New Delhi had stipulated that the U.S. would discontinue cooperation if India detonated any nuclear explosive device. The U.S. also tried to impose the CTBT on India calling it "essential" for the U.S. Congress to approve the deal.

India strongly contested both the propositions. India had a declaratory policy of voluntary, unilateral moratorium on nuclear testing but it asserted that it cannot be part of any bilateral treaty. India made it clear that it was bound only by what is contained in the 18 July statement, that is continuing its commitment to a unilateral moratorium on nuclear testing.

It must be stated that the U.S. insistence to include the provision in the 123 Agreement was uncalled for—if not futile. The U.S. Atomic Power Act already has a similar provision banning nuclear trade with nations if they carry out a nuclear test. Given all these conditions, India is not willing, still, to make a legal commitment to abjure further nuclear testing.

A voluntary moratorium can be lifted at will. Nuclear hardliners in India, including the BJP, do not want to write off the option of further tests to develop a fusion (hydrogen) bomb. India claimed it successfully tested a fusion assembly in 1998, but independent experts opine it turned out to be a dud.

The other contentious issue is a treaty to ban the production of fissile material, the fuel that goes into nuclear weapons. In early May 2006, the U.S. introduced a FMCT at the UN Conference on Disarmament (CD) in Geneva. In the past, India indeed was lukewarm towards the FMCT, because it regarded it as a measure to limit the size of its nuclear arsenal. India (like Pakistan) is still producing and stockpiling fissile material, whereas the major nuclear-weapon states have a surplus of it. But in the nuclear deal, initialled in July 2005, New Delhi had to make a concession on the issue.

"This is part of small price that India paid for the deal", says Achin Vanaik, Professor of International Relations and Global Politics at Delhi University. "The US is keen on an FMCT because it wants to freeze nuclear competition among the major states at the present level. China resists this and would like the CD to negotiate a treaty to ban an arms race in outer space before it takes up the FMCT." China is especially anxious about Washington's plans for "Star Wars"-style ballistic defence (BMD). Beijing believes the BMD programme is targetted primarily at China.

By committing itself to "work with" Washington on getting the FMCT passed, New Delhi has signalled that it stands by the U.S., not with China. India has nevertheless entered a minor caveat by emphasizing the issue of verification of the FMCT.

At the end of the day, while the government maintains it has not surrendered its strategic sovereignty on the issue of nuclear testing, merely maintaining the voluntary ban, the opposition BJP accuses it of having sold India's interests short. After all, it was the BJP Government that, in 1998, conducted a series of tests and declared India a nuclear weapons state. It deserves a mention that it was the BJP's Vajpayee-led NDA Government +that had offered the voluntary moratorium in the wake of the 1998 nuclear tests.

This introductory is a brief delineation of events, starting with joint statement of 18 July 2005 and two nations affixing their signatures on the 123 Agreement of 10 October 2008. It was a roller coaster journey extending over three years. In a manner of speaking, it was a thriller, full of suspense and uncertainties at every nook and corner. Fruition of this enterprise looked doubtful so very doubtful at every turn. This was so not only because there was opposition to it from within the two countries engaged in this exercise, the entire world, led by the non-proliferation die-hards—christened ayatollahs, by some—was ranged against the agreement. After a strenuous and tortuous journey, it seemed stuck in the last mile hamstrung by the tight legislative calendar of the U.S. Congress. The presiding persons of the two Houses had to cut corners on the urgings of the President to ensure its passage before 110th Congress ended its term in 2008. The cause of concern was that the 111th Congress might have more Democrats in its ranks who might not show the same accommodation towards these nuclear agreements as the Republicans.

Some facts, like the duplicitous conduct of the Chinese at the NSD plenary, which are not generally in the public domain have been included in this backgrounder. At the end, President George W. Bush and Prime Minister Manmohan Singh deserve a compliment for their single-minded determination, perseverence and fervour that enabled them to achieve the desideratum, their common goal, at the end of it all.

The Indo-U.S. Nuclear Deal: Struggle to Defend National Sovereignty

3

Prakash Karat

The civilian nuclear cooperation deal with the United States is only one part of the wider-ranging alliance that the UPA Government sought to forge with the United States. The strategic alliance with the United States as stated in the joint statement of July 2005 by the Indian Prime Minister and the U.S. President has four aspects. The political, which involves India joining the U.S. bandwagon of "spreading democracy" around the world; the economic, involving a strategic partnership based on a blueprint for U.S. capital; the military, expressed through the Defence Framework Agreement; and fourthly the Nuclear Cooperation Agreement.

Prior to the joint statement of July 2005, the UPA Government signed a ten-year Defence Framework Agreement with the United States. It is evident that without the defence agreement, the Americans would not have agreed for the nuclear cooperation. This seems to be part of a *quid pro quo*.

Strategic Alliance with U.S.

The Manmohan Singh Government has followed on the footsteps of the BJP-led Government in accepting the U.S. rhetoric on democracy. All the India-U.S. joint statements accord primacy to "democracy" and "freedom". This implicitly conveys the message that India is politically and ideologically with the U.S. in its crusade to project democracy and freedom as weapons to enforce regime change, prise open economies and establish U.S. hegemony in countries and regions. If the BJP-led Government enthusiastically joined the democracy bandwagon by co-sponsoring the Community of Democracies the UPA Government embraced the Global Democracy Initiative announced in the July 2005 joint statement. The UPA Government has forked out $10 million for the UN Democracy Fund, which has been set up under U.S. urging.

Two significant steps in the economic sphere were announced in the Bush-Manmohan Singh joint statement issued during the Bush visit to India in March 2006. A report of the U.S.-India CEO Forum titled "US-India Strategic Economic Partnership", which was released during the Bush visit, was welcomed in the joint statement "agreeing to consider its recommendations". Secondly, a U.S.-India Agricultural Knowledge Initiative, which was announced during Manmohan Singh's U.S. visit, was formally launched. The unequal nature of the strategic economic partnership between the American and Indian corporates can be gauged from the fact that 21 out of the 30 recommendations of the CEO Forum were exclusively meant for India, most of them in the form of demands for policy changes related to specific sectors of the Indian economy to the obvious benefits of the U.S. corporates. This includes liberalization of norms for infrastructure investments, market-driven reforms in the power and oil & gas sector, further liberalization of the telecom sector and ensuring a "level playing field" between the private and public sector telecom companies, raising the FDI cap in the Insurance sector, liberalization of norms for FDI in banking, liberalization of FDI norms in retail trade, removal of FDI caps in sectors such as print media, broadcasting, cable and satellite systems and e-commerce, liberalizing restrictions on FDI in the real estate and initiating urban reforms like removal of urban land ceiling, reducing stamp duty, etc. liberalization of defence procurement norms, liberalization of FDI in higher education and so on. The Deputy Chairman of the Planning Commission, who also co-chairs India-U.S. Economic Dialogue, had promptly announced the formation of 24 committees to take the recommendations of the CEO Forum forward. While such alacrity to serve the interests of the U.S. corporates met with domestic opposition, the Report of the CEO Forum continues to be displayed in the official website of the Planning Commission. The CEO Forum recommendations have since been earnestly pursued by the UPA Government, often overriding the NCMP.

The vision of foreign and domestic agri-business driven agriculture underlying the Agricultural Knowledge Initiative is inappropriate for a country like India dominated by peasant agriculture. The efforts by the UPA Government to allow large scale procurement of foodgrain by corporates, promote contract farming and futures trading in foodgrain and open up retail trade to FDI are influenced by such a distorted vision, which is in conflict with the commitments made in the NCMP.

Defence Agreement

The ten-year Defence Framework Agreement was signed in June 2005. It was a precursor to the joint statement issued in July, just three weeks later. Such a wide-ranging military collaboration agreement has not been signed by India with any country since independence. The agreement provides for joint operations by the two armed forces in military operations outside the auspices of the United Nations; the agreement aims "interoperability" of the armed forces; the two sides will work for missile defence cooperation; sale of US weapons to India and co-production is another feature.

Under this pact, India has agreed to work out a Logistics Support Agreement (otherwise known as the Acquisition and Cross Servicing Agreement) with the United States and a Maritime Security Cooperation between the two navies. Regular joint exercises and military training of Indian officers in the United States are already underway. This Defence Framework Agreement alone is sufficient to change the entire security and strategic orientation of India.

Following the announcement of the bilateral nuclear cooperation agreement in July 2007, Nicholas Burns, the Under Secretary of State, who was responsible for negotiating the bilateral agreement, in the official briefing after the 123

Agreement was reached, said: "And I think now that we have consummated the civil nuclear trade between us, if we look down the road in the future, we're going to see far greater defence cooperation between the United States and India: training; exercises; we hope, defence sales of American military technology to the Indian armed forces."

Implications of the Hyde Act

The intentions of the Bush Administration in working out a nuclear cooperation deal with India have unfolded since the July 2005 announcement. The discussions on the draft legislation in House of Representatives and the Senate, the briefings given by the Administration to the subcommittees of both Houses and the Hyde Act, which was eventually adopted, make one fact clear. The United States sees the nuclear cooperation deal as a key instrument to bind India to the U.S. global strategy.

However, the situation changed after the U.S. Congress adopted the final legislation to give a waiver for nuclear cooperation with India. This legislation known as the Hyde Act runs contrary to most of the assurances given by the Prime Minister in August 2006. The Act includes provisions imposing restrictions on transfer of technology and barring access to dual use technologies, thus denying India a full nuclear fuel cycle. The U.S. President has to report to the Congress every year on how India is complying with the provisions set out in the Hyde Act. The Act enjoins on the administration to prevent fuel supplies and equipment from other countries to India if the U.S. terminates the bilateral agreement. The argument that the bilateral text overrides the clause cannot be accepted, as the text also states that "national laws" will prevail. To say that the Hyde Act is not binding on India is irrelevant. The point is that it is binding on the United States.

Impact on Foreign Policy

Outside the sphere of nuclear cooperation, the Hyde Act contains directions on India's foreign policy and other security related matters. There are repeated references to India's role having to be one of support and complicity with the U.S. designs on Iran. The demand in the Hyde Act that India should have a foreign policy "congruent" to that of the United States, the expectation that India would join the Proliferation Security Initiative, and other demands, reveal how the U.S. expects India to conform as an ally.

The joint statement in September 2005 and February 2006 was followed immediately by India's *volte-face* on Iran in the International Atomic Energy Authority (IAEA), on two occasions. These moves against Iran at the IAEA, to which India became a party, set the stage for imposing immediate sanctions and later, an armed attack on Iran. Bush officials have now made public that India succumbed to the U.S. pressure in IAEA. U.S. Senator Richard G. Lugar in his opening remarks in the Senate Foreign Relations Committee had noted, approvingly, "We have already seen strategic benefits from our improving relationship with India. India's votes at the IAEA on the Iran issue last September and this past February demonstrate that New Delhi is able and willing to adjust its traditional foreign policies and play a constructive role on international issues."

The bilateral 123 Agreement that was finally concluded in July 2007 has failed to adhere to the assurances given by the Prime Minister. The text makes it clear that there will be a bar on transfer of technology dealing with enrichment, reprocessing and heavy water; there will be restrictions on access to dual use technology for these purposes, thus denying what the Prime Minister assured of cooperation for the full nuclear fuel cycle. Moreover, the assurance of an uninterrupted fuel supply is worded in such a manner which allows the "national law" to prevail, in this case the Hyde Act.

Nuclear Deal and Energy

The major argument advanced by the UPA Government is that the nuclear agreement is vital for India to end its nuclear isolation, without which it will not be possible to meet the country's energy requirements in the future. This ignores the very limited contribution that nuclear power makes to our overall energy generation which is less than 3 per cent. It cannot exceed 7 per cent even if the ambitious plans for expansion to 20,000 MW are implemented by 2020.

While talking about energy security, the cost of nuclear power has to be factored in. We should continue to develop nuclear technology based on the three-phased programme. But the expansion of nuclear power cannot become the central focus for energy security. The cost of power per unit generated for imported nuclear reactor will be twice that of a coal-based plant. The capital required to set up a plant with an imported reactor will be thrice that of a coal-based plant. So, what does it mean in terms of investment to set a target of 20,000 MW of nuclear power by 2020, or the more ambitious 40,000 MW target set out by the Prime Minister? The government has not conducted any techno-economic study on the feasibility and cost of nuclear power.

The implementation of the nuclear cooperation agreement will hamper the pursuit of an self-reliant nuclear technology policy for peaceful purposes based on the three-phase nuclear energy programme. There will be an unacceptable price to be paid. While negotiating for the nuclear deal, the United States simultaneously opposed India going ahead with the Iran pipeline project. The strategic alliance with the U.S. will constrain India from accessing energy from Iran and working for an Asian energy security grid which will link Central Asia, West Asia and South Asia.

After the Hyde Act was adopted in December 2006, the CPI(M) had stated that it contains provisions which are contrary to the assurances given by the Prime Minister to Parliament on August 17, 2006. The CPI(M) had repeatedly asked the government not to proceed with the bilateral negotiations for the 123 Agreement, till this matter was cleared up. But the government did not heed this advice too.

CPI(M) Stand: Strategy

Keeping all these factors regarding the nuclear deal in view, how did the CPI(M) formulate its stand and act? The CPI(M) programme, i.e. strategy, sets out the anti-imperialist task as a basic one along with the anti-feudal and anti-monopoly tasks. The fight against imperialist globalisation is to be carried on along with the fight against imperialist penetration within our country. As the programme states: "The imperialist driven globalisation and the policies of liberalisation adopted by the Indian ruling classes have heightened the imperialist penetration in all spheres in our country" (Para 3.25). The growing collaboration of the ruling classes in India with imperialism has also found its reflection in foreign policy. As the Programme points out: "The turn away from self reliance and recourse to foreign capital and liberalisation helped imperialism to further pressurise India which has manifested in several policy positions." Further, "The danger to foreign policy is real as the United States has long term plans to draw India into a strategic alliance to subserve its global designs against China and Russia" (Para 4.4).

This strategic perspective states that "A major struggle lies ahead for the Left and democratic forces to fight back the pro-imperialist direction in foreign policy and ensure that foreign policy retains its non-aligned basis and orientation to ward off imperialist pressures" (Para 4.6).

Forging a strategic alliance with the United States is a major step towards aligning India with U.S. imperialism. Being a basic issue of strategy concerning the fight against U.S. imperialism, the CPI(M) is irrevocably against this step.

Tactical Line

It is based on this strategic perspective that the Political Resolution of the 18th Congress of the Party while analysing the dangers of the current situation stated:

> The Party and the Left have to be vigilant about the role of imperialism, which the bourgeois parties ignore. But in domestic economic and political affairs and in foreign policy, the influence of imperialism and particularly the USA has grown. Here again, except for some shift in emphasis, the strategic collaboration with the US and its deep inroads remain. (Para 2.80)

It further underlined the link between the struggle against communalism, economic policies and imperialism by defining the present task as:

> The struggle against communalism and the economic policies are in fact connected to the anti-imperialist task, as both the Hindutva forces and the liberalisers are distinguished by their pro-imperialism. (Para 2.97)

The Party was enjoined to:

> take up the issue of foreign policy, oppose the succumbing to the pressure from imperialist finance capital and to work to check the imperialist influence penetrating different spheres of society. (Para 2.92)

In conclusion, the political resolution gave four major slogans to provide a direction to the Party. Alongwith an all-sided struggle against communalism; building a strong movement against the harmful economic policies of the central government and for alternative policies; the third slogan called upon the Party to oppose U.S. imperialist aggression globally and imperialist penetration in the country. Finally, all these three slogans are to be taken forward to strengthen the Left and democratic forces in the country.

Thus, based on the strategic understanding, the current political-tactical line of the Party has given importance to the struggle against the growing influence of U.S. imperialism in the country and the task of the Party and the working class to unite all anti-imperialist and progressive forces to fight back this trend.

Confrontation with UPA Government

The confrontation with the UPA Government on the strategic alliance with the United States and foreign policy did not come about suddenly with the finalisation of the nuclear deal. The Party Polit Bureau and the Central Committee had been noting since July 2005 the dangers inherent in the "strategic partnership" announced during the visit of the Prime Minister to Washington in July 2005. The Central Committee had noted in March 2006:

> In the last nine months, one of the main issues between the UPA government and the Left that came to the fore is the Indo-US strategic alliance and India's foreign policy. On the Iran nuclear issue, the government once again voted for reporting the matter to the Security Council in February 4,

> 2006. The whole situation will be changing with the new Indo-US equation and the strategic tie up. Our Party must understand the serious danger posed by this orientation of the UPA government. It will have serious repercussions for our economic sovereignty, independent foreign policy and lives of the working people.

When the UPA Government went ahead and finalised the 123 Agreement for nuclear cooperation with the United States in the third week of July 2007, the Party was faced with the question of what to do with an agreement that would cement the emerging Indo-U.S. strategic alliance that would have profound implications on our foreign policy and national sovereignty. The Party was faced also with the issue of how a government supported by the Left can be allowed to go ahead to forge such a strategic alliance with U.S. imperialism.

No Compromise on Strategic Tie-Up

The decision of the Polit Bureau which was endorsed by the Central Committee to block the agreement from going ahead was also governed by the fact that if U.S. imperialism succeeded in making India its strategic ally, it would have its impact on the international correlation of forces. India getting integrated into U.S. global strategy would be a "strategic gain" for the United States, in the words of the U.S. Secretary of State, Condoleezza Rice.

As a Party committed to fighting against imperialist hegemony and promoting multipolarity in international relations, it was inconceivable for the CPI(M) to support a government which facilitated such an alliance. The nuclear deal is the centre-piece of the overarching alliance the U.S. is keen to draw India into. Once such an agreement is operationalised India would be locked into a strategic tie-up which would have a long lasting impact on India's foreign policy and strategic autonomy.

Therefore, taking all the factors into account both external and internal, the CPI(M) Central Committee took a considered decision that all measures should be adopted, including if necessary, withdrawal of support, to prevent the UPA Government from going ahead with operationalising the deal.

After two months of sustained campaign and mounting pressure on the UPA Government, the Congress leadership finally decided to shelve the operationalisation of the nuclear deal. The stand of the CPI(M) and the Left also convinced the other partners of the UPA that it was not worthwhile to risk the fall of the government on this issue. This has been a significant step forward in the ongoing struggle to defend national sovereignty and an independent foreign policy. The Left succeeded in making foreign policy and strategic relations with the U.S. the main issue in national politics. In the process, the BJP was exposed as a pro-imperialist party. It began to reiterate that while it objects to certain features of the nuclear deal, it is for a strategic alliance with the United States.

Carry on Struggle against U.S. Imperialism

The CPI(M) conducted an extensive campaign amongst the people explaining how the strategic alliance and the nuclear deal will affect national sovereignty, an independent foreign policy and adversely impact on the livelihood of the people and their economic rights.

The united stand of the Left parties, the support it received from scientists, intellectuals, professional and the working people have opened up the possibilities for widening and deepening the struggle against imperialist penetration and defence of national sovereignty.

Economics of Nuclear Power from Heavy Water Reactors

4

M.V. Ramana, Antonette D'Sa and *Amulya K.N. Reddy*

The Department of Atomic Energy (DAE) has been promoting nuclear power as the "obvious choice for India to solve its energy problems in the long-term" (Bhoje, 2001). Such promises that nuclear power would play an important role in satisfying India's energy needs have been routinely offered since the 1950s, but the actual growth of nuclear power in the country has been extremely modest. As of January 2005, the total installed nuclear power generation capacity is 2,770 MW, less than 3 per cent of the total installed electricity generation capacity in the country.[1]

The promise offered by DAE is not only that nuclear power would form an important component of India's electricity supply, but that it would be cheap. As early as 1958, barely a few years after the DAE was set up, Homi Bhabha, the chief architect of the programme, projected "the contribution of atomic energy to the power production in India during the *next 10 to 15 years*" and concluded that "the costs of (nuclear power would) compare *very favourably* with the cost of power from conventional sources in many areas" (emphases added) (Bhabha and Prasad, 1958). The 'many areas' referred to regions that were remote from coal-fields. In the 1980s the DAE stated that the cost of nuclear power "compares quite favourably with coal fired stations located 800 km away from the pithead and in the 1990s would be even cheaper than coal fired stations at pithead" (Srinivasan, 1985b). This projection was not fulfilled. A more recent Nuclear Power Corporation (NPC) internal study comes to the less optimistic conclusion that the "cost of nuclear electricity generation in India remains competitive with thermal (electricity) for plants located about 1,200 km away from coal pithead, when full credit is given to long-term operating cost especially in respect of fuel prices".[2]

Despite its inability to live up to its promises, the DAE has always received high levels of financial support from the government, which have increased over the last few years (Table 1).[3] This government support has once again revived the hopes of the DAE for large-scale expansion; the DAE envisions having a total installed capacity of 20,000 MW of nuclear power by the year 2020 (Joseph, 1999). The largest component of this would be in the form of Pressurised Heavy Water Reactors (PHWR) (Chidambaram, 2001).[4]

This anticipated increase in nuclear power capacity, in particular the focus on PHWRs, makes an assessment of the economics of electricity generation in these reactors particularly relevant and urgent. Over a decade ago, a comparison of energy technologies had concluded that other options like coal and hydroelectric power were cheaper than nuclear power under realistic assumptions and "even if the projections and scenarios indicate large demand-supply gaps in the future, the most expensive way of bridging these gaps is through nuclear power plants" (Reddy et al., 1990).

The present study was undertaken with the hope that over the last decade more information on the expenditures actually incurred would have become publicly available, allowing a better and more reliable estimate of the costs of electricity generated in recently constructed and proposed reactors. This hope has been only partially realised. While the total expenditure on various reactors is available, details about operational and maintenance expenditure, the cost of producing heavy water, and so on, are not available in the public domain. Nevertheless, using the available current information, and making reasonable assumptions or extrapolations from other countries, we have calculated the 'busbar' cost of generating electricity (i.e. not including transmission and distribution costs) that is delivered to the grid (i.e. taking auxiliary or in-plant consumption of electricity into account).[5]

In order to assess the economics of nuclear power, one has to weigh these costs against the corresponding costs of generating power through some roughly comparable technology. For this purpose we follow the DAE's analyses and choose coal-based thermal power plants, which constitute 58 per cent of India's generation capacity (CEA, 2003). Like nuclear reactors, these provide base-load electricity.

Methodology

The conventional accounting procedure adopted often by Indian energy planners is the return-on-investment (ROI) approach. Here the unit energy cost includes four components: return on (capital) investment, depreciation of capital, annual costs of fuel and other materials, and operational and maintenance costs. Though widely used, this approach has important shortcomings. In particular, it ignores the time value of money and the gestation period of the project. For example, the total capital cost of the project is calculated by adding up capital expenditure figures from various years.[6] This means that a project that takes many years to build and generate electricity would appear equivalent to one with which delivers power in a shorter time but with the same total investment.

We, therefore, use the discounted cash flow (DCF) approach that is widely used in investment analysis (Brealey and Myers, 2000). This has been applied to earlier studies of the costs of nuclear power (Reddy et al., 1990), but we have fine-tuned it for this study by taking into account many of the sub-processes involved in nuclear power production. The principle underlying this approach is that money received today is worth more than the same amount of money received later, e.g. at an effective annual interest (or discount) rate of 10 per cent, today's one rupee would be equivalent to Rs 1.10 a year from now.[7] Therefore, the timing of cash inflows and outflows is important. In the DCF approach, all costs are discounted to some arbitrary but fixed reference date; the total cost reckoned at this reference point is the sum of the present values (PV) or future values (FV) of costs discounted to this date. Similarly one can calculate the present value of the revenues from the expected sale of electricity from the project. The levelised cost of electricity is then determined by setting the sum of discounted costs equal to the sum of discounted revenues.

We will express all costs in 2002 (fixed year) rupees. Our results will therefore be in terms of real discount rates rather than nominal rates. However, the two are equivalent. To convert costs from one year to another, we use the ratio of GDP deflators for the respective years as specified by the World Bank.[8] These are listed for the last 22 years in Table 2.

The cost of generating electricity consists of three main components: the capital cost of constructing the generating facility, the annual fuelling and operations and maintenance (O&M) costs, which must be incurred as long as the facility is running, and the waste management expenses from the running of the facility in an environmentally acceptable manner. One other component in the case of nuclear power is that of decommissioning the reactors. Though this is an expensive process, because it is done only many years into the future, its discounted cost will be small. In mathematical terms:

$$\text{PV (Costs)} = \sum_{1=-M}^{0} \frac{C_1}{(1+i)^1} + \sum_{k=1}^{N} \left[\frac{O_k + F_k}{(1+i)^k} \right] + \sum_{j=P+1}^{N+P+1} \frac{W_j}{(1+i)^j} + \sum_{q=N}^{N+T} \frac{D_q}{(1+i)^q}$$

where C_1 = capital cost in year 1; M = total number of years of construction before reactors becomes commercial; i = real discount rate; N = number of years of operation; O_k = operations and maintenance (O&M) cost in year k of operation; F_k = fuel cost in year k of operation; W_j = waste disposal cost in year j; P = cooling time for spent fuel; D_q = decommissioning cost; T = number of years after completion of operations before decommissioning is expected to take place. Note that in the first term on the right hand side of the equation, all of the exponents

Table 1: Government Outlay for DAE
(in Crores of Rupees)

	1997-98	1998-99	1999-2000	2000-01	2001-02	2002-03	2003-04	2004-05	2005-06
Budget estimate	1,836.53	2,608.06	2,962.01	2,750.57	2,779.39	3,868.95	3,800.09	4,469.97	4,995.86
Revised budget	1,996.33	2,418.12	2,682.04	2,745.21	2,768.59	3,351.69	3,738.77	4,240.46	

Source: Union Expenditure Budgets 1998 through 2005 (Plan + Non-plan expenditure)

Table 2: GDP Deflator Data for India
(Base Year: 1993)

Year	1981	1982	1983	1984	1985	1986	1987	1988	1989	1990	1991
Deflator	36.1	38.9	42.3	45.5	48.7	52.0	56.8	61.6	66.7	73.7	83.9
Year	1992	1993	1994	1995	1996	1997	1998	1999	2000	2001	2002
Deflator	91.3	100.0	109.7	119.5	128.2	136.5	147.3	153.0	159.9	165.4	172.0

Source: The World Bank database (available on the Internet to subscribers)

in the denominator are non-positive since the index runs from –M to 0.

The present value of the revenue generated by selling electricity is given by

$$\text{PV}(\text{Revenues}) = C_e \sum_{k=1}^{N} \frac{E_k}{(1+i)^k}$$

where C_e = levelised cost per kilowatt hour (kWh), and E_k = energy in kWh generated in year k.

When calculating the price of electricity from a power plant that is yet to be constructed, it is normal to assume that annual energy production is constant. It is also assumed that the O&M, fuel, and waste management costs will increase due to inflation, but are constant in real terms. Since we will be working in fixed year rupees, they will be constant in our calculations.

We will find that the results of our analysis depend sensitively on the discount rate used. There is no consensus on what this rate should be since it is an expression of how planners wish to allocate resources and how they value future benefits in comparison with current sacrifices. The Central Electric Authority has been using a 12 per cent discount rate in their calculations for planning and evaluation of projects (Bose, 2000). So has the Planning Commission. However, this is a nominal discount rate and translates to a real discount rate of about 6-7 per cent at the prevalent 5-6 per cent inflation rates. Our calculations will use a real discount rate, which we vary in order to test the results.

Capital Costs

The largest component of the cost of producing electricity in the case of nuclear reactors is the capital cost of the reactor. Operating costs typically constitute only a small part of the cost of generating electricity in nuclear reactors. The capital cost consists of the construction cost, and the costs of the initial loading of fuel and heavy water. Within the DCF methodology, one does not include the interest during construction (IDC) that is often mentioned as part of the cost of reactors, since interest results from the need to borrow money and is not relevant when comparing alternative investments.[9] Inclusion of the interest component would make nuclear power projects more unattractive since they are capital intensive and take longer to construct; hence, this is a conservative assumption (i.e. favourable to nuclear power).

Capital costs can vary considerably. We consider two specific cases, one set of two reactors already commissioned, and another set being constructed.[10] In the first case, we use the actual costs of the two 220 MW reactors at Kaiga Nuclear Power Station (Kaiga I and II) that were commissioned in 1999. Along with the RAPS III and IV reactors, these are the newest reactors; thus, one expects that these would have incorporated the lessons of the DAE's experiences with earlier reactors and also be indicative of the future as far as similar reactors are concerned. In the second, we use the projected costs of the two 220 MW reactors at the same site (Kaiga III and IV) that are scheduled to be commissioned in December 2006 and 2007.

Construction Costs

The initial cost estimate of Kaiga I and II, which were originally scheduled to be completed in 1994 (Srinivasan, 1985a); reprinted in (Srinivasan, 1990: 127-37), was Rs. 730.72 crore (DAE, 1996: 67). However, these plants became critical only in 1999.[11] At the time of criticality, the cost of the project was estimated at Rs. 2,896 crore (DAE, 1996: 67).[12] The year-wise expenditure on the project is given in Table 3. In our calculations, we convert the expenditure for each year to 2002 rupees using the ratio of GDP deflators in Table 2.

Table 3: Expenditure Pattern (without IDC) for Construction of Kaiga I and II

Year	1983-84	1984-85	1985-86	1986-87	1987-88	1988-89	1989-90	1990-91	1991-92
Base cost (Rs crore)	3.45	7.95	15.33	26.52	14.42	35.31	65.12	118.62	149.53
Year	**1992-93**	**1993-94**	**1994-95**	**1995-96**	**1996-97**	**1997-98**	**1998-99**	**1999-2000**	**2000-01**
Base cost (Rs crore)	137.76	207.83	186.60	185.05	171.87	134.83	113.96	177.85	64.01

Source: DAE, 2002b

One reason for the long delay and cost-overrun in the case of the Kaiga I and II reactors was that the containment dome—the structure that is supposed to prevent the escape of radioactivity into the environment should an accident occur—of one of the units collapsed in May 1994.[13] But all the reactors built by the DAE have had cost overruns (Table 4).

Table 4: Capital Costs of Operating Reactors

Station	Capacity (MW)	Original Cost (Crore)	Revised Cost (Crore)	Criticality Year
TAPS I and II	2 × 160	92.99	—	1969
RAPS I	1 × 100[14]	33.95	73.27	1972
RAPS II	1 × 200	58.16	102.54	1980
MAPS I	1 × 220	61.78	118.83	1983
MAPS II	1 × 220	70.63	127.04	1985
NAPS I and II	2 × 220	209.89	745[15]	1989 and 1991
Kakrapar I and II	2 × 220	382.5	1,335	1992 and 1995
Kaiga I and II	2 × 220	730.72	2,896	1999 and 2000
RAPS III and IV	2 × 220	711.57	2,511	2000

Sources: DAE, 1996: 67; DAE, 2002b

A 1988 study by the Comptroller and Auditor General of India (CAG) of the Narora reactors listed 10 major heads of expenditure that had cost overruns of 188 per cent or more (CAG, 1988). The CAG concluded that the revision of costs by 95 per cent in 1982 and 64 per cent in 1985 indicates that the project got "approved on unrealistic cost estimates. Unrealistic cost estimates and optimistic time schedules make financial allocations and controls less meaningful." Cost increases, though not of such a large magnitude, have occurred with nuclear reactors in other countries as well.[16] There is, therefore, the strong likelihood that capital costs are likely to increase. Despite this, in order to be conservative, we will use the stated estimated costs for all upcoming reactors.

The financial sanction for Kaiga III and IV, the reactors being constructed at the same site as Kaiga I and II, is Rs. 4,213 crore, including an interest during construction (IDC) component of Rs. 534 crore, or about 12.7 per cent of the total (DAE, 2002b: 94). Later reports suggest that the NPC anticipates a shorter gestation time and has lowered the estimated cost to Rs. 3,282 crore (Lal, 2002). The reduction of the estimated costs are due not only to lower gestation times but also due to a reduction in the prevailing rates of inflation and interest, and government concessions given to mega projects (DAE, 2002a). It is not clear how much of the estimated cost is IDC. In line with the earlier DAE (2002b) estimate, we will assume that IDC constitutes 12.7 per cent of the total cost, or Rs. 416 crore.

Plant excavation work for these reactors started in March 2001 and they are scheduled to become critical in 2006 and 2007 respectively (NPC, 2004a). However, advance procurement for these reactors began as early as 1990-91 (DAE, 1991: 14). Up to March 2000, Rs. 394.05 crore had been spent on the project (DAE, 2002b: 94). Once again, we assume that 12.7 per cent of this constitutes IDC. We also assume that the expenditure was uniform over these years. For the remaining period and amount we assume a different pattern of annual expenditure, shown in Table 5, anticipating shorter construction times. This follows the pattern of expenditure for Canadian PHWRs (NEA, 1998: 60).

Table 5: Expenditure Pattern Assumed for Kaiga III and IV

Year before commissioning	–5	–4	–3	–2	–1	0
Fraction spent (per cent)	1.9	9.7	20.2	30.9	27.3	10

Source: NEA, 1998

Heavy Water Inventory Costs

Heavy Water (HW) reactors, as the name suggests, require heavy water—water with the hydrogen replaced by deuterium, a heavier isotope of hydrogen. The HW is used both as moderator (to slow down neutrons emitted during fission so that they have a higher probability of being captured by other fissile nuclei) and as coolant (to carry away the heat produced).

The initial coolant and moderator inventory requirements for each 220 MW PHWR are 70 and 140 tonnes of HW respectively (NEI, 1994). The NPC reportedly treats the initial HW requirements as a non-depreciating asset and calculates lease charges at 8 per cent per annum to be paid to the DAE

(Muralidharan, 1988). Within the DCF methodology, the correct way to include the cost is to treat the initial HW inventory as an up-front capital cost. However, at the end of the economic lifetime of the reactor when the ('leased') HW is returned to the DAE, there is a cash inflow, which must be discounted to the time of commissioning.

There are practically no public figures available for the amount of HW produced in the DAE's heavy water plants (HWP). The DAE annual performance budgets list, for example, the annual electricity production at various reactors; however, they conspicuously avoid giving any numbers for HW production. In the past, the DAE has claimed that because of its strategic value, it would not disclose the production levels.

What little information is available is suggestive of poor performance. In 1992, *The Times of India* reported that only 273 tonnes of HW were produced in all the HWP put together (Fernandez, 1992), implying an average capacity factor of about 50 per cent. The CAG report for 1988 reported that the "Tuticorin (heavy water) plant produced 20.6 per cent of the installed capacity in the last eight years" (i.e. between July 1978 and March 1986). The best production was 42.7 per cent of the design capacity. The plant has "been able to operate on an average for about 150 days...per annum" and "the consumption of spares and maintenance cost was high and Rs. 190 lakhs had been spent per annum on an average" (CAG, 1988).

The performance of HWPs appears to have improved; in 1998, 100 tonnes of HW were exported to South Korea (Anonymous, 1997).[17] In part, this surplus availability of HW is because the expected growth in nuclear power did not take place. Even in recent years, however, a number of plants have had prolonged outages. The Talcher plant, in particular, has been suspended for many years since the associated fertiliser plant has not been operating satisfactorily (DAE, 2000: 24-25). Similarly, during 2002-03 the plant at Tuticorin was affected by frequent outages of the connected fertiliser plant (DAE, 2003: 5). The Thal plant had extended outages in 1998-99, whereas the Hazira and Kota plants had prolonged outages in 1997-98 (DAE, 2000: 24; DAE, 1999: 20). Consequently in both years, the total target production in HW was not met.

The cost of HW produced in the DAE's plants has been a matter of dispute. For example, in 1983 the AEC quoted a price of Rs. 3,875/kg, whereas the CAG calculated that it should be Rs. 13,800/kg (Reddy, 1990). Since these estimates relied on the earlier plants, and newer plants appear to be performing better, we look at the case of the most recently commissioned HWP at Manuguru.

Sanctioned in 1982, the Manuguru HWP has an annual capacity of 185 metric tonnes (MT) of HW. The estimated cost of the Manuguru HWP when it was sanctioned was Rs. 421.60 crore. In 1989, the plant cost was revised to Rs. 661.58 crore. The plant finally started production in December 1991 (CAG, 1994). According to the CAG, the "total capital cost including interest during construction and excluding cost of spares came to Rs. 983.38 crore and the increase, with reference to the original estimated cost...was...133 per cent." When questioned about the cost escalation, DAE stated that "the grounds for sanction of this project was strategic and not commercial".

The DAE's initial estimate of the cost of production was Rs. 5,176 per kg of HW (Rs./kgHW). However, due to slippages in the project schedules and consequential delay in commencement of production, the cost of HW worked out to Rs. 7,529/kgHW as of February 1986 (CAG, 1994). This translates to about Rs. 24,880/kgHW at 2002 prices, in the same ballpark as the 1983 figure of Rs. 6,635/kgHW (Rs. 26,960/kgHW when inflated to 2002 prices) cited by the then head of the DAE (Ramanna, 1985). However, in its 1994 report on Manuguru, the CAG pointed out that "Due to further escalation, the cost would have gone up further—the figures for costing after commencement of production in December 1991 were not produced to Audit" (December 1993). There appear to be no further public estimates of the cost of the project. In order to be conservative, we will use the figure of Rs. 24,880/kgHW.

One can understand the rather high cost of HW from not only the high capital costs but also the extremely energy intensive nature of the processes involved in producing heavy water. Therefore, over the last few years, the DAE has been trying to implement energy efficiency measures. According to the DAE, during the period 2001-02, energy consumption was reduced by about 6 per cent, thereby effecting savings of around Rs. 85 crore (Anonymous, 2002).[18] Therefore, the total energy consumption bill was Rs. 1,416.67 crore. Excluding the Talcher plant where operations have been suspended, the total production capacity of all HW plants at that time was about 490 tonnes per annum. Even assuming an optimistic 80 per cent capacity factor, the energy cost of producing one unit of heavy water is Rs. 18,070/kgHW. Therefore, a total cost of Rs. 24,880/kgHW is quite plausible.

When calculating the cost of the initial loading of HW, one small but pertinent detail is that there is usually a period of about six months or more between the reactor becoming critical and starting commercial operations. For example, Kaiga II became critical on September 24, 1999 but started operating commercially only on March 16, 2000 (Anonymous, 1999b; NPC, 2004b). The reactor is loaded with fuel and HW well before criticality. To be conservative, we assume that the total time between loading with HW and uranium, and the reactor producing electricity commercially is six months. Therefore, just as there is a credit for the HW returned at the end of the reactor life, there will be an additional component in the initial capital cost.

Uranium Fuel Inventory

Another component of expenditure in setting up a nuclear reactor is the initial uranium loading. A 220 MW reactor uses 3,672 fuel assemblies, each containing 15.2 kg of uranium oxide. The cost of each assembly is reported to be Rs. 2,50,000 (Subramanian, 2002b).[19] This translates to Rs. 16,450/kg of uranium fuel. This is comparable to, but less than, the 1983 price of Rs. 4,545 per kg of uranium fuel cited by the then head of the DAE, when translated to 2002 rupees (Ramanna, 1985).

The NPC obtains its fuel from the Nuclear Fuel Complex. Rather than pay the production costs plus a reasonable rate of return, the fuel is reportedly 'hired' at an administrative price set by the DAE (Wood, 1991). However, the true cost of nuclear electricity must include this cost. A 1985 paper by the DAE suggests that 50 per cent of the cost of initial uranium fuel loading is already included in the capital cost estimates (Srinivasan, 1985a); reprinted in (Srinivasan, 1990: 127-37). Even assuming this to be true, within the DCF methodology we have used, the remaining 50 per cent of the cost has to be included as part of the initial capital costs. Again, because of the assumed six-month period between fuel loading and the commercial delivery of electricity, there is an additional component to the fuel cost.

We will also assume that the nuclear plant stores about 1.5 months worth of uranium (at the assumed capacity factor) and HW (to account for expected losses) and incorporate this as a capital cost.[20]

Decommissioning Costs

Within the DCF methodology, the cost of decommissioning a reactor, which is done at the end of the economic life of the reactor and a long period of cooling, which we assume to be 40 years, should be incorporated as a capital expense. While there is little experience with actually decommissioning nuclear reactors and how much it costs, agencies that promote nuclear energy typically assume that decommissioning would cost between 9 per cent and 15 per cent of the initial capital cost of a nuclear power plant (UIC, 2001). There are other estimates. The US Nuclear Regulatory Commission estimates the cost of decommissioning nuclear reactors to be about $300-450 million (NRC, 2004). Since the typical US nuclear reactor costs about $1,500/kW and has a capacity of 1,000 MW, this is equivalent to 20-30 per cent of capital costs or $300-450 per kW. On the higher side, decommissioning the 1,240 MW Superphenix is estimated to cost $4,000 per kW.

Though based on some limited experience, the numbers cited above are only estimates. Actual experiences have often been significantly more expensive. Decommissioning the 100 MW Niederaibach HW reactor cost $1,910 per kW while the 45 MW Japan Power Demonstration boiling water reactor cost $3,180 per kW (WISE, 1998).

Nevertheless, in order to be conservative, we will assume that decommissioning expenses are 10 per cent of the initial capital cost. Decommissioning is usually divided into three stages (Saddington, 1983). In rough correspondence with these stages we assume that 40 per cent of the decommissioning expenses occur when the reactor is shutdown at the end of the economic life of the reactor, another 20 per cent at 20 years following shutdown, and the remaining 40 per cent, 40 years after shutdown.

As mentioned earlier, there is no consensus on what the discount rate should be chosen for calculations of economics of electricity generation. This debate is most intense when it comes to costs that are borne by future generations.[21] Choosing a large discount rate would mean that future expenditures are given very little weight in economic calculations. Some economists have proposed that in the interests of intergenerational equity, such activities should be valued at a zero or a very low discount rate (Howarth and Norgaard, 1993). One suggested approach is to use two discount rates, one for the near term expenditures and one for long-term expenditures. For example, the Charpin report on the future of nuclear energy in France chooses a 6 per cent discount rate for expenses in the first 30 years and a 3 per cent discount rate for expenditures thereafter (Charpin et al., 2000). Decommissioning expenses would fall in the latter category. For simplicity and in order to be conservative (i.e. favourable to nuclear power), we choose the same discount rate for all expenditures, which, as mentioned earlier, is varied in our calculations.

Recerring Costs

Rvel Load Costs

The amount of fuel needed to produce a unit of electric power is given by the formula:

$$\text{Fuel Used} = \frac{\text{Electrical power generated}}{[(\text{thermal efficiency}) \times (\text{burn up})]}$$

The thermal efficiency is the electricity generated per unit thermal power output. The burn up is the heat liberated per unit mass of fuel irradiated; it depends on the reactor type, the fuel used (level of uranium enrichment), and fuelling practices. In the case of the PHWRs we are considering, the average burn up is 7,000 MWD/tU (megawatt-day per tonne of uranium) (Hibbs, 1997a; Changrani et al., 1998). The thermal efficiency for PHWRs is taken to be the design efficiency of 0.29 (Balakrishnan, 1999). In terms of gross generation, the uranium utilisation is 20.5 mg/kWh (milligram per kilowatt-hour).

Heavy Water Make-up Costs

There are also routine losses of heavy water in PHWRs. This is due to many reasons. For example, during the initial years at the Rajasthan Power Station, there were several failures involving heat exchangers (Ghosh, 1996). These have HW on one side and cooling water on the other. Thus, when they fail, the HW could get mixed with cooling water and escape. There have also been a number of HW leaks and spills—in 1997 alone, such leaks occurred at the Kakrapar I, MAPS II and Narora II reactors (IAEA, 1998: 301-20). Such leaks could occur due to various causes. For example, on April 15, 2000, vibration caused the failure of a gasket in the moderator system piping of the Narora II reactor and 7 tonnes of HW leaked out (AERB, 2001: 13).

Typically some of the HW that is spilt or has otherwise escaped is collected, purified and reused but the rest is discharged into the atmosphere. This creates a radiation hazard to workers and potentially the general public due to the tritium build-up in the HW (Ramana, 1999).[22]

In the early years of RAPS-I operations, routine escape and losses were fairly high (Table 6). These have since reduced. In the 1980s, the DAE estimated that the annual HW make-up requirement for two 235 MW reactors (subsequently de-rated to 220 MW) was 16 tonnes/year (Ramanna, 1985). More recently, the first managing director of the NPC states that the annual make-up of HW in a 220 MW reactor is 7 tonnes/year (Kati, 2003: 39). Another report mentions that average

Table 6: RAPS-I Heavy Water Escape and Losses

Year	Escape (kg/day)	Loss (kg/day)	Annual Loss (Tonnes)
1972	135	31	11.3
1973	197	69	25.2
1974	249	57	20.8
1975	386	77	28.1

Source: Srinivasan, 1990, p. 24

HW losses for the Kakrapar reactors were "between 500 and 600 kg/month", or about 6 to 7.2 tonnes per year (Hibbs, 1997b). We will assume that each 220 MW reactor loses 7 tonnes/year.

Operations and Maintenance Cost

Operating and maintaining a nuclear power plant involves a number of expenses including paying the many trained professionals needed to run the plant, materials for maintenance, site monitoring, operating waste management facilities, collecting and purifying heavy water that escapes, and so on. Once again there is little data available publicly. We will assume that this is 2 per cent of the capital cost.[23]

Waste Management

The problem of dealing with radioactive nuclear wastes has been one of the most contentious aspects of nuclear power programmes around the world (NEA, 1996 and Berkhout, 1991). Since some of these wastes are extremely long lived, the generation of these wastes represents a burden to future generations who do not utilise the electricity produced in these nuclear reactors but may have to undertake measures to ensure that these radioactive materials do not enter their food chain, water resources, and so on. Any attempt at quantifying the costs involved is bound to have enormous uncertainties. Nevertheless, the approach used by nuclear power advocates has been to use the cost of setting up a structure that is expected to contain the radioactive materials within it for a long period of time as the cost of waste management. Despite the controversies involved, we shall follow this approach.

Most of the radioactivity produced is contained in the spent fuel, i.e. fuel after irradiation in nuclear reactors. Besides this, large quantities of low-level solid and liquid wastes are also produced during reactor operation and maintenance.[24] These are largely treated on-site and we will assume that the expenses incurred therein are included in the operations and maintenance costs.

Countries around the world have adopted one of two approaches to deal with the highly radioactive spent fuel. In the first, the spent fuel is 'directly disposed' by keeping them first in intermediate storage and eventually storing them in geological repositories. The other approach is to 'reprocess' the spent fuel to extract plutonium and the unused uranium, and concentrate the most highly radioactive components in the spent fuel into liquid 'high level waste'. Though controversies remain, it is generally accepted that direct disposal is the cheaper method of dealing with nuclear wastes at current uranium prices on the international market (Berkhout, 1997; NEA, 1994; Bunn et al., 2003). At current uranium prices, (Bunn et al., 2003) estimate that reprocessing adds "more than an 80 per cent increase in the costs attributable to spent fuel management (after taking account of appropriate credits or charges for recovered plutonium and uranium from reprocessing)" and the difference in costs "is likely to persist for many decades."

The DAE has adopted the more expensive route of reprocessing to deal with spent fuel. The rationale offered for this choice has been the three-stage programme envisioned by the DAE. The first stage involves the use of uranium fuel in PHWRs, the second stage involves fast breeder reactors that use plutonium from reprocessed spent fuel from PHWRs and thorium to produce uranium-233, and the third stage involves reactors using uranium-233 and thorium (Kakodkar, 2000). Since the second stage of the programme requires plutonium, reprocessing is needed to proceed with this programme. This requirement is used by the NPC to neglect the cost of waste disposal from PHWRs. In the NPC's analysis of the economics of PHWRs, "the cost of waste disposal has been assumed to have trade off with the amount of reprocessed fuel generated for next stage of nuclear power programme" (Nema, 1999).

Even if one were to follow the NPC's logic and assume that the hugely expensive infrastructure needed for reprocessing is a part of the second stage of the nuclear power programme, there is still the cost involved in dealing with the spent fuel prior to reprocessing. Because the spent fuel as it comes out of the reactor is highly radioactive and produces a lot of heat, it is initially kept under water for cooling. In India, this is done for a minimum of 430 days (Changrani et al., 1998). In practice it may be more, even up to 5 to 10 years, which would increase the waste management costs at the nuclear power plant (Srinivasan, 1995). Then it has to be shipped to the reprocessing plant.[25] Once again because of the high radiation levels (even after cooling), spent fuel shipping containers must be heavily shielded, and must be designed to stringent safety standards. For these reasons the cost of spent fuel shipping is not an insignificant component of the fuel cycle cost (Graves, 1979: 261). The OECD's Nuclear Energy Agency quotes a price of $13 per kilogram (1991 US dollars) for transporting spent fuel from PHWRs (NEA, 1994: 78). Converting this to 2002 rupees, this is equivalent to Rs. 878/kg of spent fuel.

To estimate the cost of waste management, we will assume that the spent fuel is simply handed over to the reprocessing plant and the only cost incurred as part of the fuel cycle of the PHWR is the cost of transportation. This is a very conservative assumption when calculating the electricity price from PHWRs. A fairer evaluation would attribute at least part of the reprocessing expenditures to the electricity generation costs at PHWRs.

Performance

The cost of electricity depends on the efficiency, measured in terms of load factor or capacity factor, with which the generation facility operates. This cost varies inversely as the capacity factor. For long, the DAE's reactors were among the poorest performers in the world. In December 1994 *Nuclear Engineering International*, a standard trade journal, found that the average lifetime load factor for Indian reactors was 36.08 per cent, the lowest among the 18 countries with four or more nuclear reactors; only Brazil, with just one reactor, fared worse (Howles, 1995). Four years later, this position was unchanged with the lifetime average load factor still the lowest (Anonymous, 1999c). However, the performance of the NPC's reactors has been improving over the last few years. This suggests that the NPC is over its teething problems. But it also reflects the recent dramatic increases in funding for the DAE (Table 1). Further, at the level of individual reactors, performance has remained erratic. For example, in 2002-03, the Kakrapar-I reactor had a record 98 per cent capacity factor, but it decreased to 78 per cent in 2003-04, and has deteriorated further in the 2004-05 (NPC, 2004c).

This improved performance of nuclear reactors must be balanced with two factors. First is the fact that similar improvements in performance have also been noted in many other sources of power. The average load factor in thermal power plants, for example, has increased from 54 per cent in 1990-91 to 69.97 per cent in 2001-02, with plants of capacity greater than 250 MW having an average load factor of over 80 per cent (CEA, 2002). Performance of the plants run by the National Thermal Power Corporation (NTPC) has been significantly better; these increased from 70 per cent in 1992-93 to 84.4 per cent in 2003-04 (NTPC, 2004). The second factor is that with the commissioning of several reactors over the past few years—more than half of the currently installed capacity was commissioned during the 1990s—the average age of the reactor units is low. As these age, one would expect to see a deterioration of performance as well as increased costs to keep them running.

It is instructive, therefore, to look at the average lifetime load factors of the DAE's PHWRs (Table 7). The average of these is 65.1 per cent. To accommodate the possibility of improved performance and to be favourable to nuclear power, we will assume a capacity factor of 80 per cent as the base figure in our calculations. This is much higher than the value of 68.5 per cent (or 70 per cent) commonly assumed in setting tariffs in power purchase agreements. Such a high capacity factor partially offsets the capital-intensive nature of nuclear power.

Table 7: PHWR Load Factors Until 2003
(in Per Cent)

Station	Cumulative Load Factor
RAPS I	23.31
RAPS II	52.65
MAPS I	52.82
MAPS II	52.92
NAPS I	60.62
NAPS II	67.82
Kakrapar I	70.91
Kakrapar II	84.14
Kaiga I	80.70
Kaiga II	80.91
RAPS III	77.98
RAPS IV	79.20

Source: Power Reactor Information System (PRIS) Database, International Atomic Energy Agency, available on the Internet at http://www.iaea.org

Another aspect of plant performance is the amount of electricity consumed by the power plant itself. The official in-plant consumption for all electricity-generating plants is 7-8 per cent (NTPC, 2004; CSO, 1999). However, looking at actual figures for gross generation and net exports at the DAE's nuclear reactors, the in-plant consumption figures in per cent, are 13.4, 12.4, 11.5, 11.3, 12, 11.7, and 11.9 for each of the years between 1994-95, and 2000-01 respectively (DAE, 1997: 10; DAE, 1998: 14; DAE, 1999: 12; DAE, 2000: 13; DAE, 2002b: 27). We will, therefore, assume 12 per cent for the in-plant consumption in the case of the Kaiga reactors.

Costs of Coal Power

For calculating the cost of producing electricity from coal, we chose the case of the Raichur VII Power Station (RTPS VII). Like the Kaiga I and II reactors, RTPS VII is also a relatively recent plant. It has a capacity of 210 MW, roughly the same as each of the Kaiga reactors, and is an example of multiple projects at the same location (just as Kaiga III and IV are co-located with Kaiga I and II). Being in the same geographical region, it feeds into the same grid and therefore faces roughly similar problems from grid instabilities.

The RTPS VII project was sanctioned on March 4, 1999 and the plant was synchronised to the grid on December 10, 2002; till March 2003, the total expenditure came to Rs. 491.33 crore (CEA, 2004a).[26] This is less than the sum often quoted as the expenditure on the plant because it does not include IDC. The annual expenditures during the four years 1999, 2000, 2001, and 2002 are assumed to be 10 per cent, 40 per cent, 40 per cent, and 10 per cent of the total. As with nuclear plants, we will assume that the plant stores about 1.5 months' supply of coal and furnace oil and incorporate this into the capital cost.

Operation and maintenance expenses at thermal plants are usually set at 2.5 per cent of the capital cost and we will follow that practice (Mahalingam, 2001). Based on actual generation data at the Raichur units (CEA, 2002), we use an auxiliary consumption rate of 8.5 per cent. We will assume that the RTPS VII station has an economical lifetime of 30 years (as opposed to 40 years for the Kaiga reactors).

The main expense in producing electricity from thermal power stations is the fuel. The fuel cost depends on the amount of coal used to generate one unit of power. At the other Raichur stations (RTPS I to VI), the coal consumption for 2001-02 was 0.63 kg/Wh (CEA, 2002). We assume the same consumption rate for RTPS VII.

The two primary qualities of coal that are of interest to thermal power plants are the calorific (energy) content and the proportion of ash. Inferior grade varieties of coal have lower calorific content and higher ash content. Since the quality of coal used varies from plant to plant and over time, we follow the expert committee on fuels for power generation and assume a standardised coal grade with calorific content of 3,750 kCal/kg (CEA, 2004b). The basic cost of this grade of coal at the pithead including taxes, duties and royalty is estimated by the expert committee to be Rs. 517/tonne; the distance from Raichur to the coal producing regions of Eastern India is about 1200 km and the cost of freight for distances above 1,200 but below 1,500 km is Rs. 894.9/tonne (CEA, 2004b).[27] Thus, the effective cost of domestic coal at the Raichur plant works out to be about Rs. 1,412/tonne.

The corresponding cost for imported coal with calorific content of 5,400 kCal/kg at the port is about Rs. 1,925/tonne; the distance from Raichur to Mangalore port is about 450 km and the cost of freight for distances between 300 and 500 km is Rs. 251/tonne. Thus, the effective cost of imported coal at the Raichur plant works out to about Rs. 2,175/tonne. With these figures, the levelised cost of electricity using imported coal is about Rs. 0.03/kWh higher than when using domestic coal. Thermal plants also use furnace oil, whose consumption at the Raichur plant is about 2 ml/kWh. Its price is about Rs. 18/litre (NTPC, 2005).

All these prices are, of course, subject to market fluctuations and standard inflationary increases. In principle, the price of uranium would also be subject to similar changes.[28] We will ignore the fluctuations since these should get averaged over the long lifetime of the plant. The inflationary increases are implicitly taken into consideration by working in fixed-year Rupees.

Just as we included the cost of waste disposal in the case of nuclear power, here we include the cost of disposal of ash. Typical ash content in Indian coal is about 40 per cent, of which about 80 per cent is fly ash and the balance 20 per cent is bottom ash (CPCB, 2000). In 1999, the ministry of environment and forests stipulated that all coal thermal power plants should utilise the fly ash generated for manufacturing bricks, road laying, making embankments, in landfills, and so on. The same notification also ordered brick manufacturers, public works departments, the National Highway Authority, and other agencies to use ash generated in coal plants. The ash is, at least initially, to be provided free of cost. However, there are definite savings for the end-users in terms of reduced requirements for various inputs.[29]

In the case of the Raichur thermal plant, the fly ash generated is used for the manufacture of portland pozzolona cement (PPC) by the Associated Cement Companies, which has exclusive rights to collect fly ash for free from three of the seven plants at that site (Giriprakash, 2001). The use of fly ash for PPC manufacture lowers the costs of cement production due to reduced requirements for thermal and electrical energy, and lower consumption of clinker. Therefore, in general, PPC manufacturers have been willing to pay the costs of transporting the fly ash from thermal plants (Shah, 1999). In some cases, they have even been willing to purchase the fly ash.

Both fly ash and bottom ash can be used to manufacture bricks, in landfills, and to build roads and embankments. The cost of using fly ash for brick manufacture have been estimated (Bhattacharjee and Kandpal, 2002a). Using these numbers, and assuming the same figures for the case of bottom ash as well, we estimate an ash disposal cost of not more than Rs. 174/tonne (Table 8).

At Rs. 174 per tonne of ash, the disposal cost for coal with 40 per cent ash content is Rs. 0.05/kWh. It should be emphasised that this is costlier than current practice because it assumes that the power plant bears part of the cost for a more environmentally benign way of disposing waste. This is also more expensive than using the ash for cement manufacture. However, in order to be conservative, i.e. favourable to nuclear power, we use this figure.

In line with the current government policy, we have not imputed any economic costs for the air pollution resulting from coal-based thermal plants. Though such pollution has gained in policy relevance with the heightened concern about global warming, inclusion of pollution costs remains problematic for many reasons, especially in the context of a comparison with nuclear power. This is because the pollution externalities for nuclear power are difficult to quantify for many reasons. Two proximate ones are the scientific and political controversies surrounding the health impacts of low level radiation and the lack of reliable data on radioactive emissions from nuclear facilities and the impossibility of independent verification of the scarce data available in the Indian context (Ramana and Gadekar, 2003). Finally, unlike carbon dioxide, which has substantial sinks in the terrestrial and marine ecosystems, there is no way to render radioactive materials benign. Hence, the environmental and public health impacts of long-lived radioactive wastes could occur well into the future, possibly tens of thousands of years from now. There are inherent problems with quantifying these. Thus, it is all but impossible to make a fair comparison of environmental externalities between coal power and nuclear power.

Table 8: Cost of Making Fly Ash Bricks

	Percentage I	Percentage II
Fly ash bricks cost differential (Rs. per 1000 bricks)	100	100
Volume per brick (cm^3)	1795.4	1795.4
Density of brick (kg/m^3)	1770	1770
Mass of 1000 bricks (kg)	3177.8	3177.8
Fly ash utilisation in fly ash clay brick	0.25	0.25
Fly ash utilisation in fly ash sand lime brick	0.6	0.6
Percentage of fly ash clay bricks as fraction of total fly ash based bricks (assumed)	50	30
Percentage of fly ash sand lime brick (assumed)	50	70
Fly ash used in 1000 fly ash based bricks (tonnes)	1.35	1.57
Cost of fly ash utilisation (Rs./tonne-fly ash)	74.0	63.6
Transportation cost (Rs./km/tonne)	2	2
Assumed distance of transport to brick kiln (km)	50	50
Cost of fly ash utilisation including transport costs (Rs./tonne)	174	163.6

Results and Comparison

We now compare the costs of nuclear power from the Kaiga I/II and Kaiga III/IV reactors and cost of thermal electricity from RTPS VII using domestic coal. Table 9 summarises the figures used in our calculations.

As mentioned earlier, the cost of electricity is calculated as a function of discount rate. We begin with the comparison for a (real) discount rate of 1 per cent. As seen in Table 10, the

Table 9: Figures Used in Calculations

	Kaiga I and II	Kaiga III and	RTPS IV VII (D)
Sum of annual construction costs[30] (Rs. Crore)	1,816	2,866.88	491.3
Power plant capacity (MW)	440	440	210
In-plant consumption (per cent)	12	12	8.5
Economic lifetime (years)	40	40	30
Uranium fuel price (Rs./kg)	16,450	16,450	
Initial uranium loading (tonnes)	111.6	111.6	
Fraction of initial fuel cost included in Capital Cost	0.5	0.5	
Assumed burn-up (MWD/tU)	7,000	7,000	
Uranium utilisation (kg/kWh (gross))	2.05E-05	2.05E-05	
Heavy water price (Rs./kg)	24,880.00	24,880.00	
Initial heavy water loading (tonnes)	420	420	
Heavy water losses (kg/year)	14,000	14,000	
Transport of spent fuel (Rs./kg)	878	878	
Decommissioning cost (fraction of capital cost) (per cent)	10	10	
Coal cost (Rs./tonne)			1,412
Coal calorific content (kCal/kg)			3,750
Coal Consumption (kg/kWh)			0.63
Coal ash fraction (per cent)			40
Ash disposal cost (Rs./tonne)			174
Furnace oil consumption (ml/kWh)			2
Furnace oil cost (Rs./litre)			18
O and M cost (fraction of capital cost) (per cent)	2	2	2.5

Table 10: Levelised Costs (in Rs./kWh) of Different Options for Discount Rate of 1 Per Cent, Capacity Factor of 80 Per cent, Economic Lifetime of 40 Years for Nuclear Reactors, 30 Years for Thermal Plant

	Kaiga I and II	Kaiga III and	RTPS IV VII (D)
Capacity cost (including O&M) Rs./kWh	0.65	0.67	0.27
Heavy water make-up cost (Rs./net kWh)	0.13	0.13	0
Fuel cost (Rs./net kWh)	0.38	0.38	1.01
Waste disposal cost (Rs./net kWh)	0.02	0.02	0.05
Total levelised cost (Rs./kWh)	1.18	1.20	1.33

levelised cost of electricity from nuclear reactors is lower than the case of RTPS VII (using domestic coal). The cost of nuclear power is dominated by the capacity cost whereas that of thermal power is dominated by the fuel cost.

Since only the capacity cost varies with discount rate, for other values of the discount rate we only list the total levelised cost. These are listed in Table 11. The last row lists levelised costs for a real discount rate of 6 per cent, which, as mentioned earlier, roughly corresponds to the discount rate assumed by the Planning Commission and the Central Electric Authority.

Table 11: Total Levelised Costs (in Rs./kWh) of Different Options for Different Discount Rates, Capacity Factor of 80 Per cent, Economic Lifetime of 40 years for Reactors, 30 Years for Thermal Plant

Discount Rate (Per Cent)	Kaiga I and II	Kaiga III and IV	RTPS VII (D)
2	1.32	1.32	1.36
2.5	1.39	1.39	1.37
3	1.48	1.46	1.39
4	1.66	1.62	1.42
5	1.87	1.79	1.45
6	2.10	1.98	1.49

The exact value of the discount rate (i.e. the crossover point) at which the cost of thermal power becomes cheaper than nuclear power from Kaiga I and II stations is about 2.33 per cent (levelised cost of Rs. 1.366). While there is debate on the appropriate discount rate for public investments, few would argue that 2.33 per cent is a high rate for long-term investments, especially in a country with multiple demands for capital. The crossover point determined by Reddy (1990) varied from 5 to 7.5 per cent (nominal discount rate).

As mentioned earlier, the utilisation of a power plant (expressed through the capacity factor) is a determinant of the price of electricity generated. Since nuclear power is capital intensive, lower capacity factors would reduce its competitiveness. This is shown in Table 12 that lists the crossover point in discount rates for three different capacity factors. If the capacity factor is only 75 per cent, then nuclear power is cheaper than coal power only for discount rates lower than 1.7 per cent.

Table 12: Variation with Capacity Factor
(in Per cent)

Capacity factor	75	80	85
Crossover point between Kaiga I and II and RTPS VII (D)	2.0	2.33	2.65
Crossover point between Kaiga III and IV and RTPS VII (D)	1.93	2.33	2.7

The crossover point also varies with the assumed lifetimes of the power plants. If one were to assume that the economic lifetime of the coal plant is the same as that of the nuclear plant, i.e. 40 years, the crossover point (at 80 per cent capacity factor) between Kaiga III and IV and RTPS VII becomes 2.01 per cent, and that between Kaiga I and II and RTPS VII becomes 2.06 per cent. As mentioned earlier, all of these crossover points are unrealistically low values. Therefore, for realistic values of discount rates, nuclear power from the Kaiga reactors is more expensive than electricity generated in RTPS VII.

Conclusions

Our primary goal in this paper was to calculate in detail, dealing exhaustively with many of the sub-processes involved and using updated data, the cost of producing electricity from the DAE's pressurised heavy water reactors. We have done so in a transparent manner laying out the methodology and assumptions explicitly. This allows for the possibility that it can be corrected, should better data become available; given the limited amount of data publicly available, this is quite likely.

Our analysis demonstrates that electricity from PHWRs is more expensive for real discount rates above about 2-3 per cent, under most reasonable assumptions. Such rates may not be realistic over the decades that these plants are to operate.

One criticism of this study is that we have considered nuclear plants of smaller capacities, namely 220 MW, even though it is expected that electricity from larger capacity nuclear plants would be cheaper. And therefore, the argument goes, if one were to compare such larger sized plants, then electricity from nuclear reactors would be cheaper than electricity from similar sized coal based thermal power plants. There are two problems with this argument. First, the experience of the last five decades of nuclear power suggests that early predictions of costs are frequently wrong. This is especially true in the case of the DAE. In all the reactors constructed so far, final cost figures have been higher than originally estimated.[31] Thus, without experience with actually constructed reactors at lower prices, any claims about their cost should be viewed with some scepticism.

Second, a fair comparison would also include the effects of cost-cutting measures at coal based thermal plants, including both capital cost reductions and fuel cost reductions.[32] In this regard, RTPS-7 can be counted as an example of a plant that has reduced capital costs and construction times successfully. However, this reduced capital cost does not make the comparison of Kaiga nuclear plants with RTPS-7 an unfair one because its distance from coal mines is somewhat large, thereby increasing its fuel costs, which dominate the cost of producing electricity at thermal plants.

Considering that electricity from the 220 MW Kaiga plants is costlier than thermal power for a large range of parameters, the conclusion that nuclear power is more expensive than thermal power from coal is robust. This contradicts numerous claims by the DAE that nuclear power is cheaper than coal based thermal power at sites which are 800-1,000 km away from coal mines. Nuclear power plants, therefore, have been and remain a costlier way of trying to address India's electricity needs than coal based thermal plants.

NOTES

1. Two 540 MW reactors are due to become commercial soon raising the total nuclear capacity to 3,850 MW.
2. The summary of this study was published as (Nema, 1999). When asked for a copy of the full study, the NPC's spokesperson told one of the authors (MVR) that it was not available to the public.
3. For comparison, the final (revised) budget for the Ministry of Non-Conventional Energy Sources that is in charge of developing solar, wind, small hydro and biomass based power in 2002-03 was Rs. 473.56 crore. These sources between them comprise 4,800 MW of generating capacity (MNES, 2004), as compared to the 2,770 MW of nuclear power. Their contribution to actual electricity generation would, of course, be smaller because these are intermittent sources of power.

4. Pressurised Heavy Water Reactors use heavy water (in which the hydrogen atoms are replaced by deuterium, a heavier isotope of hydrogen).
5. This compares the economics of generating electricity from two different sources of power. Transmission and distribution costs are external to the production process itself and their inclusion would make the comparison dependent on the locations of the power plant and the load centres.
6. Even ignoring the time value of money, this is inconsistent because it adds rupees from different years without considering differences in purchasing power due to inflation.
7. The discount rate used here can be either a nominal discount rate d_n or a real (i.e. inflation corrected) discount rate d_r with the two options being related as: $d_r = (d_n - i)/(1 + i)$ or approximately $d_r = (d_n - i)$, subject to an error of $1/(1 + i)$. If inflation has already been taken into account (for example, when prices for one year are adjusted for another year using inflation rates), then the discount rate is a real discount rate.
8. The data is available on the internet to subscribers at http://www.worldbank.org/
9. In other words, the comparison is for an investor who already has the required funds.
10. The DAE typically constructs two nuclear reactors at one time at each site. This is why we treat the two reactors as one unit.
11. A nuclear plant is said to become critical when it starts sustaining a chain reaction. There is usually a period reserved for safety checks and other operational matters before the reactor actually starts supplying electricity to the grid.
12. This is in mixed year rupees, and cannot be directly compared with future reactors whose costs are given in present day rupees.
13. The collapse is usually termed "delamination" in official documents (Mohan, 1994). There was also a less publicised fire on the same dome (Anonymous, 1999a).
14. This was derated from 200 MW.
15. The revised cost estimates for NAPS, Kakrapar and Kaiga includes interest during construction.
16. For nuclear power cost increases in the case of the US, see Komanoff, 1981.
17. From the reported value of 20 million dollars for the 100 tonnes of heavy water exported, it would seem that the heavy water was probably sold below cost of production.

18. Elsewhere the savings have been quoted as being Rs. 100 crore (Anonymous 2001).
19. The article itself mentions a price of "about Rs. 25 lakh" for a fuel assembly. However, this appears to be a misprint or an error. When asked for clarification, the author confirmed that the engineers at the Nuclear Fuel Complex had actually mentioned a price of Rs 2.5 lakh (Subramanian, 2002a).
20. This is sometimes called working capital.
21. See the discussion in Bunn et al., 2003.
22. In the case of the leak at Narora-II on April 15, 2000, one worker received an internal dose of 47.12 mSv, well in excess of the 30 mSv annual limit on radiation doses to workers.
23. We thank the anonymous reviewer for suggesting this.
24. For an estimate of the quantities involved see Ramana et al., 2001.
25. Like most of the DAE's nuclear power stations, the Kaiga nuclear reactors do not have a reprocessing plant on-site. Therefore, if its spent fuel is to be reprocessed, it must be shipped to either Tarapur or Kalpakkam.
26. Expenses after that are considered part of O&M expenses.
27. We are being somewhat unfavourable to the cost of coal power since the kind of inferior grade coal that we have assumed for RTPS is available from points closer to Raichur.
28. In the case of uranium, however, one would expect to see an increase in the price over and above inflation in the not-too-distant future because of diminishing domestic reserves. We ignore this increase in order to be conservative.
29. For an estimate see Bhattacharjee and Kandpal, 2002b.
30. This is the sum of the actual expenditures incurred (or projected to be incurred, in the case of the Kaiga III and IV) and does not include interest during construction (IDC).
31. Even in the case of the 540 MW reactors coming up at Tarapur, the initial cost estimate was only Rs. 2,427.51 crore. The final cost estimate is of the order of Rs. 6,000 crore.
32. One way to lower fuel costs would be through coal washing, which decreases ash content, which in turn reduces transportation costs and increases plant efficiencies.

REFERENCES

AERB (2001): "Annual Report 2000-2001", Atomic Energy Regulatory Board, Mumbai.

Anonymous (1997): "India to Export Heavy Water to S. Korea", *Business Line*, November 1.

——(1999a): "Fire Breaks Out in Kaiga Plant Dome", *The Times of India*, November 13.

——(1999b): "Kaiga Goes Critical, to Generate Power from January 2000", *The Times of India*, September 25.

——(1999c): "Load Factors to End September 1998", *Nuclear Engineering International*, March, pp. 22-25.

——(2001): "India: Three-pronged Strategy for Enhancing N-power", *The Hindu*, April 26.

——(2002): "Heavy Water Board Performs Exceedingly Well", *Nuclear India*, July-August, p. 11.

Balakrishnan, Kamala (1999): "Alternate Fuel Cycles in the Indian PHWR", *BARC Newsletter*, April.

Berkhout, Frans (1991): *Radioactive Waste: Politics and Technology*, Routledge, London.

——(1997): "The Economics of Reprocessing", *Energy and Security*, October 2.

Bhabha, Homi J. and N.B. Prasad (1958): "A Study of the Contribution of Atomic Energy to a Power Programme in India" in *Proceedings of the Second United Nations International Conference on the Peaceful Uses of Atomic Energy*, Geneva, pp. 89-101.

Bhattacharjee, Ujjwal and Tara Chadra Kandpal (2002a): "Financial Evaluation of Coal Thermal Power Generation Costs in India: Effect of Incremental Costs of Fly Ash Utilisation" in *Proceedings of the World Renewable Energy Congress VII.*

——(2002b): "Potential of Fly Ash Utilisation in India", *Energy*, 27, pp. 151-66.

Bhoje, S.B. (2001): "Atomic Energy Obvious Choice for India: Interview with S.B. Bhoje, Director, IGCAR", *Frontline*, March 30, pp. 84-85.

Bose, Deb Kumar (2000): "Nuclear Power for Eastern India: No Basis for Choice", *Economic and Political Weekly*, September 23, pp. 3480-84.

Brealey, Richard A. and Stewart C. Myers (2000): *Principles of Corporate Finance*, 6 ed, Irwin McGraw-Hill, Boston.

Bunn, Matthew, Steve Fetter, John P. Holdren and Bob van der Zwaan (2003): "The Economics of Reprocessing vs Direct Disposal of Spent Nuclear Fuel", *Project on Managing the Atom*, Harvard University, Cambridge.

CAG (1988): "Report by the Comptroller and Auditor General of India", *Comptroller and Auditor General*, New Delhi.

——(1994): "Report by the Comptroller and Auditor General of India", *Comptroller and Auditor General of India.*

CEA (2002): "Performance Review of Thermal Power Stations 2001-02", Central Electricity Authority, http://www.cea.nic.in/opm/anu0102/31index.pdf, accessed on November 16, 2004.

——(2003): "All India Electricity Statistics, General Review 2002-03", Central Electric Authority, http://www.cea.nic.in/ge_re/2002-03/genrev4561.pdf, accessed on March 4, 2005.

——(2004a): "Broad Status of Thermal Power Projects in Karnataka", Central Electric Authority, http://www.cea.nic.in/data/opt2_const_mon_th_ index.htm, accessed on November 16, 2004.

——(2004b): "Report of the Expert Committee on Fuels for Power Generation", Central Electric Authority, Planning Wing, New Delhi, also available at http://www.cea.nic.in/Rep_fuels_gen.pdf.

Changrani, R.D., D.D. Bajpai and S.S. Kodilkar (1998): "Storage of Spent Fuel from Power Reactor in India: Management and Experience" in *Proceedings of the Storage of Spent Fuel from Power Reactors*, pp. 65-72, International Atomic Energy Agency, Vienna.

Charpin, Jean-Michel, Benjamin Dessus and René Pellat (2000): "Economic Forecast Study of the Nuclear Power Option", Office of the Prime Minister, Paris, also available at http://fire.pppl.gov/eu_fr_fission_plan.pdf

Chidambaram, R. (2001): "Nuclear Energy Needs and Proliferation Misconceptions", *Current Science*, July 10, 81(1), pp 17-21.

CPCB (2000): "Benefits of Beneficiated Coal in Coal Based Power Generation in India", Central Pollution Control Board, http://www.cleantechindia.com/bishtml/210301.18.htm, accessed on November 16, 2004.

CSO (1999): *Statistical Abstract: India, 1998*, Central Statistical Organisation, Department of Statistics and Programme Implementation, New Delhi.

DAE (1991): "Annual Report 1990-1991", Department of Atomic Energy, Mumbai.

——(1996): "Performance Budget 1995-96", Department of Atomic Energy, Mumbai.

——(1997): "Performance Budget 1996-97", Department of Atomic Energy, Mumbai.

——(1998): "Performance Budget 1997-98", Department of Atomic Energy, Mumbai.

——(1999): "Performance Budget 1998-99", Department of Atomic Energy, Mumbai.

——(2000): "Performance Budget 1999-2000", Department of Atomic Energy, Mumbai.

——(2002a): "Nuclear Power Generation: Targets and Achievements, 25th Report Presented to the Lok Sabha", Department of Atomic Energy/Lok Sabha Secretariat, New Delhi, also available at http:// 164.100.24.208/ ls/committeeR/Energy/25th.pdf.

——(2002b): "Performance Budget 2001-2002", Department of Atomic Energy, Mumbai.

——(2003): "Annual Report 2002-2003", Department of Atomic Energy, Mumbai.

Fernandez, Clarence (1992): "Heavy Going for Heavy Water Board", *The Times of India*, March 25, p. 7.

Ghosh, G. (1996): "Operational Experiences: Nuclear Power Stations", *Electrical India*, August 15, pp. 29-33.

Giriprakash, K. (2001): "ACC's New Cement Plant at Wadi Commissioned in Record Time", *The Indian Concrete Journal*, May: 307-310.

Graves, Harvey W., Jr. (1979): *Nuclear Fuel Management*, John Wiley, New York and Santa Barbara.

Hibbs, Mark (1997a): "First Separation Line at Kalpakkam Slated to Begin Operations Next Year", *Nuclear Fuel*, December 1, p. 8.

——(1997b): "NPC says Kakrapar Peer Review Should Dispel Foreign Safety Fear", *Nucleonics Week*, December 4, 38(49), p. 8.

Howarth, Richard and Richard Norgaard (1993): "Intergenerational Transfers and the Social Discount Rate", *Environmental and Resource Economics*, 3, pp. 337-58.

Howles, Laurie (1995): "Load Factors: 1994 Annual Review", *Nuclear Engineering International*, April, pp. 26-30.

IAEA (1998): "Operating Experience with Nuclear Power Stations in Member States in 1997", International Atomic Energy Agency, Vienna.

Joseph, Anto (1999): "India Plans to be Nuke Powerhouse by 2020, Sets a 20,000 MW Target", *The Economic Times*, September 16.

Kakodkar, Anil (2000): "Neutron Bomb Capability Exists: Interview with Anil Kakodkar", *Frontline*, December 22, pp. 89-91.

Kati, S.L. (2003): "Conceptual Design of Heavy Water Moderated Organic Cooled Reactor", *Nu-Power*, 17(4), pp. 36-39.

Komanoff, Charles (1981): *Power Plant Cost Escalation: Nuclear and Coal Capital Costs, Regulation and Economics*, Komanoff Energy Associates, New York.

Lal, M.M. (2002): "Slashing Construction Times and Pre-project Activities in Indian Nuclear Power Projects" in *Proceedings of the 13th Annual Conference of the Indian Nuclear Society* (INSAC 2002), INSAC, Mumbai.

Mahalingam, Sudha (2001): "A Worrisome Tariff Order", *Frontline*, February 2.

MNES (2004): "Annual Report 2003-2004", Minstry of Non-Conventional Energy Sources, Delhi, also available at http://mnes.nic.in/annualreport/ 2003_2004_English/index.html

Mohan, M. Madan (1994): "Kaiga Questions: A Gaping Hole in Safety Standards", *Frontline*, June 17, pp. 84-85.

Muralidharan, Sukumar (1988): "Birth of Nuclear Power Corporation", *Economic and Political Weekly*, January 30, pp. 190-92.

NEA (1994): "The Economics of the Nuclear Fuel Cycle", *Nuclear Energy Agency*, OECD, Paris.

——(1996): "Radioactive Waste Management in Perspective", *Nuclear Energy Agency*, OECD, Paris.

——(1998): "Projected Costs of Generating Electricity: Update 1998", Nuclear Energy Agency, OECD, Paris.

NEI (1994): "Power Reactors: Main Data for Individual Units", *World Nuclear Industry Handbook*, pp. 71-94.

Nema, A.K. (1999): "Nuclear Generation Cost in India", *Nu-Power*, 13(1).

NPC (2004a): "Kaiga Atomic Power Project 3 & 4", Nuclear Power Corporation, http://www.npcil.org/kapp3&4.asp, accessed on November 16.

——(2004b): "Kaiga Atomic Power Station", *Nuclear Power Corporation*, http://www.npcil.org/kaigaaps.asp, accessed on November 16.

——(2004c): "Kakrapar Atomic Power Station", *Nuclear Power Corporation*, http://www.npcil.org/kaps.asp, accessed on November 16.

NRC (2004): "Reactor Decommissioning Funding", US Nuclear Regulatory Commission, http://www.nrc.gov/reactors/decommissioning/funding.html, accessed on November 16.

NTPC (2004): "Power Plant Operations", National Thermal Power Corporation, http://www.ntpc.co.in/operations/operations.shtml, accessed on November 16.

——(2005): "Ramagundam Super Thermal Power Station—Stage III (500 MW): Tariff Petition for the Period 01.03.2005 to 31.03.2009", National Thermal Power Corporation, http://www.ntpc.co.in/bidsnotices/docs/ Ramagundam.pdf, accessed on March 9.

Ramana, M.V. (1999): "Disturbing Questions", *Frontline*, June 4, pp. 119-20.

Ramana, M.V. and Surendra Gadekar (2003): "The Price We Pay: Environmental and Health Impacts of Nuclear Weapons Production and Testing" in M.V. Ramana and C. Rammanohar Reddy, (eds), Prisoners of the Nuclear Dream, Orient Longman, New Delhi.

Ramana, M.V., Dennis George Thomas and Susy Varughese (2001): "Estimating Nuclear Waste Production in India", *Current Science*, December 10, 81(11), pp 1458-62.

Ramanna, Raja (1985): "Can Nuclear Energy Claim to be the Only Source of Power in the Future?" C.C. Desai Memorial Lecture, Administrative Staff College of India, March 4.

Reddy, Amulya Kumar N. (1990): "Nuclear Power: Is It Necessary or Economical?", Seminar, June, (1), pp. 18-26.

Reddy, Amulya Kumar N., Gladys D. Sumithra, P. Balachandra and Antonette D'Sa (1990): "Comparative Costs of Electricity Conservation, Centralised and Decentralised Electricity Generation", *Economic and Political Weekly*, June 2, 35(22).

Saddington, K. (1983): "Decommissioning of Nuclear Facilities" in W. Marshall (ed), *Nuclear Power Technology*, Clarendon Press, Oxford, pp. 335-67.

Shah, S.N. (1999): "Prism Cement Pins Hopes on Higher Net Cement Realisation", *Financial Express*, October 22.

Srinivasan, M.R. (1985a): "Economic Case for Small and Medium Power Reactors in India" in *Proceedings of the International Atomic Energy Agency General Conference*, International Atomic Energy Agency, Vienna.

——(1985b): "The Indian Nuclear Power Programme" in *Proceedings of the Indo-French Seminar on Nuclear Energy*, pp. 9-21, Department of Atomic Energy, Bombay.

Srinivasan, M.R. (ed) (1990): *Selected Lectures of Dr M.R. Srinivasan*, Department of Atomic Energy, Bombay.

Srinivasan, V.S. (1995): "Design, Planning and Siting of Spent Fuel Storage Facilities in India" in *Proceedings of an International Symposium on Safety and Engineering Aspects of Spent Fuel Storage*, International Atomic Energy Agency, Vienna, pp. 57-69.

Subramanian, T.S. (2002a): E-mail Communication, June 11.

——(2002b): "Fuelling Power", *Frontline*, March 29.

UIC (2001): "The Economics of Nuclear Power", Nuclear Issues Briefing Paper No. 8, Uranium Information Centre, Sydney, also available at http://www.uic.com.au.

WISE (1998): "Problems of Decommissioning Nuclear Facilities", *WISE News Communique*, January 23, p. 485.

Wood, Janet (1991): "Can Nuclear Pay Its Way in India?", *Nuclear Engineering International*, December, pp 52-53.

5

Feeding the Nuclear Fire

Zia Mian and *M.V. Ramana*

The July 18 joint statement by U.S. President George Bush and Prime Minister Manmohan Singh has attracted a great deal of comment. The focus has been the possible consequences of U.S. promises to support India's nuclear energy programme in exchange for India clearly separating its military and civilian nuclear facilities and programmes, and opening the latter to international inspection.

Much of the debate on the deal has been between what can be broadly called the nuclear hawks and the nuclear nationalists. The nuclear hawks believe India's nuclear programme is a great success and more than able to take care of itself. They see the deal as imposing unnecessary constraints on the programme and making more difficult the creation of the large nuclear arsenal, including thermonuclear weapons (hydrogen bombs), that they believe is essential for India to be a 'great power'.

The clearest expression of this has come from former Prime Minister Atal Behari Vajpayee and the BJP, who seek the largest possible nuclear weapons capability. Vajpayee has already argued that "Separating the civilian from the military would be very difficult, if not impossible.... It will also deny us any flexibility in determining the size of our nuclear deterrent." When he refers to "flexibility" in determining the size of an Indian nuclear arsenal, he does not mean that it should be possible to make it much smaller (if not eliminate it altogether).

He is expressing the fear that separating civil and military facilities may stop the arsenal from becoming as big as he and others like him might like it to be.

Nuclear nationalists have the less ambitious, more traditional perspective that sees the nuclear programme as a great national technological achievement and necessary for India's economic and social development. They see the deal as offering a way to sustain and expand the nuclear energy programme, while not unduly restricting the building of what they see as a 'minimum' nuclear weapons arsenal.

The government has embraced this view, as have many defenders of the deal. The Prime Minister laid it out most clearly to Parliament on July 29, saying "Our nuclear programme ...is unique. It encompasses the complete range of activities that characterise an advanced nuclear power...our scientists have done excellent work and we are progressing well on this programme as per the original vision outlined by Pandit Jawaharlal Nehru and Dr Homi Bhabha." He went on to argue that "nuclear power has to play an increasing role in our electricity generation plans" and the deal offers a way where "our indigeneous nuclear power programme based on domestic resources and national technological capabilities would continue to grow." The expected international support, both as nuclear fuel and nuclear reactors, would help "enhance nuclear power production rapidly." At the same time, he made it clear that "there is nothing in the joint statement that amounts to limiting or inhibiting our strategic nuclear weapons programme."

These two positions have by and large dominated the debate so far. There are many problems with both views. The first is their shared belief in the success of India's nuclear energy programme and the need to continue with and expand this effort. They fail to recognise that the deal is actually testament to the long-standing, expensive, and large-scale failure of the department of atomic energy (DAE) and its tremendous but largely hidden costs, in terms of health, safety, environment, and local democracy.

The second belief shared by the nuclear hawks and the nuclear nationalists is that nuclear weapons are a source of security. This belief has been extensively debunked.[1] Those who persist in this belief also ignore the essential moral, legal, and criminal questions of what it means to have and be prepared to use nuclear weapons. The only difference between the two camps is on the character and size of the genocidal weapons they aspire to, and how many people in how many cities they are prepared to threaten to kill.

A History of Failure

The establishment of the Atomic Energy Commission (AEC) in 1948 was framed by the rhetoric of indigenous national development. Led by Homi Bhabha, the AEC portrayed India as forging its own path in the new nuclear age. That was not to be. There was no progress until the UK offered the design details and enriched uranium fuel for the first Indian nuclear reactor, Apsara.[2] In what was to become a pattern, the official announcements when the Apsara reactor went critical declared it a "purely indigenous affair" (Abraham, 1997).

Similarly, the CIRUS reactor, which provided the plutonium used in the 1974 nuclear test (and quite likely some used in the 1998 tests as well), was supplied by Canada while the heavy water used in it came from the U.S. An American firm, Vitro International, was awarded the contract to prepare blueprints for the first reprocessing plant at Trombay. The first power reactors at Tarapur and Rawatbhata were supplied by the U.S. and Canada respectively. It was not just reactors. Many of India's nuclear scientists were made in America and elsewhere. Between 1955 and 1974, over 1,100 Indian scientists were sent to train at various U.S. facilities (Perkovich, 1999: 30, 482).

Extensive foreign support to the nuclear programme ended only after the 1974 nuclear test. The international community, led by Canada and the U.S., who were incensed by India's use of plutonium from CIRUS that had been given to the country for purely peaceful purposes, cut-off most material transfers relating to the nuclear programme. However, a little advertised fact is that various nuclear facilities still procured components from abroad and foreign consultants continued to be hired for projects.[3] DAE personnel still had access to nuclear literature and participated in international conferences where technical details were freely discussed.

Even with all this help, DAE's failures were many and stark. In 1962, Homi Bhabha predicted that by 1987 nuclear energy would constitute 20,000 to 25,000 MW of installed electricity generation capacity (Hart, 1983:61). His successor as head of the DAE, Vikram Sarabhai, predicted that by 2000 there would be 43,500 MW of nuclear power (Sarabhai, 1974: 89). In 1984, the 'Nuclear Power Profile' drawn up by the DAE suggested the more modest goal of 10,000 MW by 2000 (Ramachandran, 2000). None of these goals ever came close to being met.

After over 50 years of generous government funding, nuclear power amounts to only 3,400 MW, barely 3 per cent of India's installed electricity capacity. This capacity is expected go up by nearly 50 per cent over the next few years, but not because of the DAE. The largest component of this expansion will be two 1,000 MW reactors purchased from and being built by Russia.

This history of failure explains why the demands from the DAE and other nuclear advocates to gain access to international nuclear markets have became louder and louder over the last decade. It is only with international help that the DAE can ever hope to achieve its latest promised goal of 20,000 MW by the year 2020.

The other pressure driving this deal has been the DAE's extraordinary failure to manage its actually existing nuclear programme. In its determination to build more and more reactors, something to show for all the money that it gets, the DAE has failed to take account of the need to fuel them. This was evident in the statement from an unnamed official to British Broadcasting Corporation soon after the U.S.-India deal was announced, when he said: "The truth is we were desperate. We have nuclear fuel to last only till the end of 2006. If this agreement had not come through we might have as well closed down our nuclear reactors and by extension our nuclear programme" (Srivastava, 2005). The former head of the atomic energy regulatory board has reported that this is not a new problem, he notes that "uranium shortage" has been "a major problem for the officials of NPCIL and the Nuclear Fuel Complex (NFC) for some time" (Gopalakrishnan, 2005).

The issue is simple. Apart from Tarapur I and II, all DAE reactors are fuelled using uranium from the Jaduguda region of Jharkand. The total electric capacity of the heavy water based power reactors is 2,450 MW. At 75 per cent capacity, these require nearly 330 tonnes of uranium every year.[4] The reactors that are supposedly dedicated to making plutonium for nuclear weapons, CIRUS and Dhruva, consume perhaps another 30-35 tonnes. When mining started in Jaduguda, the average ore grade was about 0.067 per cent (Sarkar, 1984: 193). Now it is reportedly less than half that. The current mining capacity is around 2,800 tonnes of uranium ore per day. This means the DAE may only be producing about 300 tonnes of uranium a year. This falls well short of the fuelling requirements. DAE has been able to continue to operate its reactors by using stockpiled uranium from earlier days when the nuclear capacity was much smaller. Our estimates are that this stockpile would be exhausted by 2007.

The DAE has been desperately trying to open new uranium mines in the country. But it has been met with stiff public resistance everywhere (Dias, 2005). This local resistance stems from the widely documented impacts of uranium mining and milling on public and occupational health.

The limits on domestic uranium reserves have been known since the nuclear programme was started. This concern was the justification for the three-phase nuclear power programme that Bhabha originally had put forward and continues to be pursued (Bhabha and Prasad, 1958). This programme involves separating plutonium from the spent fuel produced in natural uranium reactors and setting up breeder reactors, which in turn could be used to utilise India's thorium resources for energy production. The three phases are far from being realised. DAE has failed to build and sustain enough natural uranium fuelled reactors for the first phase. The second phase is still experimental and the first plutonium fuelled power reactor is yet to be completed. Even if it becomes fully functional, breeder reactors are unlikely to be a significant source of electricity for several more decades at least (Tongia and Arunachalam, 1998). The thorium fuel cycle, the third phase, is still far in the future.

Implications of the Agreement for Nuclear Energy in India

If the deal goes through, the DAE will be free to purchase uranium from the international market for its safeguarded reactors. This has some important consequences. The first of these is that it will reduce pressure on domestic uranium reserves. Since imported uranium will be much cheaper than Indian uranium, it may also marginally reduce the operating costs of Indian nuclear plants. Although DAE hides its actual costs, there is little doubt that nuclear electricity is more expensive than other major sources of power in India (Ramana et al., 2005).

At the same time, access to cheap imported uranium will remove what has been DAE's primary justification for a large part of its long-term nuclear plan. For decades, the DAE has offered the shortage of domestic uranium as justification for the breeder programme. This is despite the fact that poor economics and countless engineering problems have effectively killed such breeder reactor programmes in the U.S., France and Germany. The high costs of breeder reactors stem from the need to have plutonium to fuel them. This plutonium is produced at reprocessing plants by chemically treating spent (i.e. used) nuclear fuel from ordinary reactors. The separated plutonium is then made into breeder fuel at special and costly fabrication plants. There are enormous economic costs, environmental damage, and potential public health risks that are associated with this whole scheme.

With cheap uranium being available to India, there will be no need for any of this. It can all be abandoned. Despite all this, DAE may not agree to give up its breeder reactor programme. It may choose to try to follow the example of Japan, which imports uranium to power its nuclear reactors and, ignoring the costs and risks, continues to pursue its breeder reactor. This will show, again, how DAE's institutional interests have triumphed again over economic good sense and concerns about health and environment.

The existing nuclear capacity and any increases in it, domestic or foreign, that the deal makes possible should not to be considered a benefit. Nuclear electricity is expensive and it would be far better to invest in other cheaper sources of power as well as energy conservation measures (Ramana et al., 2005). There are also important safety concerns associated with nuclear power. At least one of the DAE's nuclear reactors has come close to a major accident (Chanda, 1999: 1363). One can barely imagine the consequences of a Chernobyl-like accident involving the release of large quantities of radioactive materials at a reactor in a densely populated country like India.[5] Other facilities associated with the nuclear fuel cycle have also had accidents, though these have primarily affected workers within the plant (Anand, 2003: 100).

Apart from extreme accidents, there are many environmental and public health consequences associated with the many facilities that make up the nuclear complex (Ramana and Gadekar, 2003). A scientific study of the health consequences on the local population around the Rajasthan Atomic Power Station (RAPS) located at Rawatbhata near Kota observed statistically significant increases in, inter alia, the rates of congenital deformities, spontaneous abortions, stillbirths and one day deaths of new born babies, and solid tumours (Gadekar, 1996: 384).

And, to cap it all, there is the so far unsolved problem of managing large amounts of radioactive waste for many tens of thousands of years. The question that really needs to be discussed but has hardly figured in the debate is whether India needs any nuclear power plants at all. There are many who believe India would be better off giving up this costly and dangerous technology and finding ways to meet the needs of its people that do not threaten their future or their environment.

How Many Bombs are Enough

The nuclear energy and nuclear weapons programme have been linked from the beginning. This will continue under the nuclear deal. Access to the international uranium market to fuel its power reactors will further free up domestic uranium for the nuclear weapons programme and other military uses. This may allow a significant expansion in India's nuclear weapons capabilities.

There are several ways in which India could use its freed-up domestic uranium. It could choose to build a third reactor dedicated to making plutonium for its nuclear weapons. There have been proposals for a larger reactor to add to CIRUS and Dhruva at the Bhabha Atomic Research Centre in Bombay (Anonymous, 1999). India could also start to make highly-enriched uranium for nuclear weapons—Pakistan has used such highly-enriched uranium, produced at Kahuta, for its weapons. Both paths, which need not be exclusive, would allow India to increase its fissile materials stockpile at a much faster rate. A third use for domestic uranium would be in supplying the fuel for the nuclear submarine that has been under development since the 1970s (Rethinaraj, 1998). Limited uranium availability, and the need to keep the power reactors running, is quite likely to have restricted all such plans in the past.

India can use both its current stockpile of weapons-grade plutonium and future production from the CIRUS and Dhruva and other future plutonium production reactors to make nuclear weapons. The current stockpile is estimated to be perhaps 400-500 kg, sufficient for about 100 simple fission weapons. (It is usually assumed that 5 kg may be needed for a simple weapon. More sophisticated designs would typically require less plutonium.) CIRUS and Dhruva could continue to produce about 25 to 35 kg of plutonium a year. This means that by 2010 the potential arsenal size could be about 130.

The above estimate is purely on the basis of existing facilities known to be making weapons useable fissile material. There could be other sources. Power reactors could have been or could be used to make weapons-grade plutonium by limiting the time the fuel is irradiated. Run this way, a typical 220 MW power reactor could produce between 150-200 kg/year of weapons-grade plutonium when operated at 60-80 per cent capacity.

Another source of weapons useable material is the stockpile of plutonium in the spent fuel of power reactors. Though it has a slightly different mix of the plutonium isotopes from the special weapons-grade plutonium normally used for weapons, it can be used to make a nuclear explosive (Mark, 1993). The U.S. conducted a nuclear test in 1962 using plutonium that was not of weapons-grade. One of India's May 1998 nuclear tests is also reported to have involved such material (Perkovich, 1999: 428-31).

Over the years, some 8,000 kilograms of reactor-grade plutonium may have been produced in the power reactors that are not under safeguards. Only about 8 kg of such plutonium are needed to make a simple nuclear weapon. If this spent fuel is not put under safeguards, i.e. declared to be for military purposes, as part of the deal, India would have enough plutonium from this source alone for an arsenal of about 1,000 weapons, larger than that of all the nuclear weapons states except the U.S. and Russia.

Lastly, there is the plutonium that is produced in Kalpakkam in the small fast breeder test reactor. Much more plutonium will be produced by the 500 MW prototype FBTR now under construction. It is curious that ever since the 1960s, DAE has resisted placing the breeder programme under international safeguards. This is despite that fact that both Germany and Japan, neither of them nuclear weapon states, ran their breeder reactor programmes under such safeguards. The purpose of these safeguards is to prevent plutonium or uranium from civil nuclear facilities from being used to make nuclear weapons. DAE's resistance to safeguards begs the question as to whether the breeder programme is, or ever was, only for civilian purposes.

A.N. Prasad, former director of the Bhabha Atomic Research Centre (BARC), has argued that these large stocks of weapons-useable material are beside the point. The deal should be rejected because "Our military activities are not aimed at stockpiling nuclear weapons." He suggests that this was to overcome the problem that "the weapons become old, their materials degrade, they have to be dismantled and replaced" (Varadarajan, 2005).

This is disingenuous. It is estimated the plutonium used in U.S. nuclear weapons may not need to be replaced for somewhere between 45 and 60 years. The material can then be recycled and reused again in making new nuclear weapons. Moreover, many of the aging effects that the plutonium experiences can be avoided with proper storage. Therefore, existing stocks of plutonium can probably last indefinitely far into the future. All other nuclear weapons states have stopped producing new material for their nuclear weapons programmes—only India, Pakistan, and Israel seem to be still producing new weapons material.

Another nuclear weapons material is tritium, a gas used to boost the yield of fission weapons many fold. The DAE claims to have tested such a tritium boosted weapon in 1998. However, tritium decays relatively quickly (half of it will decay in just over 12 years). Thus, to maintain a stockpile of tritium for a long time requires either a very large initial amount or that it be produced at a rate that balances its decay. Tritium is produced as a by-product in the nuclear reactors dedicated to producing plutonium for weapons. These reactors can also be used specifically to produce more tritium.

In short, the nuclear deal promises not just to leave India's nuclear weapons capability intact but allows for a rapid and large expansion of the nuclear arsenal, and for it to be sustained for the indefinite future. It takes for granted that this a good thing.

The effects of the use of both the smaller yield fission weapons and the more destructive thermonuclear weapons in the arsenal are well known (Rajaraman et al., 2004). Put simply, the smaller weapons will kill almost everyone within 1.5 km of the explosion, the larger weapons will kill most people out to distances of 3.5 km. The effects of radioactive fallout would spread many tens of kilometres further. Either kind of bomb would be enough to destroy a modern city. The question that needs to be asked is how many cities do India's leaders wish to be able to destroy?

There are many who believe India, and no one else for that matter, should have any nuclear weapons. They are instruments to create fear through the threat of genocide. Moreover, the lessons of the 60 years since Hiroshima should be enough to make clear to anyone that there is no security to be found in the threat to kill millions.

Conclusion

The nuclear agreement between the U.S. and India has many problems. But there are two fundamental questions at its core. The first is whether India needs nuclear energy for its development and the well-being of its people. A good case can be made that it does not.

The second question is whether India needs nuclear weapons if it actually wants to live in peace with its neighbours and with the world. Many believe, with good reason, that it does not.

The answer t › both questions that is offered by the deal is a future in which a nuclear-powered and nuclear-armed India swaggers along in the shadow of the US. The choice could not be more stark.

NOTES

1. See for example the essays in (Kothari and Mian, 2001) and (Ramana and Reddy, 2003). The drastic deterioration in south Asia's security after the 1998 nuclear tests is documented in (Ramana and Mian, 2003).
2. In 1951 India and France signed an agreement to collaborate but it was not followed by any collaboration (Abraham, 2004).
3. For example, the initial financial sanction in 1982 for the Manuguru heavy water plant indicated the project cost as Rs. 421.60 crore with a foreign exchange component of Rs. 50.00 crore. This was revised to Rs. 661.58 crore in 1989, with a foreign exchange component of Rs. 78.59 crore (CAG, 1994). Similarly, between 1985 and 1993, two foreign consultancy contracts were awarded for "various works" relating to the 540 MW reactors (CAG, 1999).

4. This estimate assumes a burnup of 7,000 MWd/tU and a thermal efficiency of 0.29.
5. For a study of the consequences of a potential major nuclear accident in Pakistan see (Mian and Nayyar, 1999).

REFERENCES

Abraham, Itty (1997): "Science and Secrecy in Making of Postcolonial State", *Economic and Political Weekly*, August 16-23, pp. 2136-46.

——(2004): "Notes Toward a Global Nuclear History", *Economic and Political Weekly*, November 20, 39(46 and 47), pp. 4997-5005.

Anand, S. (2003): "India's Worst Radiation Accident", *Outlook*, July 28, 43(29): pp. 18-20.

Anonymous (1999): "Questions in Lok Sabha: Government Proposes to Build Another Nuclear Reactor", *Hindustan Times*, December 16.

Bhabha, Homi J. and N.B. Prasad (1958): "A Study of the Contribution of Atomic Energy to a Power Programme in India" in *Proceedings of the Second United Nations International Conference on the Peaceful Uses of Atomic Energy*, Geneva, pp. 89-101.

CAG (1994): "Report by the Comptroller and Auditor General of India", Comptroller and Auditor General of India.

——(1999): "Report by the Comptroller and Auditor General of India", Comptroller and Auditor General of India.

Chanda, Nayan (1999): "The Perils of Power", *Far Eastern Economic Review*, February 4.

Dias, Xavier (2005): "DAE's Gambit", *Economic and Political Weekly*, August 6, 40(32), pp. 3567-69.

Gadekar, Sanghamitra and Surendra N. Gadekar (1996): 'Rawatbhata' in Vinod Gaur (ed), *Nuclear Energy and Public Safety*, Indian National Trust for Art and Cultural Heritage, New Delhi, pp. 57-87.

Gopalakrishnan, A (2005): "Indo-US Nuclear Cooperation: A Nonstarter?" *Economic and Political Weekly*, July 2.

Hart, David (1983): *Nuclear Power in India: A Comparative Analysis*, George Allen and Unwin, London.

Kothari, Smitu and Zia Mian (2001): *Out of the Nuclear Shadow, Lokayan*, Rainbow Publishers and Zed Books, Delhi, and London; New York.

Mark, J. Carson (1993): "Explosive Properties of Reactor-Grade Plutonium", *Science and Global Security*, 4(1): 111-24.

Mian, Zia and A.H. Nayyar (1999): "Pakistan's Chashma Nuclear Power Plant: A Preliminary Study of Some Safety Issues and Estimates of the Consequences of a Severe Accident", Report No. 321, Center for Energy and Environmental Studies, Princeton University, Princeton.

Perkovich, George (1999): *India's Nuclear Bomb: The Impact on Global Proliferation*, University of California Press, Berkeley.

Rajaraman, R., Zia Mian and A.H. Nayyar (2004): "Nuclear Civil Defence in South Asia: Is It Feasible?" *Economic and Political Weekly*, November 20, 39 (46 and 47):5017-26.

Ramachandran, R. (2000): "Thwarted Nuclear Ambitions", *Frontline*, January 21, pp. 90-93.

Ramana, M.V., Antonette D'Sa and Amulya, K.N. Reddy (2005): "Economics of Nuclear Power from Heavy Water Reactors", *Economic and Political Weekly*, April 23, 40(17): 1763-73.

Ramana, M.V. and Zia Mian (2003): "The Nuclear Confrontation in South Asia" in *SIPRI Yearbook 2003: Armaments, Disarmament and International Security*, Oxford University Press, New York.

Ramana, M.V. and C. Rammanohar Reddy (eds) (2003): *Prisoners of the Nuclear Dream*, Orient Longman, New Delhi.

Ramana, M.V. and Surendra Gadekar (2003): "The Price We Pay: Environmental and Health Impacts of Nuclear Weapons Production and Testing" in M.V. Ramana and C. Rammanohar Reddy (eds), *Prisoners of the Nuclear Dream*, Orient Longman, New Delhi.

Rethinaraj, T.S. Gopi (1998): "ATV: All at Sea Before it Hits the Water", *Jane's Intelligence Review*, June 1: 31-35.

Sarabhai, Vikram (1974): *Science Policy and National Development*, Macmillan, Delhi.

Sarkar, Sanjib Chandra (1984): *Geology and Ore Mineralisation of the Singhbhum Copper-Uranium Belt*, Eastern India, Jadavpur University, Calcutta.

Srivastava, Sanjeev (2005): "Indian PM Feels Political Heat", British Broadcasting Corporation, http://news.bbc.co.uk/go/pr/fr/-/2/hi/south_asia/4715797.stm, accessed on July 26.

Tongia, Rahul and V.S. Arunachalam (1998): "India's Nuclear Breeders: Technology, Viability and Options", *Current Science*, September 25, 75(6).

Varadarajan, Siddharth (2005): "Nuclear Bargain May Prove Costly in Long Tun", *The Hindu*, July 20.

U.S.-India Civil Nuclear Cooperation Initiative: Fact Sheet, Bureau of South and Central Asian Affairs, Washington DC

6

(September 14, 2008)

President Bush and Indian Prime Minister Singh announced the U.S.-India Civil Nuclear Cooperation Initiative in their Joint Statement on July 18, 2005. This initiative simultaneously provides a process for developing civil nuclear cooperation to help meet India's growing energy requirements and strengthens the nonproliferation regime by welcoming India into internationally accepted nonproliferation standards and practices.

With approval of the Safeguards Agreement by the International Atomic Energy Agency, and the Nuclear Suppliers Group exception now agreed, two of three key steps have been accomplished in bringing civil nuclear cooperation to fruition. The locus of the initiative has now shifted from Vienna and New Delhi to Washington for the third and final step—approval by the U.S. Congress. Congressional approval would be the culmination of an unprecedented three-year effort by the U.S. and India, working together as they have never before—in a way that deepens our strategic partnership and strengthens global nonproliferation principals while providing trade and investment opportunities that will assist India to meet its energy requirements in an environmentally responsible way.

Current Status/Background

Several key objectives were accomplished to bring us to this moment in history. In December 2006, the U.S. Congress passed the Henry J. Hyde U.S.-India Peaceful Atomic Energy Cooperation Act (Hyde Act), which provides a framework in U.S. law for facilitating civil nuclear cooperation with India. In July 2007, the United States and India concluded negotiations on the Agreement for Cooperation between the U.S. and India concerning peaceful uses of nuclear energy (or "123 Agreement"), which must be approved by the U.S. Congress. The Board of Governors of the International Atomic Energy Agency (IAEA) in Vienna, Austria approved the India Safeguards Agreement on August 1, 2008. Another key pre-requisite for submitting the 123 Agreement also took place in Vienna, with the Nuclear Suppliers Group (NSG) consensus decision on September 6, 2008 to grant an exception to its full-scope safeguards requirement to permit civil nuclear supply to India. These historic events have welcomed India into the nonproliferation regimes and formed a firm foundation for the U.S. and India to strengthen our efforts in the future to prevent WMD proliferation and to combat terrorism.

On September 10, 2008, the President submitted the 123 Agreement, to Congress for its review and approval. This agreement would provide the legal framework for the U.S. to engage in civil nuclear cooperation with this key strategic partner. President Bush has made the requisite determinations on India's progress on a number of commitments it made in the 2005 Joint Statement, as provided for under the Hyde Act and the Atomic Energy Act. We believe the 123 Agreement package is consistent with the requirements Congress set out with strong bipartisan support in its passage of the Hyde Act in 2006, and we look forward to continuing our work with Congress to bring the agreement into force.

Benefits of the Initiative

There are powerful security, political, economic, and environmental reasons to support this initiative. The U.S.-India Initiative provides significant gains: (1) deepens our strategic partnership with India—the world's largest democracy and a rising economic power; (2) enhances energy security by helping India's large and growing population meet its rising energy needs; (3) helps protect the environment (since nuclear energy presents a cleaner alternative than other available options); (4) increases trade, creates new jobs and investment opportunities for U.S. companies; and (5) welcomes India into the nonproliferation mainstream. With respect to the last point, India's enhanced nonproliferation commitments strengthen the nuclear nonproliferation framework and constitute a net gain for the global nonproliferation regime.

Under this initiative, India remains outside the Non-Proliferation Treaty (NPT) but assumes important nonproliferation responsibilities and obligations, including separating its civil and military nuclear facilities, accepting IAEA safeguards at its civil nuclear facilities, and signing and implementing an Additional Protocol. India has created a robust national export control system, including through harmonization with and adherence to the Nuclear Suppliers Group (NSG) and the Missile Technology Control Regime (MTCR) guidelines and annexes. Additionally, India has pledged to continue its unilateral moratorium on nuclear testing and is working with the United States to conclude a multilateral Fissile Material Cutoff Treaty—a long-standing objective of the international community.

Individually, each of these activities helps strengthen the global nonproliferation regime. Together, they constitute a dramatic change in moving India into closer conformity with international nonproliferation standards and practices.

International Atomic Energy Agency (IAEA) Safeguards

On August 1, 2008, the IAEA Board of Governors approved the India Safeguards Agreement. The Safeguards Agreement provides for appropriate, effective safeguards in perpetuity, based on accepted IAEA safeguards principles, while taking into account India's unique circumstances. India also has pledged to sign and implement an IAEA Additional Protocol, which will provide IAEA inspectors with additional tools for safeguards inspections in India, as well as contribute to the universality of the Protocol and help establish it as the new international safeguards standard—an important nonproliferation goal for the United States, many other NPT States Party, and the IAEA.

India has made public a plan to separate its civil and military facilities, in which 14 reactors, including the four presently safeguarded reactors, and other facilities would be offered for safeguards under the agreement. The Agreement is based on INFCIRC/66, the IAEA safeguards system utilized for states not under NPT full-scope safeguards. The Safeguards Agreement provides that, once safeguards are put in place, they must remain in place until the IAEA and India jointly determine that the facility is no longer usable for nuclear activities. We have made clear to the Government of India that there will be no cooperation on unsafeguarded facilities. As its future civilian thermal power and civilian breeder reactors will be placed under safeguards, we expect that the proportion of India's nuclear industry subject to such controls will increase over time.

These steps, which will bring more than 65 per cent of India's reactors under safeguards, have brought India closer to the nonproliferation mainstream, and the United States believes the India Safeguards Agreement represents an important step toward realizing the economic and energy benefits foreseen by the initiative.

Nuclear Suppliers Group (NSG)

On September 6, 2008, the Nuclear Suppliers Group reached a consensus policy decision to grant an exception to its full-scope safeguards requirement to permit civil nuclear supply to India. This historic achievement brings us closer to realizing the important benefits—including nonproliferation benefits—that successful implementation of the U.S.-India Civil Nuclear Cooperation Initiative will bring about.

The United States thanks the participating governments in the NSG for their outstanding efforts and cooperation in forging this consensus on welcoming India closer to the international nonproliferation regime. We also congratulate the people of India on its accomplishments in carrying out the initiative. India's commitments will strengthen the international nonproliferation regime and the NSG consensus policy decision has brought us another step closer to realizing full civil nuclear cooperation with India, thus helping the world's largest democracy gain access to environmentally responsible energy supplies.

Peaceful Nuclear Cooperation

The U.S.-India Initiative is about civil nuclear cooperation, not about India's strategic weapons program. It seeks to enable civil nuclear cooperation with India, a state that faces real and growing energy needs, has a solid nuclear nonproliferation export record, has an established and widespread nuclear infrastructure, and has made enhanced nonproliferation commitments which strengthen the global nonproliferation regime. India's commitment to continue its unilateral moratorium on nuclear testing, along with the others India made under the joint statement, made this initiative achievable.

Peaceful nuclear cooperation does not fundamentally differ from other forms of energy cooperation (e.g. oil supply, clean coal technology, alternative fuels). The NPT allows for such nuclear energy cooperation with non-parties that do not have full-scope safeguards, so long as such cooperation is under safeguards. And a successfully implemented Civil Nuclear Cooperation Initiative will create strong energy and economic incentives for India to ensure that its civil nuclear energy sector is properly separated.

This initiative establishes a firm foundation for additional nonproliferation and counter-proliferation cooperation, areas we fully intend to advance through the course of our strategic partnership. We will do everything we can to ensure that the 123 Agreement is reviewed and approved before the end of this Congressional session, and we look forward to working with Congress to bring the initiative to fruition.

7

Agreement for Cooperation Between the Government of the United States of America and the Government of India Concerning Peaceful Uses of Nuclear Energy

(August 1, 2007)

The Government of India and the Government of the United States of America, hereinafter referred to as the Parties,

Recognizing the significance of civilian nuclear energy for meeting growing global energy demands in a cleaner and more efficient manner;

Desiring to cooperate extensively in the full development and use of nuclear energy for peaceful purposes as a means of achieving energy security, on a stable, reliable and predictable basis;

Wishing to develop such cooperation on the basis of mutual respect for sovereignty, non-interference in each other's internal affairs, equality, mutual benefit, reciprocity and with due respect for each other's nuclear programmes;

Desiring to establish the necessary legal framework and basis for cooperation concerning peaceful uses of nuclear energy;

Affirming that cooperation under this Agreement is between two States possessing advanced nuclear technology, both Parties having the same benefits and advantages, both committed to preventing WMD proliferation;

Noting the understandings expressed in the India-U.S. Joint Statement of July 18, 2005 to enable full civil nuclear energy cooperation with India covering aspects of the associated nuclear fuel cycle;

Affirming their support for the objectives of the International Atomic Energy Agency (IAEA) and its safeguards system, as applicable to India and the United States of America, and its importance in ensuring that international cooperation in development and use of nuclear energy for peaceful purposes is carried out under arrangements that will not contribute to the proliferation of nuclear weapons or other nuclear explosive devices;

Noting their respective commitments to safety and security of peaceful uses of nuclear energy, to adequate physical protection of nuclear material and effective national export controls;

Mindful that peaceful nuclear activities must be undertaken with a view to protecting the environment;

Mindful of their shared commitment to preventing the proliferation of weapons of mass destruction; and

Desirous of strengthening the strategic partnership between them;

Have agreed on the following:

ARTICLE 1—Definitions

For the purposes of this Agreement:

(A) "By-product material" means any radioactive material (except special fissionable material) yielded in or made radioactive by exposure to the radiation incident to the process of producing or utilizing special fissionable material. By-product material shall not be subject to safeguards or any other form of verification under this Agreement, unless it has been decided otherwise by prior mutual agreement in writing between the two Parties.

(B) "Component" means a component part of equipment, or other item so designated by agreement of the Parties.

(C) "Conversion" means any of the normal operations in the nuclear fuel cycle, preceding fuel fabrication and excluding enrichment, by which uranium is transformed from one chemical form to another—for example, from uranium hexafluoride (UF_6) to uranium dioxide (UO_2) or from uranium oxide to metal.

(D) "Decommissioning" means the actions taken at the end of a facility's useful life to retire the facility from service in the manner that provides adequate protection for the health and safety of the decommissioning workers and the general public, and for the environment. These actions can range from closing down the facility and a minimal removal of nuclear material coupled with continuing maintenance and surveillance, to a complete removal of residual radioactivity in excess of levels acceptable for unrestricted use of the facility and its site.

(E) "Dual-Use Item" means a nuclear related item which has a technical use in both nuclear and non-nuclear applications.

(F) "Equipment" means any equipment in nuclear operation including reactor, reactor pressure vessel, reactor fuel charging and discharging equipment, reactor control rods, reactor pressure tubes, reactor primary coolant pumps, zirconium tubing, equipment for fuel fabrication and any other item so designated by the Parties.

(G) "High enriched uranium" means uranium enriched to twenty per cent or greater in the isotope 235.

(H) "Information" means any information that is not in the public domain and is transferred in any form pursuant to this Agreement and so designated and documented in hard copy or digital form by mutual agreement by the Parties that it shall be subject to this Agreement, but will cease to be information whenever the Party transferring the information or any third party legitimately releases it into the public domain.

(I) "Low enriched uranium" means uranium enriched to less than twenty per cent in the isotope 235.

(J) "Major critical component" means any part or group of parts essential to the operation of a sensitive nuclear facility or heavy water production facility.

(K) "Non-nuclear material" means heavy water, or any other material suitable for use in a reactor to slow down high velocity neutrons and increase the likelihood of further fission, as may be jointly designated by the appropriate authorities of the Parties.

(L) "Nuclear material" means (1) source material and (2) special fissionable material. "Source material" means uranium containing the mixture of isotopes occurring in nature; uranium depleted in the isotope 235; thorium; any of the foregoing in the form of metal, alloy, chemical compound, or concentrate; any other material containing one or more of the foregoing in such concentration as the Board of Governors of the IAEA shall from time to time determine; and such other materials as the Board of Governors of the IAEA may determine or as may be agreed by the appropriate authorities of both Parties. "Special fissionable material" means plutonium, uranium-233, uranium enriched in the isotope 233 or 235, any substance containing one or more of the foregoing, and such other substances as the Board of Governors of the IAEA may determine or as may be agreed by the appropriate authorities of both Parties. "Special fissionable material" does not include "source material". Any determination by the Board of Governors of the IAEA under Article XX of that Agency's Statute or otherwise that amends the list of materials considered to be "source material" or "special fissionable material" shall only have effect under this Agreement when both Parties to this Agreement have informed each other in writing that they accept such amendment.

(M) "Peaceful purposes" include the use of information, nuclear material, equipment or components in such fields as research, power generation, medicine, agriculture and industry, but do not include use in, research on, or development of any nuclear explosive device or any other military purpose. Provision of power for a military base drawn from any power network, production of radioisotopes to be used for medical purposes in military environment for diagnostics, therapy and sterility assurance, and other similar purposes as may be mutually agreed by the Parties shall not be regarded as military purpose.

(N) "Person" means any individual or any entity subject to the territorial jurisdiction of either Party but does not include the Parties.

(O) "Reactor" means any apparatus, other than a nuclear weapon or other nuclear explosive device, in which a self-sustaining fission chain reaction is maintained by utilizing uranium, plutonium, or thorium or any combination thereof.

(P) "Sensitive nuclear facility" means any facility designed or used primarily for uranium enrichment, reprocessing of nuclear fuel, or fabrication of nuclear fuel containing plutonium.

(Q) "Sensitive nuclear technology" means any information that is not in the public domain and that is important to the design, construction, fabrication, operation, or maintenance of any sensitive nuclear facility, or other such information that may be so designated by agreement of the Parties.

ARTICLE 2—Scope of Cooperation

1. The Parties shall cooperate in the use of nuclear energy for peaceful purposes in accordance with the provisions of this Agreement. Each Party shall implement this Agreement in accordance with its respective applicable treaties, national laws, regulations, and license requirements concerning the use of nuclear energy for peaceful purposes.

2. The purpose of the Agreement being to enable full civil nuclear energy cooperation between the Parties, the Parties may

pursue cooperation in all relevant areas to include, but not limited to, the following:

(a) Advanced nuclear energy research and development in such areas as may be agreed between the Parties;

(b) Nuclear safety matters of mutual interest and competence, as set out in Article 3;

(c) Facilitation of exchange of scientists for visits, meetings, symposia and collaborative research;

(d) Full civil nuclear cooperation activities covering nuclear reactors and aspects of the associated nuclear fuel cycle including technology transfer on an industrial or commercial scale between the Parties or authorized persons;

(e) Development of a strategic reserve of nuclear fuel to guard against any disruption of supply over the lifetime of India's reactors;

(f) Advanced research and development in nuclear sciences including but not limited to biological research, medicine, agriculture and industry, environment and climate change;

(g) Supply between the Parties, whether for use by or for the benefit of the Parties or third countries, of nuclear material;

(h) Alteration in form or content of nuclear material as provided for in Article 6;

(i) Supply between the Parties of equipment, whether for use by or for the benefit of the Parties or third countries;

(j) Controlled thermonuclear fusion including in multilateral projects; and

(k) Other areas of mutual interest as may be agreed by the Parties.

3. Transfer of nuclear material, non-nuclear material, equipment, components and information under this Agreement may be undertaken directly between the Parties or through authorized persons. Such transfers shall be subject to this

Agreement and to such additional terms and conditions as may be agreed by the Parties. Nuclear material, non-nuclear material, equipment, components and information transferred from the territory of one Party to the territory of the other Party, whether directly or through a third country, will be regarded as having been transferred pursuant to this Agreement only upon confirmation, by the appropriate authority of the recipient Party to the appropriate authority of the supplier Party that such items both will be subject to the Agreement and have been received by the recipient Party.

4. The Parties affirm that the purpose of this Agreement is to provide for peaceful nuclear cooperation and not to affect the unsafeguarded nuclear activities of either Party. Accordingly, nothing in this Agreement shall be interpreted as affecting the rights of the Parties to use for their own purposes nuclear material, non-nuclear material, equipment, components, information or technology produced, acquired or developed by them independent of any nuclear material, non-nuclear material, equipment, components, information or technology transferred to them pursuant to this Agreement. This Agreement shall be implemented in a manner so as not to hinder or otherwise interfere with any other activities involving the use of nuclear material, non-nuclear material, equipment, components, information or technology and military nuclear facilities produced, acquired or developed by them independent of this Agreement for their own purposes.

ARTICLE 3—Transfer of Information

1. Information concerning the use of nuclear energy for peaceful purposes may be transferred between the Parties. Transfers of information may be accomplished through reports, data banks and computer programs and any other means mutually agreed to by the Parties. Fields that may be covered include, but shall not be limited to, the following:

(a) Research, development, design, construction, operation, maintenance and use of reactors, reactor experiments, and decommissioning;

(b) The use of nuclear material in physical, chemical, radiological and biological research, medicine, agriculture and industry;

(c) Fuel cycle activities to meet future world-wide civil nuclear energy needs, including multilateral approaches to which they are parties for ensuring nuclear fuel supply and appropriate techniques for management of nuclear wastes;

(d) Advanced research and development in nuclear science and technology;

(e) Health, safety, and environmental considerations related to the foregoing;

(f) Assessments of the role nuclear power may play in national energy plans;

(g) Codes, regulations and standards for the nuclear industry;

(h) Research on controlled thermonuclear fusion including bilateral activities and contributions toward multilateral projects such as the International Thermonuclear Experimental Reactor (ITER); and

(i) Any other field mutually agreed to by the Parties.

2. Cooperation pursuant to this Article may include, but is not limited to, training, exchange of personnel, meetings, exchange of samples, materials and instruments for experimental purposes and a balanced participation in joint studies and projects.

3. This Agreement does not require the transfer of any information regarding matters outside the scope of this Agreement, or information that the Parties are not permitted under their respective treaties, national laws, or regulations to transfer.

4. Restricted Data, as defined by each Party, shall not be transferred under this Agreement.

ARTICLE 4—Nuclear Trade

1. The Parties shall facilitate nuclear trade between themselves in the mutual interests of their respective industry,

utilities and consumers and also, where appropriate, trade between third countries and either Party of items obligated to the other Party. The Parties recognize that reliability of supplies is essential to ensure smooth and uninterrupted operation of nuclear facilities and that industry in both the Parties needs continuing reassurance that deliveries can be made on time in order to plan for the efficient operation of nuclear installations.

2. Authorizations, including export and import licenses as well as authorizations or consents to third parties, relating to trade, industrial operations or nuclear material movement should be consistent with the sound and efficient administration of this Agreement and should not be used to restrict trade. It is further agreed that if the relevant authority of the concerned Party considers that an application cannot be processed within a two-month period it shall immediately, upon request, provide reasoned information to the submitting Party. In the event of a refusal to authorize an application or a delay exceeding four months from the date of the first application the Party of the submitting persons or undertakings may call for urgent consultations under Article 13 of this Agreement, which shall take place at the earliest opportunity and in any case not later than 30 days after such a request.

ARTICLE 5—Transfer of Nuclear Material, Non-nuclear Material, Equipment, Components and Related Technology

1. Nuclear material, non-nuclear material, equipment and components may be transferred for applications consistent with this Agreement. Any special fissionable material transferred under this Agreement shall be low enriched uranium, except as provided in paragraph 5.

2. Sensitive nuclear technology, heavy water production technology, sensitive nuclear facilities, heavy water production facilities and major critical components of such facilities may be transferred under this Agreement pursuant to an amendment to this Agreement. Transfers of dual-use items that could be used in enrichment, reprocessing or heavy water production facilities will be subject to the Parties' respective applicable laws, regulations and license policies.

3. Natural or low enriched uranium may be transferred for use as fuel in reactor experiments and in reactors, for conversion or fabrication, or for such other purposes as may be agreed to by the Parties.

4. The quantity of nuclear material transferred under this Agreement shall be consistent with any of the following purposes: use in reactor experiments or the loading of reactors, the efficient and continuous conduct of such reactor experiments or operation of reactors for their lifetime, use as samples, standards, detectors, and targets, and the accomplishment of other purposes as may be agreed by the Parties.

5. Small quantities of special fissionable material may be transferred for use as samples, standards, detectors, and targets, and for such other purposes as the Parties may agree.

6. (a) The United States has conveyed its commitment to the reliable supply of fuel to India. Consistent with the July 18, 2005, Joint Statement, the United States has also reaffirmed its assurance to create the necessary conditions for India to have assured and full access to fuel for its reactors. As part of its implementation of the July 18, 2005, Joint Statement the United States is committed to seeking agreement from the U.S. Congress to amend its domestic laws and to work with friends and allies to adjust the practices of the Nuclear Suppliers Group to create the necessary conditions for India to obtain full access to the international fuel market, including reliable, uninterrupted and continual access to fuel supplies from firms in several nations.

(b) To further guard against any disruption of fuel supplies, the United States is prepared to take the following additional steps:

(i) The United States is willing to incorporate assurances regarding fuel supply in the bilateral U.S.-India agreement on peaceful uses of nuclear energy under Section 123 of the U.S. Atomic Energy Act, which would be submitted to the U.S. Congress.

(ii) The United States will join India in seeking to negotiate with the IAEA an India-specific fuel supply agreement.

(iii) The United States will support an Indian effort to develop a strategic reserve of nuclear fuel to guard against any disruption of supply over the lifetime of India's reactors.

(iv) If despite these arrangements, a disruption of fuel supplies to India occurs, the United States and India would jointly convene a group of friendly supplier countries to include countries such as Russia, France and the United Kingdom to pursue such measures as would restore fuel supply to India.

(c) In light of the above understandings with the United States, an India-specific safeguards agreement will be negotiated between India and the IAEA providing for safeguards to guard against withdrawal of safeguarded nuclear material from civilian use at any time as well as providing for corrective measures that India may take to ensure uninterrupted operation of its civilian nuclear reactors in the event of disruption of foreign fuel supplies. Taking this into account, India will place its civilian nuclear facilities under India-specific safeguards in perpetuity and negotiate an appropriate safeguards agreement to this end with the IAEA.

ARTICLE 6—Nuclear Fuel Cycle Activities

In keeping with their commitment to full civil nuclear cooperation, both Parties, as they do with other states with advanced nuclear technology, may carry out the following nuclear fuel cycle activities:

(i) Within the territorial jurisdiction of either Party, enrichment up to twenty per cent in the isotope 235 of uranium transferred pursuant to this Agreement, as well as of uranium used in or produced through the use of equipment so transferred, may be carried out.

(ii) Irradiation within the territorial jurisdiction of either Party of Plutonium, uranium-233, high enriched uranium and irradiated nuclear material transferred pursuant to this Agreement or used in or produced through the use of non-nuclear material, nuclear material or equipment so transferred may be carried out.

(iii) With a view to implementing full civil nuclear cooperation as envisioned in the Joint Statement of the Parties of July 18, 2005, the Parties grant each other consent to reprocess or otherwise alter in form or content nuclear material transferred pursuant to this Agreement and nuclear material and by-product material used in or produced through the use of nuclear material, non-nuclear material, or equipment so transferred. To bring these rights into effect, India will establish a new national reprocessing facility dedicated to reprocessing safeguarded nuclear material under IAEA safeguards and the Parties will agree on arrangements and procedures under which such reprocessing or other alteration in form or content will take place in this new facility. Consultations on arrangements and procedures will begin within six months of a request by either Party and will be concluded within one year. The Parties agree on the application of IAEA safeguards to all facilities concerned with the above activities. These arrangements and procedures shall include provisions with respect to physical protection standards set out in Article 8, storage standards set out in Article 7, and environmental protections set forth in Article 11 of this Agreement, and such other provisions as may be agreed by the Parties. Any special fissionable material that may be separated may only be utilized in national facilities under IAEA safeguards.

(iv) Post-irradiation examination involving chemical dissolution or separation of irradiated nuclear material transferred pursuant to this Agreement or irradiated nuclear material used in or produced through the use of non-nuclear material, nuclear material or equipment so transferred may be carried out.

ARTICLE 7—Storage and Retransfers

1. Plutonium and uranium-233 (except as either may be contained in irradiated fuel elements), and high enriched uranium, transferred pursuant to this Agreement or used in or produced through the use of material or equipment so transferred, may be stored in facilities that are at all times subject, as a minimum, to the levels of physical protection that are set out in IAEA document INFCIRC 225/REV 4 as it may be revised and accepted by the Parties. Each Party shall record such facilities on a list, made available to the other Party. A Party's list shall be held confidential if that Party so requests. Either Party may make changes to its list by notifying the other Party in writing and receiving a written acknowledgement. Such acknowledgement shall be given no later than thirty days after the receipt of the notification and shall be limited to a statement that the notification has been received. If there are grounds to believe that the provisions of this sub-Article are not being fully complied with, immediate consultations may be called for. Following upon such consultations, each Party shall ensure by means of such consultations that necessary remedial measures are taken immediately. Such measures shall be sufficient to restore the levels of physical protection referred to above at the facility in question. However, if the Party on whose territory the nuclear material in question is stored determines that such measures are not feasible, it will shift the nuclear material to another appropriate, listed facility it identifies.

2. Nuclear material, non-nuclear material, equipment, components, and information transferred pursuant to this Agreement and any special fissionable material produced through the use of nuclear material, non-nuclear material or equipment so transferred shall not be transferred or re-transferred to unauthorized persons or, unless the Parties agree, beyond the recipient Party's territorial jurisdiction.

ARTICLE 8—Physical Protection

1. Adequate physical protection shall be maintained with respect to nuclear material and equipment transferred pursuant to this Agreement and nuclear material used in or produced

through the use of nuclear material, non-nuclear material or equipment so transferred.

2. To fulfill the requirement in paragraph 1, each Party shall apply measures in accordance with (i) levels of physical protection at least equivalent to the recommendations published in IAEA document INFCIRC/225/Rev.4 entitled "The Physical Protection of Nuclear Material and Nuclear Facilities," and in any subsequent revisions of that document agreed to by the Parties, and (ii) the provisions of the 1980 Convention on the Physical Protection of Nuclear Material and any amendments to the Convention that enter into force for both Parties.

3. The Parties will keep each other informed through diplomatic channels of those agencies or authorities having responsibility for ensuring that levels of physical protection for nuclear material in their territory or under their jurisdiction or control are adequately met and having responsibility for coordinating response and recovery operations in the event of unauthorized use or handling of material subject to this Article. The Parties will also keep each other informed through diplomatic channels of the designated points of contact within their national authorities to cooperate on matters of out-of-country transportation and other matters of mutual concern.

4. The provisions of this Article shall be implemented in such a manner as to avoid undue interference in the Parties' peaceful nuclear activities and so as to be consistent with prudent management practices required for the safe and economic conduct of their peaceful nuclear programs.

ARTICLE 9—Peaceful Use

Nuclear material, equipment and components transferred pursuant to this Agreement and nuclear material and by-product material used in or produced through the use of any nuclear material, equipment, and components so transferred shall not be used by the recipient Party for any nuclear explosive device, for research on or development of any nuclear explosive device or for any military purpose.

ARTICLE 10—IAEA Safeguards

1. Safeguards will be maintained with respect to all nuclear materials and equipment transferred pursuant to this Agreement, and with respect to all special fissionable material used in or produced through the use of such nuclear materials and equipment, so long as the material or equipment remains under the jurisdiction or control of the cooperating Party.

2. Taking into account Article 5.6 of this Agreement, India agrees that nuclear material and equipment transferred to India by the United States of America pursuant to this Agreement and any nuclear material used in or produced through the use of nuclear material, non-nuclear material, equipment or components so transferred shall be subject to safeguards in perpetuity in accordance with the India-specific Safeguards Agreement between India and the IAEA [identifying data] and an Additional Protocol, when in force.

3. Nuclear material and equipment transferred to the United States of America pursuant to this Agreement and any nuclear material used in or produced through the use of any nuclear material, non-nuclear material, equipment, or components so transferred shall be subject to the Agreement between the United States of America and the IAEA for the application of safeguards in the United States of America, done at Vienna November 18, 1977, which entered into force on December 9, 1980, and an Additional Protocol, when in force.

4. If the IAEA decides that the application of IAEA safeguards is no longer possible, the supplier and recipient should consult and agree on appropriate verification measures.

5. Each Party shall take such measures as are necessary to maintain and facilitate the application of IAEA safeguards in its respective territory provided for under this Article.

6. Each Party shall establish and maintain a system of accounting for and control of nuclear material transferred pursuant to this Agreement and nuclear material used in or produced through the use of any material, equipment, or components so transferred. The procedures applicable to India

shall be those set forth in the India-specific Safeguards Agreement referred to in Paragraph 2 of this Article.

7. Upon the request of either Party, the other Party shall report or permit the IAEA to report to the requesting Party on the status of all inventories of material subject to this Agreement.

8. The provisions of this Article shall be implemented in such a manner as to avoid hampering, delay, or undue interference in the Parties' peaceful nuclear activities and so as to be consistent with prudent management practices required for the safe and economic conduct of their peaceful nuclear programs.

ARTICLE 11—Environmental Protection

The Parties shall cooperate in following the best practices for minimizing the impact on the environment from any radioactive, chemical or thermal contamination arising from peaceful nuclear activities under this Agreement and in related matters of health and safety.

ARTICLE 12—Implementation of the Agreement

1. This Agreement shall be implemented in a manner designed:

(a) to avoid hampering or delaying the nuclear activities in the territory of either Party;

(b) to avoid interference in such activities;

(c) to be consistent with prudent management practices required for the safe conduct of such activities; and

(d) to take full account of the long term requirements of the nuclear energy programs of the Parties.

2. The provisions of this Agreement shall not be used to:

(a) secure unfair commercial or industrial advantages or to restrict trade to the disadvantage of persons and undertakings of either Party or hamper their commercial or industrial interests, whether international or domestic;

(b) interfere with the nuclear policy or programs for the promotion of the peaceful uses of nuclear energy including research and development; or

(c) impede the free movement of nuclear material, non-nuclear material and equipment supplied under this Agreement within the territory of the Parties.

3. When execution of an agreement or contract pursuant to this Agreement between Indian and United States organizations requires exchanges of experts, the Parties shall facilitate entry of the experts to their territories and their stay therein consistent with national laws, regulations and practices. When other cooperation pursuant to this Agreement requires visits of experts, the Parties shall facilitate entry of the experts to their territory and their stay therein consistent with national laws, regulations and practices.

ARTICLE 13—Consultations

1. The Parties undertake to consult at the request of either Party regarding the implementation of this Agreement and the development of further cooperation in the field of peaceful uses of nuclear energy on a stable, reliable and predictable basis. The Parties recognize that such consultations are between two States with advanced nuclear technology, which have agreed to assume the same responsibilities and practices and acquire the same benefits and advantages as other leading countries with advanced nuclear technology.

2. Each Party shall endeavor to avoid taking any action that adversely affects cooperation envisaged under Article 2 of this Agreement. If either Party at any time following the entry into force of this Agreement does not comply with the provisions of this Agreement, the Parties shall promptly hold consultations with a view to resolving the matter in a way that protects the legitimate interests of both Parties, it being understood that rights of either Party under Article 16.2 remain unaffected.

3. Consultations under this Article may be carried out by a Joint Committee specifically established for this purpose. A Joint Technical Working Group reporting to the Joint Committee will be set up to ensure the fulfillment of the requirements of the Administrative Arrangements referred to in Article 17.

ARTICLE 14—Termination and Cessation of Cooperation

1. Either Party shall have the right to terminate this Agreement prior to its expiration on one year's written notice to the other Party. A Party giving notice of termination shall provide the reasons for seeking such termination. The Agreement shall terminate one year from the date of the written notice, unless the notice has been withdrawn by the providing Party in writing prior to the date of termination.

2. Before this Agreement is terminated pursuant to paragraph 1 of this Article, the Parties shall consider the relevant circumstances and promptly hold consultations, as provided in Article 13, to address the reasons cited by the Party seeking termination. The Party seeking termination has the right to cease further cooperation under this Agreement if it determines that a mutually acceptable resolution of outstanding issues has not been possible or cannot be achieved through consultations. The Parties agree to consider carefully the circumstances that may lead to termination or cessation of cooperation. They further agree to take into account whether the circumstances that may lead to termination or cessation resulted from a Party's serious concern about a changed security environment or as a response to similar actions by other States which could impact national security.

3. If a Party seeking termination cites a violation of this Agreement as the reason for notice for seeking termination, the Parties shall consider whether the action was caused inadvertently or otherwise and whether the violation could be considered as material. No violation may be considered as being material unless corresponding to the definition of material violation or breach in the Vienna Convention on the Law of Treaties. If a Party seeking termination cites a violation of an IAEA safeguards agreement as the reason for notice for seeking termination, a crucial factor will be whether the IAEA Board of Governors has made a finding of non-compliance.

4. Following the cessation of cooperation under this Agreement, either Party shall have the right to require the return by the other Party of any nuclear material, equipment,

non-nuclear material or components transferred under this Agreement and any special fissionable material produced through their use. A notice by a Party that is invoking the right of return shall be delivered to the other Party on or before the date of termination of this Agreement. The notice shall contain a statement of the items subject to this Agreement as to which the Party is requesting return. Except as provided in provisions of Article 16.3, all other legal obligations pertaining to this Agreement shall cease to apply with respect to the nuclear items remaining on the territory of the Party concerned upon termination of this Agreement.

5. The two Parties recognize that exercising the right of return would have profound implications for their relations. If either Party seeks to exercise its right pursuant to paragraph 4 of this Article, it shall, prior to the removal from the territory or from the control of the other Party of any nuclear items mentioned in paragraph 4, undertake consultations with the other Party. Such consultations shall give special consideration to the importance of uninterrupted operation of nuclear reactors of the Party concerned with respect to the availability of nuclear energy for peaceful purposes as a means of achieving energy security. Both Parties shall take into account the potential negative consequences of such termination on the on-going contracts and projects initiated under this Agreement of significance for the respective nuclear programs of either Party.

6. If either Party exercises its right of return pursuant to paragraph 4 of this Article, it shall, prior to the removal from the territory or from the control of the other Party, compensate promptly that Party for the fair market value thereof and for the costs incurred as a consequence of such removal. If the return of nuclear items is required, the Parties shall agree on methods and arrangements for the return of the items, the relevant quantity of the items to be returned, and the amount of compensation that would have to be paid by the Party exercising the right to the other Party.

7. Prior to return of nuclear items, the Parties shall satisfy themselves that full safety, radiological and physical protection

measures have been ensured in accordance with their existing national regulations and that the transfers pose no unreasonable risk to either Party, countries through which the nuclear items may transit and to the global environment and are in accordance with existing international regulations.

8. The Party seeking the return of nuclear items shall ensure that the timing, methods and arrangements for return of nuclear items are in accordance with paragraphs 5, 6 and 7. Accordingly, the consultations between the Parties shall address mutual commitments as contained in Article 5.6. It is not the purpose of the provisions of this Article regarding cessation of cooperation and right of return to derogate from the rights of the Parties under Article 5.6.

9. The arrangements and procedures concluded pursuant to Article 6(iii) shall be subject to suspension by either Party in exceptional circumstances, as defined by the Parties, after consultations have been held between the Parties aimed at reaching mutually acceptable resolution of outstanding issues, while taking into account the effects of such suspension on other aspects of cooperation under this Agreement.

ARTICLE 15—Settlement of Disputes

Any dispute concerning the interpretation or implementation of the provisions of this Agreement shall be promptly negotiated by the Parties with a view to resolving that dispute.

ARTICLE 16—Entry into Force and Duration

1. This Agreement shall enter into force on the date on which the Parties exchange diplomatic notes informing each other that they have completed all applicable requirements for its entry into force.

2. This Agreement shall remain in force for a period of 40-years. It shall continue in force thereafter for additional periods of 10-years each. Each Party may, by giving 6 months written notice to the other Party, terminate this Agreement at the end of the initial 40-year period or at the end of any subsequent 10-year period.

3. Notwithstanding the termination or expiration of this Agreement or withdrawal of a Party from this Agreement, Articles 5.6(c), 6, 7, 8, 9, 10 and 15 shall continue in effect so long as any nuclear material, non-nuclear material, by-product material, equipment or components subject to these articles remains in the territory of the Party concerned or under its jurisdiction or control anywhere, or until such time as the Parties agree that such nuclear material is no longer usable for any nuclear activity relevant from the point of view of safeguards.

4. This Agreement shall be implemented in good faith and in accordance with the principles of international law.

5. The Parties may consult, at the request of either Party, on possible amendments to this Agreement. This Agreement may be amended if the Parties so agree. Any amendment shall enter into force on the date on which the Parties exchange diplomatic notes informing each other that their respective internal legal procedures necessary for the entry into force have been completed.

ARTICLE 17—Administrative Arrangement

1. The appropriate authorities of the Parties shall establish an Administrative Arrangement in order to provide for the effective implementation of the provisions of this Agreement.

2. The principles of fungibility and equivalence shall apply to nuclear material and non-nuclear material subject to this Agreement. Detailed provisions for applying these principles shall be set forth in the Administrative Arrangement.

3. The Administrative Arrangement established pursuant to this Article may be amended by agreement of the appropriate authorities of the Parties.

In Witness Whereof the undersigned, being duly authorized, have signed this Agreement.

Done at , this day of , 200 , in duplicate.

For the Government of the United States of America:	For the Government of India:

AGREED MINUTE

During the negotiation of the Agreement for Cooperation Between the Government of the United States of America and the Government of India Concerning Peaceful Uses of Nuclear Energy ("the Agreement") signed today, the following understandings, which shall be an integral part of the Agreement, were reached.

Proportionality

For the purposes of implementing the rights specified in Articles 6 and 7 of the Agreement with respect to special fissionable material and by-product material produced through the use of nuclear material and non-nuclear material, respectively, transferred pursuant to the Agreement and not used in or produced through the use of equipment transferred pursuant to the Agreement, such rights shall in practice be applied to that proportion of special fissionable material and by-product material produced that represents the ratio of transferred nuclear material and non-nuclear material, respectively, used in the production of the special fissionable material and byproduct material to the total amount of nuclear material and non-nuclear material so used, and similarly for subsequent generations.

By-product Material

The Parties agree that reporting and exchanges of information on by-product material subject to the Agreement will be limited to the following:

(1) Both Parties would comply with the provisions as contained in the IAEA document GOV/1999/19/Rev.2, with regard to by-product material subject to the Agreement.

(2) With regard to tritium subject to the Agreement, the Parties will exchange annually information pertaining to its disposition for peaceful purposes consistent with Article 9 of this Agreement.

For the Government of the United States of America:	For the Government of India:

Presidential Determination No. 2008-26

8

(September 10, 2008)

Memorandum for the Secretary of State and the Secretary of Energy

Subject: Proposed Agreement for Cooperation Between the Government of the United States of America and the Government of India Concerning Peaceful Uses of Nuclear Energy.

I have considered the proposed Agreement for Cooperation Between the Government of the United States of America and the Government of India Concerning Peaceful Uses of Nuclear Energy, along with the views, recommendations, and statements of interested agencies.

I have determined that the performance of the Agreement will promote, and will not constitute an unreasonable risk to, the common defense and security. Pursuant to section 123 b. of the Atomic Energy Act of 1954, as amended [42 U.S.C. 2153(b)], I hereby approve the proposed Agreement and authorize the Secretary of State to arrange for its execution.

In addition, pursuant to the authority vested in me by the Constitution and the laws of the United States of America, including the Henry J. Hyde United States-India Peaceful Atomic Energy Cooperation Act of 2006 (Public Law 109-401), I hereby determine that:

1. India has provided the United States and the IAEA with a credible plan to separate civil and military nuclear facilities, materials, and programs, and has filed a declaration regarding its civil facilities and materials with the IAEA;
2. India and the IAEA have concluded all legal steps required prior to signature by the parties of an agreement requiring the application of IAEA safeguards in perpetuity in accordance with IAEA standards, principles, and practices [including IAEA Board of Governors Document GOV/1621 (1973)] to India's civil nuclear facilities, materials, and programs as declared in the plan described in paragraph (1), including materials used in or produced through the use of India's civil nuclear facilities;
3. India and the IAEA are making substantial progress toward concluding an Additional Protocol consistent with IAEA principles, practices, and policies that would apply to India's civil nuclear program;
4. India is working actively with the United States for the early conclusion of a multilateral treaty on the cessation of the production of fissile materials for use in nuclear weapons or other nuclear explosive devices;
5. India is working with and supporting United States and international efforts to prevent the spread of enrichment and reprocessing technology to any state that does not already possess full-scale, functioning enrichment or reprocessing plants;
6. India is taking the necessary steps to secure nuclear and other sensitive materials and technology, including through (A) the enactment and effective enforcement of comprehensive export control legislation and regulations; (B) harmonization of its export control laws, regulations, policies, and practices with the guidelines and practices of the Missile Technology Control Regime (MTCR) and the Nuclear Suppliers Group (NSG); and (C) adherence to the MTCR and

the NSG in accordance with the procedures of those regimes for unilateral adherence; and

7. The NSG has decided by consensus to permit supply to India of nuclear items covered by the guidelines of the NSG.

I, therefore, hereby (1) exempt the proposed Agreement for Cooperation Between the Government of the United States of America and the Government of India Concerning Peaceful Uses of Nuclear Energy arranged pursuant to section 123 of the Atomic Energy Act of 1954 (42 U.S.C. 2153) from the requirement of subsection 123 a.(2) of such section; (2) waive the application of section 128 of the Atomic Energy Act of 1954 (42 U.S.C. 2157) with respect to exports to India; and (3) waive with respect to India the application of:

(A) subsection 129 a.(1)(D) of the Atomic Energy Act of 1954 [42 U.S.C. 2158(a)(1)(D)]; and

(B) section 129 of the Atomic Energy Act of 1954 (42 U.S.C. 2158) regarding any actions that occurred before July 18, 2005.

The Secretary of State is authorized and directed to publish this determination in the *Federal Register*.

9

Report Pursuant to Section 104(c) of the Hyde Act Regarding Civil Nuclear Cooperation with India

This report is submitted in accordance with Section 104(c) of the Henry J. Hyde United States-India Peaceful Atomic Energy Cooperation Act of 2006 (Public Law 109-401).

The U.S.-India Civil Nuclear Cooperation Initiative was announced in a Joint Statement by President Bush and Indian Prime Minister Manmohan Singh in Washington on July 18, 2005. On December 18, 2006, the President signed into law the Henry J. Hyde United States-India Peaceful Atomic Energy Cooperation Act of 2006 (the "Hyde Act"), to facilitate peaceful nuclear cooperation with India by authorizing the President to exempt the U.S.-India nuclear cooperation agreement and waive two provisions of the Atomic Energy Act of 1954 ("AEA") based on his determination that certain nonproliferation commitments have been met. Pursuant to Section 104(c) of the Hyde Act, the following report details the basis for the President's determinations and provides a available information on the areas listed in Section 104(c)(2).

Separation Plan and Declaration

Section 104(c)(2)(A) of the Hyde Act requires:

"A summary of the plan provided by India to the United States and the IAEA to separate India's civil and military nuclear facilities, materials, and programs, and the declaration made by India to the IAEA identifying India's civil facilities to be placed under IAEA safeguards, including an analysis of the credibility of such plan and declaration, together with copies of the plan and declaration."

The Government of India first made its Separation Plan public on March 7, 2006 and tabled the Separation Plan in Parliament on May 11. On July 25, 2008, the Government of India transmitted the Separation Plan to the Director General of the IAEA to be distributed "to all Member-States of the Agency". The IAEA circulated the Separation Plan to Members as IAEA document INFCIRC/731.

The Separation Plan includes a list of facilities to be designated as civil, a general description of additional facilities to be designated civil in the future, and a description of India's rationale for civil versus military designations, including a statement that the overarching criterion would be a judgement whether subjecting a facility to IAEA safeguards would adversely impact India's national security.... Designating a facility as civil marks it as not relevant to India's strategic nuclear program. The civil designation also ensures that after separation, these facilities will not be engaged in activities of strategic significance for India's military nuclear program. Facilities located in a larger hub of strategic significance, even if they do not normally engage in activities of strategic significance, will not be designated by India as civil. Also included in the Plan are dates specifying when each of the civil facilities are to be offered for safeguards according to a "phased" timeline.

The Separation Plan notes that "India has decided to place under safeguards all future civilian thermal power reactors and civilian breeder reactors, and the Government of India *retains the sole right to determine such reactors as civil*" (emphasis added). It also clarified that the "phasing of specific thermal power reactors being offered for safeguards would be indicated separately by India." And it explicitly described the distinct steps of (1) "filing a declaration regarding its civilian facilities with the IAEA" and (2) "taking a decision to place voluntarily its civilian facilities under IAEA safeguards." (See paragraph 3 of the Separation Plan)

The United States and other potential suppliers to India have international, and in many cases domestic, legal and policy requirements to ensure that items supplied under their agreements for peaceful nuclear cooperation serve exclusively the civil sector. All reactors supplied by the United States or by India's other international partners, and nuclear material used in such reactors, will be required to be designated as "civil" and subject to IAEA safeguards in perpetuity in accordance with IAEA practices. In addition, nuclear supplier nations will not be able to engage in nuclear cooperation, including fuel supply, with India's current reactors or future indigenous reactors unless they are designated as "civil" and subject to IAEA safeguards in perpetuity.

With these conditions in mind, the Plan's civil designations cover most of India's power reactors, raising the total installed thermal power capacity under safeguards from 19 per cent to 65 per cent by 2014.

India identifies 14 thermal reactors as civil, which according to the March 2006 Separation Plan were scheduled to be offered for safeguards between 2006 and 2014. These include the four existing foreign-supplied reactors (TAPS-1 and -2 (the U.S.-supplied Tarapur reactors), RAPS-1 and -2) and the two foreign-supplied reactors under construction (KK-1 and -2). These also include eight indigenous PHWRs, each with a generating capacity of 220 MWe: RAPS-3, -4, -5 and -6, KAPS-1 and -2, and NAPS-1 and -2. India further notes that safeguards will be applied in a phased manner consistent with its agreement with the IAEA. Eight indigenous PHWRs (TAPS-3 and -4, MAPS-1 and -2, Kaiga-1, -2, -3 and -4) are to remain outside of safeguards.

India opted to continue unsafeguarded operations at its operating fast breeder test reactor and also to exclude its prototype fast breeder reactor from safeguards. The fast breeder program is currently at the research and development stage and will take time to reach an advanced stage of development, according to India. India seeks to ensure that it does not face any external "encumbrances" in this process, and so chooses to exclude them from safeguards at this time. India and the United States would not be able to engage in the type of nuclear fuel cycle cooperation contemplated in the U.S.-India Agreement for Peaceful Nuclear Cooperation with regard to India's breeder reactors until India declared them "civil" and placed them under safeguards.

With regard to future reactors that India may operate, India states that it will place under IAEA safeguards "all future civilian thermal power reactors and civilian breeder reactors," retaining for itself the right to designate such reactors as civilian. While India retains the right to develop indigenous facilities for either civil or military purposes in the future, the United States expects the vast majority of future nuclear program growth to occur in India's civil sector. This expectation is based on discussions with the Government of India as well as India's need to obtain the maximum benefit from international cooperation in order to meet its enduring and expanding energy requirements.

Select research reactors and facilities are also included in the Separation Plan. India will permanently shut down the CIRUS plutonium production reactor in 2010. It will also place the foreign-supplied fuel core from the APSARA reactor under safeguards that year. India has not declared as civil the Dhruva research reactor, the Advanced Heavy Water Reactor, and activities relating to naval nuclear propulsion at Kalpakkam. India plans to declare as civil nine research facilities: the Tata Institute of Fundamental Research; the Variable Energy Cyclotron Centre; the Saha Institute of Nuclear Physics; the Institute for Plasma Research; the Institute of Mathematics Science; the Institute of Physics; the Tata Memorial Centre; the Board of Radiation and Isotope Technology; and the Harish Chandra Research Institute. India expects these civil facilities to play a "prominent role" in international cooperation. Other Indian nuclear and nuclear-related facilities—such as those in the Bhabha Atomic Research Center (BARC) or in the Indira Gandhi Center for Advanced Research (IGCAR)—were not declared as civil, presumably because they retain a military or strategic role. India has not declared as civil the Dhruva research reactor, the Advanced Heavy Water Reactor, and activities relating to naval nuclear propulsion at Kalpakkam.

The civil facilities covered under India's safeguards agreement also include all upstream and downstream facilities involved in India's civil nuclear fuel cycle. India designates as civil the following specific upstream facilities associated with the Nuclear Fuel Complex: the Uranium Oxide Plant (Block A); both the Palletizing and the Assembly Ceramic Fuel Fabrication Plants (Block A); the Enriched Uranium Oxide Plant; the Enriched Fuel Fabrication Plant; and the Gadolinia Facility. The heavy water production plants at Thal, Tuticorin, and Hazira will also be designated as civil. While India does not consider them as "relevant for safeguards purposes," at a minimum India's Additional Protocol is expected to include them. India decided not to designate for civilian uses three additional heavy water production plants, as well as other select Nuclear Fuel Complex facilities.

India plans to continue the current policy of possible "campaign-mode" safeguards with respect to downstream facilities including the Tarapur Power Reactor Fuel Reprocessing Plant (PREFRE). Moreover, both the Tarapur and Rajasthan "Away from Reactor" spent fuel storage pools will be made available for safeguards. India decided not to declare as civil its other spent fuel reprocessing facilities, as well as its indigenous uranium enrichment capability. Subsequent to India's March 2006 separation plan, the Indian government decided to pursue development of a new civil facility dedicated to reprocessing material under safeguards. Development of this facility (and agreement with the United States on arrangements and procedures related thereto) will be required to bring into effect U.S. consent to reprocessing, pursuant to Article 6 of the Agreement.

Including upstream and downstream facilities under safeguards greatly enhances the ability to ensure that India is effectively separating its civilian and military facilities and programs, safeguarding the civil nuclear program, equipment, and materials, and that no diversion of international civil nuclear assistance is taking place to further military uses. By including both upstream and downstream facilities, India's Separation Plan covers every stage in the fuel cycle process from conversion and fuel fabrication, through the end of the nuclear fuel cycle into stages including spent fuel storage.

As a whole, the United States assesses India's plan to be credible, transparent, and defensible from a nonproliferation standpoint. When implemented, the total installed nuclear capacity under safeguards will rise from 19 per cent today to 65 per cent; a percentage that will increase to more than 80 per cent as India further expands its civil infrastructure through foreign supply and indigenous development. Based on India's safeguards agreement with the IAEA (discussed below), appropriate safeguards will cover India's civil nuclear fuel cycle and provide strong assurances to supplier states that material and technology provided or generated through civil nuclear cooperation will not be diverted either to the military sphere or for unauthorized purposes. In addition, the total portion of India's spent fuel and plutonium stockpiles under safeguards will increase substantially over time (although the reprocessing consent in Article 6 of the U.S.-India Agreement for Peaceful Nuclear Cooperation, if and when the consent comes into effect, could increase modestly the quantity of separated civil plutonium stored in India).

With respect to India filing a declaration with the IAEA, as previously noted, on July 25, 2008, the Government of India transmitted the Separation Plan to the Director General of the IAEA to be distributed "to all Member-States of the Agency" (and the IAEA circulated the Separation Plan to Members as IAEA document INFCIRC/731). Paragraph 14 of the Separation Plan describes the "civil" elements of India's nuclear program, specifically naming the 14 reactors that will be declared "civil" and establishing a timetable for placing them under safeguards, as well as describing the treatment of other types of facilities (breeder reactors, research reactors, upstream facilities, downstream facilities, and research facilities). In a speech to the Indian Parliament on August 17, 2006, the Prime Minister confirmed that the "civil" facilities designated in the Separation Plan would be submitted to safeguards in a phased manner. He made similar statements to the Indian Parliament on August 13, 2007, after negotiations were completed on the 123 Agreement. In addition, in introducing the India-IAEA Safeguards Agreement, the Director General of the IAEA specifically referred to the significance of the Separation Plan (which had been recently circulated within the IAEA), noting that it described the facilities envisages as coming under safeguards by 2014.

IAEA Safeguards

Section 104(c)(2)(B) of the Hyde Act requires:

> "A summary of the agreement that has been entered into between India and the IAEA requiring the application of safeguards in accordance with IAEA practices to India's civil nuclear facilities as declared in the plan described in subparagraph (A), together with a copy of the agreement, and a description of the progress toward its full implementation."

India and the IAEA negotiated, in early 2008, a safeguards agreement, based on INFCIRC/66, the IAEA's approved safeguards system for states not party to the Treaty on the Non-Proliferation of Nuclear Weapons..... On August 1, 2008, the IAEA Board of Governors approved this agreement by consensus. Thus all legal steps required prior to signature of the safeguards agreement have been concluded. In his statement to the Board of Governors on August 1, 2008 Director General ElBaradei stated:

> "The text before you is an INFCIRC/66-type safeguards agreement based on the Agency's standard safeguards practices and procedures.... In the case of the draft before you, it is an "umbrella agreement", which provides for any facility notified by India to the Agency in the future to become subject to safeguards.... The "umbrella" nature of this agreement provides a more efficient mechanism for ensuring that safeguards requirements can be met. It satisfies India's needs while maintaining all the Agency's legal requirements.... As you can see from *India's Plan*, which has been circulated for the information of all IAEA Member States, a total of 14 reactors are envisaged to come under

Agency safeguards by 2014. As with other safeguards agreements between the Agency and Member States, the agreement is of indefinite duration. There are no conditions for the discontinuation of safeguards other than those provided by the safeguards agreement itself. The termination provisions contained in the agreement are the same as for other 66-type agreements. Naturally—as with all safeguards agreements—this agreement is subject to the general rules of international law. Therefore, the agreement should be read as an integral whole. The preamble provides for contextual background and safeguards are implemented in accordance with the terms of the agreement."

Specifically, paragraph 11 of the safeguards agreement describes the items subject to safeguards:

"11. The items subject to this Agreement shall be:

(a) Any facility listed in the Annex to this Agreement, as notified by India pursuant to paragraph 14(a) of this Agreement;

(b) Any nuclear material, non-nuclear material, equipment and components supplied to India which are required to be safeguarded pursuant to a bilateral or multilateral arrangement to which India is a party;

(c) Any nuclear material, including subsequent generations of special fissionable material, produced, processed or used in or by the use of a facility listed in the Annex or in or by the use of any nuclear material, non-nuclear material, equipment and components referred to in paragraph 11(b);

(d) Any nuclear material substituted in accordance with paragraph 27 or 30(d) of this Agreement for nuclear material referred to in paragraph 11(b) or 11(c) of this Agreement;

(e) Any heavy water substituted in accordance with paragraph 32 of this Agreement for heavy water subject to this Agreement;

(f) Any facility other than a facility identified in paragraph 11(a) above, or any other location in India, while producing, processing, using, fabricating or storing any nuclear material, non-nuclear material, equipment or components referred to in paragraph 11(b), (c), (d), or (e) of this Agreement, as notified by India pursuant to paragraph 14(b) of this Agreement."

Paragraph 14(a) provides that India shall "notify the Agency in writing" of its decision to offer a facility for safeguards, after which that facility is included on the Annex to the safeguards agreement. This step of "notifying" the Agency of a facility offered for safeguards will be preceded by India's filing a "declaration" of civil facilities to be placed under safeguards in a phased manner; this filing will occur upon entry into force of the safeguards agreement.

Once a facility is listed in the Annex, safeguards will continue indefinitely unless "India and the Agency have jointly determined that the facility is no longer usable for any nuclear activity relevant from the point of view of safeguards" (paragraph 32). While there are a number of conditions for the termination of safeguards on materials (e.g., material is diluted to the point where it is no longer usable), these termination conditions, as noted by the El Baradei statement, are in accordance with standard IAEA practices, including INFICIRC/66. Thus, the facilities and materials subject to safeguards as described by paragraph 11(a)-(c) are under "safeguards in perpetuity in accordance with IAEA standards, principles, and practices."

India has indicated that it will submit facilities to safeguards under the India-IAEA safeguards agreement "as declared in" the Indian Separation Plan. As noted by the IAEA Director General, the "umbrella"-type safeguards agreement is well-suited for placing the facilities identified in the Separation Plan under safeguards in a phased manner. In addition, it is well-suited to adding future indigenous reactors that India may construct for civil purposes, as well as reactors that India may import from international suppliers.

Full implementation of the India-IAEA safeguards agreement will require signature of the agreement by both the IAEA and India. The agreement will enter into force once India informs the IAEA that India's domestic legal requirements for entry into force have been met. The Government of India's cover letter transmitting the Separation Plan to the IAEA contained a statement of its "intention to move forward in accordance with the provisions of the Safeguards Agreement after its entry into force." In the meantime, Indian discussions with the IAEA on implementation of the safeguards agreement are ongoing.

IAEA Additional Protocol

Section 104(c)(2c) of the Hyde Act requires:

> "A summary of the progress made toward conclusion and implementation of an Additional Protocol between India and the IAEA, including a description of the scope of such Additional Protocol."

To further strengthen safeguards on India's civil nuclear facilities, consistent with its July 2005 Joint Statement commitment, India is in discussions and working closely with the IAEA to conclude an Additional Protocol that would give the IAEA expanded rights of access and additional information regarding India's civil nuclear facilities, including information on exports and imports of trigger list items. These activities, as well as others required to be reported and made available for access under an Additional Protocol, would not otherwise be subject to safeguards. Entry into force of an India-IAEA Additional Protocol could, therefore, provide even more transparency into India's civil nuclear activities.

Indian External Affairs Minister Pranab Mukherjee noted in his statement of September 5, 2008 that India was "working closely with the IAEA to ensure early conclusion of an Additional Protocol to the Safeguards Agreement." Indian officials have conveyed a letter to IAEA counterparts outlining the contours of a proposed Protocol, and the IAEA is currently reviewing India's proposal. The details included in this letter as well as substantive discussions between Indian officials and the IAEA prompted IAEA Director General Mohammed ElBaradei to conclude on September 10, 2008 that India has made substantial progress toward concluding an Additional Protocol consistent with IAEA principles, practices, and policies that would apply to India's civil nuclear program. We look forward to conclusion of this Additional Protocol at an early date.

Fissile Material Cut-Off Treaty

Section 104(c)(2)(D) of the Hyde Act requires:

> "A description of the steps that India is taking to work with the United States for the conclusion of a multilateral treaty banning the production of fissile material for nuclear weapons, including a description of the steps that the United States has taken and will take to encourage India to identify and declare a date by which India would be willing to stop production of fissile material for nuclear weapons unilaterally or pursuant to a multilateral moratorium or treaty."

In August 2006, Indian Prime Minister Singh told the Indian Parliament that India was willing to join a "non-discriminatory, multilaterally-negotiated and internationally verifiable FMCT...provided its security interests are fully addressed." Following this statement, India has publicly endorsed the negotiation of an FMCT in the Conference on Disarmament (CD) and has worked with the U.S. and its international partners to commence FMCT negotiations in that forum. In a 2007 session of the CD, although India initially posed procedural objections to the proposed Program of Work, which included among other items negotiations on an FMCT, India later dropped this objection and supported the measure after the U.S. decided to join consensus support of the Program. In a 2008 session of the CD, India was also supportive of U.S. efforts to realize an effective Program of Work for the CD; India made several constructive suggestions that were incorporated into the draft program of work presented in that session (CD/1840).

Despite the cooperative working relationship between the U.S., India, and some other countries in the CD, obstacles remain in securing consensus on a Program of Work in the CD that includes negotiations on an FMCT. Nevertheless, the U.S.,

India, and other like-minded states continue to seek a way forward. The U.S. has now given its support to work plan CD/1840 as the best, albeit not ideal, option available for forward movement on the FMCT.

In the March 2008 session of the CD, India made a statement expressing support for consensus on a program of work that took into account "the interests of all stake-holders." In July 2008, India told the U.S. that its Ambassador in Geneva would, at a July 29 CD meeting, publicly declare broad support for an FMCT and efforts to reach consensus on a work plan. At that meeting, the Indian Ambassador repeated India's support for consensus on a program of work that takes into account "the interests of all stake-holders." India followed this with a statement in an informal session on July 31, where they reiterated their long-standing support for negotiating an FMCT in the CD.

On September 5, 2008, Indian External Affairs Minister Pranab Mukherjee stated, "We are committed to work with others towards the conclusion of a multilateral Fissile Material Cut-off Treaty in the Conference on Disarmament that is universal, non-discriminatory, and verifiable."

In addition to discussions at the CD on an FMCT, the U.S. remains willing to explore other intermediate options. We continue to encourage an early end to the production of fissile material production for weapons by all states. Toward that end we have urged India as part of our bilateral dialogue to put in place a moratorium on fissile material production, as we have done. India has rejected this notion in favor of working this issue at the CD.

Preventing the Spread of Enrichment and Reprocessing Technology

Section 104(c)(2)(E) of the Hyde Act requires:

"A description of the steps India is taking to prevent the spread of nuclear-related technology, including enrichment and reprocessing technology or materials that can be used to acquire a nuclear weapons capability, as well as the support that India is providing to the United States to further United States objectives to restrict the spread of such technology."

India has a solid nonproliferation record on enrichment and reprocessing (ENR) transfers; we are aware of no Indian transfers of ENR equipment or technologies to another state. India furthermore is supportive of international efforts to limit their spread to states that do not already possess ENR.

India has been supportive of U.S. efforts to work with other states to develop incentives to encourage states without ENR not to pursue these technologies. One such effort is the IAEA fuel bank initiative. Toward that end, India sent a letter dated 18 August 2008 to IAEA Director General El Baradei indicating India's interest in participating as a supplier nation in the IAEA's effort to establish international fuel banks. In this letter, Dr. Anil Kakodkar, Chairman of India's Atomic Energy Commission, reaffirmed that "India will refrain from the transfer of enrichment and reprocessing technologies to States that do not have them, and support international efforts to limit their spread."

Indian External Affairs Minister Pranab Mukherjee reiterated that in a September 5, 2008 public statement that:

> "India will not be the source of proliferation of sensitive technologies, including enrichment and reprocessing transfers. We stand for the strengthening of the non-proliferation regime. We support international efforts to limit the spread of ENR equipment or technologies to states that do not have them. We will work together with the international community to advance our common objective of non-proliferation. In this regard, India is interested in participating as a supplier nation, particularly for Thorium-based fuel and in establishment of international fuel banks, which also benefit India."

Export Controls

Section 104(c)(2)(F) of the Hyde Act requires:

> "A description of the steps that India is taking to secure materials and technology applicable for the development,

acquisition, or manufacture of weapons of mass destruction and the means to deliver such weapons through the application of comprehensive export control legislation and regulations, and through harmonization with and adherence to MTCR, NSG, Australia Group, and Wassenaar Arrangement guidelines, compliance with United Nations Security Council Resolution 1540, and participation in the Proliferation Security Initiative."

India committed under the July 18, 2005 Joint Statement, which launched the Civil Nuclear Cooperation Initiative, to harmonize its export controls with and unilaterally adhere to the Missile Technology Control Regime (MTCR) and NSG Guidelines. Through our various discussions since then, India has assured the United States that it has taken the necessary steps to have in place and fully implement effective and comprehensive export controls to deny unlawful access by states or non-state actors. Moreover, India has given assurances of a high-level political commitment to this effort.

India's June 2005 "Weapons of Mass Destruction (WMD) and their Delivery Systems (Prohibitions of Unlawful Activities) Act" and subsequent implementing regulations bring Indian export controls further in line with widely accepted export control standards for preventing WMD proliferation and are consistent with the kinds of measures that UN Security Council Resolution 1540 requires states to implement. The WMD Act, with its stronger "catch-all" provisions, considerably strengthens the government's regulatory ability to control transfers of otherwise uncontrolled items that could contribute to a WMD or missile program of concern.

To assist India in strengthening its export control system, the U.S. held two rounds of experts-level export control talks with India (October 15-16, 2007 and August 11-12, 2008). During these talks, the U.S. gained greater understanding of India's export control laws and regulations, their history, its Special Chemicals, Organisms, Materials, Equipment, and Technologies (SCOMET) list, and how its controls are implemented and enforced. As a result of our engagement with

India on its export control system, India not only provided greater clarity on that system but also took specific steps such as issuing a revised SCOMET notification on September 7, 2007.

With respect to harmonization with the NSG and MTCR, in addition to issuing the revision to the SCOMET list in 2007, India explained how the Government of India sometimes uses broader terms than is utilized in the NSG or MTCR; this is done so as to exercise greater licensing oversight. India further explained that there are no substantial differences between its guidelines and those of the NSG and that the only linguistic differences flow from India's nonparticipation in the NSG. The U.S. assesses that India has harmonized with the MTCR and with the NSG up through the 2005 revisions, and has the means in place to make future updates to its guidelines and control lists if it chooses to do so. Furthermore, India's SCOMET list already captures some of the follow-on updates to the MTCR. We understand that this harmonization process will continue as an element of India's unilateral adherence to the NSG and MTCR. The Government of India has assured us that it has in place a process to make changes to the SCOMET list. Ongoing review and strengthening of India's export controls is built into the Indian system through regular inter-ministerial working groups as well as the Advisory Committees set up in November 2006 under the WMD Act of 2005.

India stated its adherence to the NSG and its annexes in a letter dated September 8, 2008, to Dr. Mohammed El Baradei, the Director General of the International Atomic Energy Agency. Likewise, India stated its adherence to the MTCR and its annex in a letter dated September 9, 2008, to Mr. Jacques Audibert, the MTCR Point of Contact in Paris. Taking into account these statements, the U.S. assesses that India has adhered to the guidelines and annexes of the NSG and the MTCR, and has done so in a manner consistent with the procedures and/or practices of those regimes.

As part of our strategic partnership, and in the course of a variety of dialogues, including annual nonproliferation talks, we discuss with India a wide range of nonproliferation and export control-related issues, including harmonization with and adherence to the Australia Group (AG) and Wassenaar Arrangement (WA), endorsement of the Proliferation Security Initiative, and implementation of UN Security Council Resolution 1540. We have discussed areas of differences between the SCOMET list and the AG as well as the process of adherence. With respect to the WA, India is in the process of developing a munitions list, and has welcomed outreach by the WA Chair. Discussions with India regarding PSI are ongoing. Since October 2007, India has attended as observers three PSI exercises and the PSI Fifth Anniversary Workshop for non-PSI partners. With respect to UNSCR 1540, India has submitted to the Committee established by UN Security Council Resolution 1540 its initial report as well as two subsequent reports on steps it has taken to meet its UN Security Council Resolution 1540 obligations, and continues to support the Committee's work.

Dissuading Iran from Acquiring WMD

Section 104(c)(2)(G) of the Hyde Act requires:

> "A description and assessment of the specific measures that India has taken to fully and actively participate in United States and international efforts to dissuade, isolate, and, if necessary, sanction and contain Iran for its efforts to acquire weapons of mass destruction, including a nuclear weapons capability and the capability to enrich uranium or reprocess nuclear fuel and the means to deliver weapons of mass destruction."

The Government of India has taken several steps to support the U.S. in this regard and to bring Iran back into compliance with its international obligations, particularly those pertaining to its nuclear weapons program. As a member of the IAEA Board of Governors, India voted in favor of both the resolution that found Iran in noncompliance with its IAEA Safeguards Agreement in September 2005 and the resolution that reported Iran's noncompliance to the UN Security Council in February 2006. Responding to the adoption of three Chapter VII UN Security Council Resolutions (1737 in 2006, 1747 in 2007, and 183 in 2008), India reported that it is fully implementing their provisions, including those related to preventing Iran's acquisition of sensitive technology that could facilitate its uranium enrichment program or any future action to reprocess spent fuel.

India has also maintained a strong public line of support for P5+1 and U.S. diplomatic efforts to resolve international concerns with Iran's nuclear program. Furthermore, India has stressed that it does not favor the emergence of additional nuclear weapons states in the region and that all states must adhere to commitments under international treaties and be transparent in fulfilling these commitments. In this vein, India has called on Iran to cooperate fully with the IAEA on numerous occasions and delivered the same message to the Iranians during bilateral consultations.

Nuclear Suppliers Group Exception

Section 104(c)(2)(H) of the Hyde Act requires:

> "A description of the decision of the NSG relating to nuclear cooperation with India, including whether nuclear cooperation by the United States under an agreement for cooperation arranged pursuant to section 123 of the Atomic Energy Act of 1954 (42 U.S.C. 2153) is consistent with the decision, practices, and policies of the NSG."

On September 6, 2008, the Nuclear Suppliers Group approved a policy statement by consensus excepting India from the Group's full-scope safeguards requirement for civil nuclear trade. This decision was made at the second of two Extraordinary Plenary sessions held August 21-22 and September 4-6, 2008. This historic decision by the NSG strengthens global nonproliferation principles while assisting India to meet its energy requirements in an environmentally friendly manner.

This exception involved intense scrutiny and debate by and among participating governments. On September 5, 2008, Indian External Affairs Minister (EAM) Pranab Mukherjee issued the following statement on the Civil Nuclear Cooperation Initiative, which was helpful in garnering additional momentum towards consensus:

STATEMENT BY EXTERNAL AFFAIRS MINISTER OF INDIA SHRI PRANAB MUKHERJEE ON THE CIVIL NUCLEAR INITIATIVE

05 SEPTEMBER 2008

To reiterate India's stand on disarmament and nonproliferation, EAM has made the following statement:

A Plenary meeting of the Nuclear Suppliers Group to consider an exception for India from its guidelines to allow for full civil nuclear cooperation with India is being held in Vienna from September 4-5, 2008.

India has a long-standing and steadfast commitment to universal, nondiscriminatory and total elimination of nuclear weapons. The vision of a world free of nuclear weapons which Shri Rajiv Gandhi put before the UN in 1988 still has universal resonance.

We approach our dialogue with the Nuclear Suppliers Group and all its members in a spirit of cooperation that allows for an ongoing frank exchange of views on subjects of mutual interest and concern. Such a dialogue will strengthen our relationship in the years to come.

Our civil nuclear initiative will strengthen the international nonproliferation regime. India believes that the opening of full civil nuclear cooperation will be good for India and for the world. It will have a profound positive impact on global energy security and international efforts to combat climate change.

India has recently submitted a Working Paper on Nuclear Disarmament to the UN General Assembly, containing initiatives on nuclear disarmament. These include the reaffirmation of the unequivocal commitment of all nuclear weapon States to the goal of complete elimination of nuclear weapons; negotiation of a Convention on the complete prohibition of the use or threat of use of nuclear weapons; and negotiation of a Nuclear Weapons Convention prohibiting the development, production, stockpiling and use of nuclear weapons and on their destruction, leading to the global, nondiscriminatory and verifiable elimination of nuclear weapons within a specified timeframe.

We remain committed to a voluntary, unilateral moratorium on nuclear testing. We do not subscribe to any arms race, including a nuclear arms race. We have always tempered the exercise of our strategic autonomy with a sense of global responsibility. We affirm our policy of no-first-use of nuclear weapons.

We are committed to work with others towards the conclusion of a multilateral Fissile Material cut-off Treaty in the Conference on Disarmament that is universal, non-discriminatory and verifiable.

India has an impeccable non-proliferation record. We have in place an effective and comprehensive system of national export controls, which has been constantly updated to meet the highest international standards. This is manifested in the enactment of the Weapons of Mass Destruction and their Delivery Systems Act in 2005. India has taken the necessary steps to secure nuclear materials and technology through comprehensive export control legislation and through harmonization and committing to adhere to Missile Technology Control Regime and Nuclear Suppliers Group guidelines.

India will not be the source of proliferation of sensitive technologies, including enrichment and reprocessing transfers. We stand for the strengthening of the non-proliferation regime. We support international efforts to limit the spread of ENR equipment or technologies to states that do not have them. We will work together with the international community to advance our common objective of non-proliferation. In this regard, India is interested in participating as a supplier nation, particularly for Thorium-based fuel and in establishment of international fuel banks, which also benefit India.

India places great value on the role played by the IAEA's nuclear safeguards system. We look forward to working with the IAEA in implementing the India-specific Safeguards Agreement concluded with the IAEA. In keeping with our commitment to sign and adhere to an Additional Protocol with respect to India's civil nuclear facilities, we are working closely with the IAEA to ensure early conclusion of an Additional Protocol to the Safeguards Agreement.

New Delhi

5th September 2008

With these assurances reaffirmed, NSG Participating Governments agreed by consensus on an exception for India on September 6, 2008. This decision is consistent with the cooperation envisioned under the U.S.-India peaceful nuclear cooperation agreement detailed below as well as with NSG practices and policies. This policy decision:

- exempts India from the NSG's full-scope safeguards requirement as a condition for transfer of Trigger List items for peaceful purposes and for use in IAEA safeguarded civil nuclear facilities, provided that the transfer satisfies all other provisions of the NSG Guidelines.
- contains an information exchange clause, which is consistent with current practice of the NSG.
- calls for intensified dialogue between the NSG Chair and India; this dialogue already exists. It is useful for it to be intensified not only as part of this decision, but also given India's decision to adhere to the NSG, which involves remaining abreast of and in line with changes to the NSG list and guidelines.
- addresses the desire expressed by some Participating Governments for an explicit review mechanism and/or for the ability to respond in the event that India abrogates its commitments, such as a nuclear explosive test or safeguards violation. This ability to consult in response to some problem is already provided for under Paragraph 16 of the Guidelines; any participating government may exercise this ability if they consider circumstances warrant.
- notes that Participating Governments will maintain contact and consult through regular channels to

"consider" matters related to this decision consistent with the NSG's existing authority and practice.

- provides for enhanced outreach between India and the NSG Chair following this decision and in light of India's decision to adhere to the NSG. This is consistent with enhanced outreach that we support with all adherents and is especially important in light of the civil nuclear trade with India to result from the NSG's decision.

Envisioned Scope of U.S.-India Peaceful Nuclear Cooperation

Section 104(c)(2i)

"A description of the scope of peaceful cooperation envisioned by the United States and India that will be implemented under the agreement for nuclear cooperation, including whether such cooperation will include the provision of enrichment and reprocessing technology."

Envisioned civil nuclear cooperation with India will include a number of activities, which are described in general terms in the Proposed Agreement for Cooperation Between the Government of the United States of America and the Government of India Concerning Peaceful Uses of Nuclear Energy Article 2(2). These activities are to take place in accordance with the provisions of the Agreement and each Party's applicable treaties, national laws, regulations, and license requirements and may include, but are not limited to, the following areas:

- Advanced nuclear energy research and development in areas agreed to by the Parties;
- Nuclear safety matters;
- Facilitation of exchange of scientists for visits, meetings, symposia and collaborative research;
- Full civil nuclear cooperation activities covering nuclear reactors and aspects of the associated nuclear fuel cycle including technology transfer on an industrial or commercial scale between the Parties or authorized persons;

- Development of a strategic reserve to guard against any disruption of supply over the lifetime of India's reactors;
- Advanced research and development in nuclear sciences including biological research, medicine, agriculture and industry, environment and climate change;
- Supply between the Parties, whether for use by or for the benefit of the Parties or third countries, of nuclear material;
- Alteration in form or content of nuclear material as provided for in Article 6 of the Agreement;
- Supply between the Parties of equipment, whether for use by or for the benefit of the Parties or third countries;
- Controlled thermonuclear fusion including in multilateral projects; and
- Other areas of mutual interest as may be agreed by the Parties.

Article 2(3) of the Agreement specifically provides that the Parties may undertake transfers between themselves or their authorized persons of nuclear material, non-nuclear material, equipment, components and information.

In Article 2(4) of the Agreement, the U.S. and India further delimit the scope of cooperation by affirming that the purpose of the Agreement is to provide for peaceful nuclear cooperation and not to affect the unsafeguarded nuclear activities of either Party. Nothing in the Agreement is to be interpreted as affecting the rights of the Parties to use for their own purposes nuclear material, non-nuclear material, equipment, components, information or technology produced, acquired or developed by them independent of any nuclear material, non-nuclear material, equipment, components, information or technology transferred to them pursuant to the Agreement. The Agreement is to be implemented in a manner so as not to hinder or otherwise interfere with any other activities involving the use of nuclear material, non-nuclear material, equipment, components, information or technology and military nuclear facilities produced, acquired or developed by them independent of the Agreement for their own purposes.

Article 3(1) of the Agreement again specifically provides that information may be transferred between the Parties, and that such information may cover, but need not be limited to, the following fields:

- Research, development, design, construction, operation, maintenance and use of reactors, reactor experiments, and decommissioning;
- The use of nuclear material in physical, chemical, radiological and biological research, medicine, agriculture and industry;
- Fuel cycle activities to meet future world-wide civil nuclear energy needs, including multilateral approaches to which they are parties for ensuring nuclear fuel supply and appropriate techniques for management of nuclear wastes;
- Advanced research and development in nuclear science and technology;
- Health, safety and environmental considerations related to the foregoing;
- Assessments of the role that nuclear power may play in national energy plans;
- Codes, regulations and standards for the nuclear industry;
- Research on controlled thermonuclear fusion including bilateral activities and contributions toward multilateral projects such as the International Thermonuclear Experimental Reactor (ITER); and
- Any other field mutually agreed to by the Parties.

Article 3(2) provides that the above cooperation may include training, exchange of personnel, meetings, exchange of samples, materials and instruments for experimental purposes and a balanced participation in joint studies and projects.

Article 3(3) states that the Agreement does not require the transfer of any information outside the scope of the Agreement, or information that the Parties are not permitted under their respective treaties, national laws or regulations to transfer.

Article 3(4) provides that Restricted Data, as defined by each Party, shall not be transferred under the Agreement.

Article 4(1) provides *inter alia* for the Parties to facilitate nuclear trade between themselves in the mutual interests of their respective industry, utilities and consumers and also, where appropriate, trade between either Party and a third country of items obligated to the other Party.

Article 4(2) provides *inter alia* that authorizations, including export and import licenses as well as authorizations or consents to third parties relating to trade, industrial operations or nuclear material movement, should be consistent with the sound and efficient administration of the Agreement and should not be used to restrict trade.

Article 5(1) provides that nuclear material, non-nuclear material, equipment and components may be transferred for applications consistent with the Agreement. However, any special fissionable material transferred shall be limited to low enriched uranium, except for "small quantities," which may be transferred pursuant to Article 5(5) for use as samples, standards, detectors and targets, and the accomplishment of other purposes as agreed by the Parties.

In considering the scope of civil nuclear cooperation with India, the issue of spreading sensitive technologies is often raised. The requirement of section 123a.(9) pertains to situations that may result when sensitive nuclear technology is transferred pursuant to a section 123 agreement for cooperation. Article 5(2) of the Agreement provides that sensitive nuclear technology shall only be transferred under the Agreement if provided for by an amendment to the Agreement, and Article 5(2) further provides that sensitive nuclear facilities and major critical components thereof shall only be transferred under the Agreement if provided for by an amendment to the Agreement. Accordingly, the requirement in section 123a.(9) is not relevant to the proposed Agreement, and the requirement in section 402(b) of the NNPA precluding the transfer of major critical components of facilities for uranium enrichment, nuclear fuel reprocessing, or heavy water production unless an agreement for cooperation "specifically designates such components as items to be exported pursuant to [such] agreement" is also satisfied.

Article 5(4) provides that the *quantity* of nuclear material transferred under the Agreement shall be consistent with any of the following purposes: use in reactor experiments or the loading of reactors, the efficient and continuous conduct of such reactor experiments or operation of reactors for their lifetime, use as samples, standards, detectors and targets, and other purposes as the Parties may agree.

Article 5(6) records verbatim certain political assurances relating to reliable supply of nuclear fuel given to India by the United States in March 2006. The Agreement language does not have the effect of converting these political assurances into legally binding commitments.

Articles 5(2), 6-10, and 14 address the specific requirements of section 123a. of the Atomic Energy Act of 1954 (AEA).

Article 11 provides that the Parties shall cooperate in following the best practices for minimizing the impact on the environment from any radioactive, chemical or thermal contamination arising from activities under the Agreement and in related matters of health and safety.

Article 12 contains additional provisions with regard to implementation of activities falling within the scope of the Agreement.

Article 13 provides for consultations at the request of either Party regarding implementation of the Agreement and the development of further cooperation in the field of peaceful uses of nuclear energy on a stable, reliable and predictable basis. It further provides that the Parties shall endeavor to avoid taking any action that adversely affects cooperation under Article 2, which is the general "Scope of Cooperation" article.

Article 15 provides for dispute settlement through negotiations between the Parties.

Article 16 provides for the Agreement to have an initial duration of 40 years and to continue in force for additional periods of 10 years each, subject to a proviso that either Party may terminate the Agreement by giving written notice to the other Party six months prior to the close of a period. It also provides for continuation in effect of key nonproliferation provisions of the Agreement in the event of its termination.

Ensuring Cooperation does not in any Way Assist India's Nuclear Weapons Program

Section 104(c)(2)(J) of the Hyde Act requires:

> "A description of the steps taken to ensure that proposed United States civil nuclear cooperation with India will not in any way assist India's nuclear weapons program."

As previously described, India has developed a Separation Plan (INFCIR/731) to separate civil and military nuclear facilities. The India-IAEA safeguards agreement, which was unanimously approved by the IAEA Board of Governors on August 1, 2008, establishes procedures for applying safeguards to India's "civil" nuclear facilities in accordance with IAEA standards, principles, and practices. The stated purpose of the safeguards agreement is to ensure that no safeguarded item is "used for the manufacture of any nuclear weapon or to further any other military purpose and that such items are used exclusively for peaceful purposes." To this end, IAEA safeguards are designed to detect and prevent diversion from civil to military facilities, making the conclusion of this safeguards agreement the key to ensuring that civil nuclear cooperation could not be used to advance a nuclear weapons program. The U.S. does not in any way support India's nuclear weapons program.

Under the Safeguards Agreement, the IAEA will verify that all of India's current and future civil nuclear facilities and material, as well as certain upstream and downstream facilities, are used only for peaceful purposes. Once a reactor is under IAEA safeguards, those safeguards will remain in place on an unconditional basis until the reactor is jointly determined by the IAEA and India to be no longer usable for nuclear activities relevant from the point of view of safeguards. This initiative will only allow for nuclear cooperation to proceed with facilities subject to IAEA safeguards, monitoring, and inspections to ensure that the civilian nature of the work therein is not compromised. This also provides an incentive for India to declare any future reactors as civil and thus bring them into this framework of nuclear cooperation; otherwise no foreign material and technology would be available for their construction and operation.

For dual-use nuclear exports administered by the Department of Commerce, there are several ways the U.S. is assured that exports are going to reliable recipients of U.S. origin items and have not been diverted to unauthorized end users or end uses. As part of the license application package, we require certification that the item(s) will not be used in any of the prohibited activities described in 744.2(a) of the Export Administration Regulations (EAR). Through the licensing process, the intelligence and enforcement communities provide information on the bona fides of prospective end-users. Commerce determines the bona fides of the transaction and suitability of the end-user through the use of pre-license checks. This information is then used to make licensing decisions. As part of the approval process, export licenses normally have conditions attached that prohibit re-export, retransfer, or use in sensitive nuclear, chemical, biological, or missile end uses. We require applicants to inform end-users of the licensing conditions. In addition, the U.S. has an end use assurance letter from the Government of India that commits it to ensure that items are not transferred from or through India for use in prohibited unsafeguarded nuclear, WMD, or WMD delivery programs. Also, through post-shipment verifications, the U.S. visits recipients of U.S.-origin items to ensure that the items have actually been delivered to the authorized ultimate consignee or end-user and those items are being used as stated on the export license application.

The transfer of nuclear fuel technology requires authorization by the Secretary of Energy under Section 57(b) of the Atomic Energy Act of 1954 as amended. The regulations that implement Section 57(b) are found in 10 CFR Part 810, which require that prior to such approval, government-to-government assurances outlining the controls/conditions that will be used for securing this technology must be in place. This includes the requirement that the transfer, anything derived from the transfer, and anything that is produced or modified in a facility constructed as a result of the transfer will be used for peaceful purposes. Further, the United States places additional conditions on an authorization to transfer the technology that limits access and prohibits the retransfer of the technology.

Conclusion

As great progress has been made in bringing the U.S.-India Civil Nuclear Cooperation Initiative to fruition, India has been brought closer to the nonproliferation mainstream. India has completed a Separation Plan, negotiated a safeguards agreement, and made substantial progress towards an Additional Protocol. India has greatly improved its export controls and pledged to maintain the highest international standards on restricting the transfer of sensitive technologies. The U.S.-India bilateral relationship has been revamped and has facilitated cooperation on many key regional and global issues, such as dissuading Iranian attempts to acquire WMD and completing an FMCT in the CD, and this close cooperation is expected to continue in the future, advancing U.S. strategic interests and increasing U.S. national security. Civil nuclear trade with India will increase global energy security and advance U.S. and Indian economic interests while at the same time strengthening the global nonproliferation regime. In meeting its nonproliferation commitments under the Hyde Act, India has made a great step forward in taking its place as a strategic partner for the U.S. now and in the future.

10 Nuclear Proliferation Assessment Statement Pursuant to Section 123a. of the Atomic Energy Act of 1954, as Amended, with Respect to the Proposed Agreement for Cooperation between the Government of the United States of America and the Government of India Concerning Peaceful Uses of Nuclear Energy

This Nuclear Proliferation Assessment Statement ("NPAS") relates to the proposed Agreement for Cooperation Between the Government of the United States of America and the Government of India Concerning Peaceful Uses of Nuclear Energy (the "Agreement"). The Agreement is being submitted to the President jointly by the Secretary of State and the Secretary of Energy for his approval.

Section 123a. of the Atomic Energy Act, as amended (the "Atomic Energy Act" or "the AEA"), provides that an NPAS be submitted by the Secretary of State to the President on each new or amended agreement for cooperation concluded pursuant to that section. Pursuant to section 123a., the NPAS must analyze the consistency of the text of the proposed agreement with all the requirements of the AEA, with specific attention to whether the proposed agreement is consistent with each of the criteria set forth in that subsection, and address the adequacy of the safeguards and other control mechanisms and the peaceful use assurances contained in the agreement for cooperation to ensure that any assistance furnished thereunder will not be used to further any military or nuclear explosive purpose.

With this statutory mandate in mind, this NPAS: (a) provides background information on India's civil nuclear program and the military nuclear program from which it is being separated (Part I); (b) describes the nature and scope of the cooperation contemplated in the proposed Agreement (Part II); (c) reviews the applicable substantive requirements of the AEA and the Nuclear Non-Proliferation Act of 1978 ("NNPA") and details how they are met by the proposed Agreement (Part III); (d) addresses additional relevant policy issues (Part IV); and (e) sets forth the net assessment, conclusions, views and recommendations of the Department of State as contemplated by section 123a. of the AEA (Part V).

INTRODUCTION: THE U.S.-INDIA CIVIL NUCLEAR COOPERATION INITIATIVE

The U.S.-India Civil Nuclear Cooperation Initiative, of which the proposed U.S.-India Agreement for Peaceful Nuclear Cooperation is the central element, was announced in a Joint Statement by President Bush and Indian Prime Minister Manmohan Singh in Washington on July 18, 2005 ("Joint Statement"). For the United States the Initiative is premised on its contribution to U.S. national security interests by establishing a broad strategic partnership with India that encourages India's emergence as a positive force on the world scene. India is a rising global power and an important democratic partner for the United States. The United States and India are bound together by a strong congruence of interests and values. For example, the United States is seeking to work with India to win the global War on Terrorism, to prevent the spread of weapons of mass destruction and the missiles that could deliver them, to enhance peace and stability in Asia, and to advance the spread of democracy. In the context of this growing partnership, the United States and India issued a landmark Joint Statement in July 2005 to work toward full civil nuclear cooperation while at the same time strengthening global nonproliferation efforts.

India believes, and the United States agrees, that it needs nuclear power to sustain dynamic economic growth and to address its growing energy requirements in an affordable and environmentally-responsible manner. The U.S. goal—in the context of the Joint Statement—is to provide India access to the technology it needs to build a safe, modern and efficient infrastructure that will provide clean, peaceful nuclear energy.

At the same time, India has clearly demonstrated over the past several years its desire to work with the United States and the international community to fight the spread of sensitive nuclear and other technologies. As part of an effort launched with India during the Administration's first term—the Next Steps in Strategic Partnership—India took a number of significant steps to strengthen export controls and to ensure that Indian companies would not be a source of future proliferation. Not only did India pledge to bring its export control laws, regulations, and enforcement practices in line with international export control standards, but it also passed an extensive export control law and issued an upgraded national control list that will help it achieve this goal. India is a signatory to the Biological and Toxin Weapons Convention and the Chemical Weapons Convention, and reports annually to the UN Register of Conventional Arms. In addition, India has become a party to the Convention on the Physical Protection of Nuclear Material, ratified the International Convention for the Suppression of Acts of Nuclear Terrorism, and supports the IAEA Code of Conduct on Safety and Security of Radioactive Sources. India is also a partner in the Global Initiative to Combat Nuclear Terrorism. With respect to its UNSCR 1540 obligations, India has submitted a national report and two addenda to the Committee and currently is represented on the UNSCR 1540 Experts Committee.

With respect to strategic trade enforcement, India has bilateral customs cooperation agreements in place with a number of countries, including with the United States, and has announced its intent to join the Department of Homeland Security's Container Security Initiative. In addition, India participates in the Department of Energy's Megaports Initiative radiation portal monitor program and has deployed advanced scanners at seaports to screen container cargo for arms, explosives, WMD, and other contraband. India also has participated as an official observer of Proliferation Security Initiative regional interdiction exercises.

The additional nonproliferation commitments India has made as part of the Joint Statement go even further and will bring it into closer conformity with international nuclear nonproliferation standards and practices. While the United States will continue to work with India to encourage it to do more over time, India's implementation of its commitments will, on balance, enhance global nonproliferation efforts. The United States expects that the international nuclear nonproliferation regime will emerge stronger as a result.

Through the Joint Statement, India publicly committed to take the following important nonproliferation steps:

- Identify and separate its civilian and military nuclear facilities and programs and file a declaration with the International Atomic Energy Agency (IAEA) regarding its civilian facilities;
- Place voluntarily its civilian nuclear facilities under IAEA safeguards;
- Sign and adhere to an Additional Protocol with the IAEA with respect to its civilian nuclear facilities;
- Continue its unilateral moratorium on nuclear testing;
- Work with the United States for the conclusion of a multilateral Fissile Material Cut-Off Treaty (FMCT) to halt production of fissile material for nuclear weapons;
- Refrain from the transfer of enrichment and reprocessing technologies to states that do not have them, and support efforts to limit their spread; and
- Secure nuclear and missile materials and technologies through comprehensive export control legislation and through harmonization and adherence to the Missile Technology Control Regime (MTCR) and the Nuclear Suppliers Group (NSG) guidelines.

India's commitment to separate its civil and military facilities and place its civil facilities and activities under IAEA safeguards demonstrates its willingness to assume full responsibility for preventing proliferation from its civil nuclear program. It will also help protect against diversion of nuclear material and technologies to India's nuclear weapon program.

By adopting an Additional Protocol with the IAEA, India will commit to reporting to the IAEA on exports of all NSG Trigger List items. This will help the IAEA track potential proliferation elsewhere, and bolster U.S. efforts to encourage all states to adopt an Additional Protocol as a condition of supply.

By committing to adopt strong and effective export controls, including adherence to NSG and MTCR Guidelines, India will help ensure that its companies do not transfer sensitive weapons of mass destruction and missile-related technologies to countries of concern.

In July 2005, India took an important step by harmonizing its national control list with the NSG Guidelines and by adding many items that appear on the MTCR Annex.

India has also committed to work with the United States toward the conclusion of a multilateral FMCT, which, if successfully negotiated and ratified, will ban the production of fissile material for use in nuclear weapons or other nuclear explosive devices.

India's pledge to maintain its nuclear testing moratorium contributes to nonproliferation efforts by making its ending of nuclear explosive tests one of the conditions of full civil nuclear cooperation. Since to date Pakistan has test-exploded nuclear weapons only in response to Indian nuclear tests, this commitment may help diminish the prospects for future nuclear testing in South Asia.

By committing not to export enrichment and reprocessing technology to states that do not already have such fully-functioning capabilities, India will help the United States achieve its goal of preventing the further spread of such proliferation sensitive equipment and technology.

Each of these steps is significant. Together, they constitute a substantial shift in moving India into closer conformity with international nonproliferation standards and practices. Their successful implementation will help to strengthen the global nonproliferation regime.

On a reciprocal basis with India's commitments, the United States committed to work to achieve full civil nuclear cooperation with India. The proposed U.S.-India Agreement for Peaceful Nuclear Cooperation constitutes a core element of that commitment.

I. India's Nuclear Programs and Policies

India's Energy Needs

India, a nation of more than one billion people today, with an economy growing in the range of 8 per cent per year, faces real and growing energy needs. Substantial population growth, expanding industrial production, economic development, urbanization, and growth in transportation sector energy consumption are all driving strong energy demand. Between 1980 and 2001, demand increased by 208 per cent. By contrast, China, often thought of as the world's next big energy consumer, saw a 130 per cent increase over the same period. In 2003, India was the sixth largest consumer of energy in the world behind only the United States, China, Russia, Japan, and Germany.

To meet these growing demands, the Indian Government plans to double its capacity to produce electricity within the next seven years. At present, almost 55 per cent of India's 127 gigawatt (GW) total installed energy generating capacity is derived from coal; roughly 26 per cent from hydro-electric power; 11 per cent from natural gas; and almost 5 per cent from renewable sources. Just 3 per cent of India's total power generation comes from nuclear energy.

Indian energy officials project that by 2031-32, roughly a quarter century from now, India will have a total energy requirement of 700 GW, of which the nuclear component is expected to comprise 63 GW, or approximately nine per cent. India will also require large-scale infrastructure investments and upgrades, including transmission and distribution, as a result of a fivefold increase in electrical power consumption.

Nuclear Energy in India

India has a substantial and growing nuclear infrastructure. Its current capabilities span the nuclear fuel cycle. Indian nuclear facilities include various uranium processing capabilities (uranium mining and milling, copper mine tailing extraction, uranium conversion, fuel fabrication, enrichment); thermal and breeder reactors; research reactors; heavy water production facilities; and spent fuel reprocessing facilities. As of early 2007, the Nuclear Power Corporation of India, Ltd. (NPCIL) operated 16 power reactors, and an additional six are currently under construction. Bharatiya Nabhikiya Vidyut Nigam, Ltd. (Bhavini) operates a 40 MWe fast breeder test reactor and is currently building a 500 MWe prototype fast breeder reactor.

India's operating civil nuclear power plants currently have approximately 3,900 megawatts (MWe) of installed electricity generation capacity, based on the 14 pressurized heavy water reactors (PHWRs) and two boiling water reactors (BWRs) currently on-line. An additional four PHWRs, two light water reactors (LWRs), and the prototype fast breeder reactor (FBR) currently under construction should add an additional 3,380 MWe when operational, bringing the total installed nuclear energy generating capacity to approximately 7,280 MWe. Indian officials have stated their intent to increase the installed nuclear capacity to 20,000 MWe by 2020—a fivefold increase over present output and a goal that cannot be obtained absent substantial foreign assistance.

Over time, the Indian Government intends to increase the nuclear component of its energy output to approximately 20 per cent of India's total energy production, thus significantly decreasing the growth in its reliance on fossil fuels. Senior officials in India's atomic energy establishment have indicated their desire to exceed the 20,000 MWe target through the accelerated import of high-unit capacity foreign reactors.

To this end, Indian officials have begun to discuss their long-term plans with American, Russian, French, and other potential vendors. In early 2007, India and Russia announced a statement of intent to field an additional four LWRs at

Kudankulam, one of three planned "nuclear parks" set aside for international supply. While Russia is already supplying two LWRs at Kudankulam—a "grandfathered" arrangement dating to a time prior to establishment of the Nuclear Suppliers Group (NSG) full-scope safeguards export guideline—the expanded deal is predicated on positive NSG action to enable civil nuclear cooperation with India. American companies would similarly like the chance to compete, on a level playing field, to supply India's civil nuclear program. The recent NSG decision by consensus to except India from the full-scope safeguards export condition is a principal enabling step for potential suppliers. Positive Congressional action on the proposed U.S.-India Agreement for Peaceful Nuclear Cooperation is an additional step necessary to open the Indian civil nuclear market to U.S. industry.

India's Three-Stage (Thorium) Program

India has long sought to implement a three-stage nuclear power programme to meet its growing energy needs. The Department of Atomic Energy (DAE) argues that in the context of India's "modest" uranium reserves but substantial thorium reserves, large scale deployment of nuclear energy is best realized through eventual use of thorium. According to a report issued by the IAEA, India has limited uranium reserves, consisting of approximately 54,636 tons of "reasonably assured resources," 25,245 tons of "estimated additional resources," 15,488 tons of "undiscovered conventional resources," and 17,000 tons of "speculative" resources.

India's known and recoverable uranium resources are insufficient to generate, on a sustainable basis, a capable civil nuclear energy program. According to NPCIL, India's uranium reserves are sufficient to generate perhaps 10,000 MW of electricity for 40 years. Together with India's current installed capacity, once the seven reactors currently under construction come on-line India's total installed nuclear capacity will rise to more than 70 per cent of this sum. This is inadequate to meet India's energy requirements.

By contrast, India has roughly one-third of the world's known thorium reserves. Natural uranium is a source material that can be used in a nuclear reactor to produce energy through nuclear fission. Thorium must first be converted to a fissile material, uranium-233, in a reactor. For more than four decades DAE has sought to develop the capability to use thorium, based on a closed nuclear fuel cycle, for large-scale nuclear energy production. The three-stage program it has sought to implement involves: (1) natural uranium-fueled pressurized heavy water reactors (PHWRs); (2) fast breeder reactors using plutonium-based fuel; and (3) advanced nuclear power systems based on a thorium-uranium-233 cycle. In theory, DAE argues, breeder reactors, using plutonium produced through domestic uranium sources, could generate perhaps 500 GW of electricity.

Despite years of effort, however, India's three-stage program has advanced slowly. India's Atomic Energy Commission projected in 1954 that India would achieve a target of 3 GWe by 1975 and 8 GWe by 1980; instead it hit 540 MWe through 1980, and produces roughly 3 GWe today. As noted above, India is also far short of achieving its goal of 20 GWe of installed capacity by 2020 or its projections that upwardly revise this target. While Indian officials continue to seek the long-term energy independence that, in principle, could be achieved through successful implementation of its three-stage nuclear program, in practice it is clear that India must import fuel, reactors, and other technologies that it has been denied for more than three decades under international export control policies to meet its nuclear electricity-generating targets. With the NSG decision to enable supply of Trigger List items to India, prospective international suppliers now have the ability to supply nuclear-related items to India for peaceful uses.

Civil vs. Military

India's existing nuclear infrastructure is today largely unsafeguarded: only four (rising to six, once Kudankulam-1 and -2 come on-line) power reactors and related nuclear material are currently under International Atomic Energy Agency safeguards. This accounts for approximately 19 per cent of India's total current nuclear energy output. India's existing nuclear infrastructure is today fundamentally intertwined, serving both civil and military or strategic purposes; the Indian government states that its strategic program is an "offshoot" of its research on civil nuclear power, and consequently "it is embedded in a larger undifferentiated programme." In the July 2005 U.S.-India Joint Statement, India committed to identify and separate its civil and military nuclear facilities and programs in a phased manner, placing the civil aspects under safeguards and an Additional Protocol with the IAEA. In this context, India has undertaken to ensure that any international civil nuclear cooperation would not be diverted from civil purposes or transferred to third countries without safeguards or on an otherwise unauthorized basis.

Overview of India's Separation Plan

The Indian Government released its plan to separate India's civil and military nuclear facilities on March 7, 2006; it updated this document on May 11, 2006 and asked the IAEA to circulate it to Member States on July 25, 2008 (IAEA document INFCIRC/731). Because India's existing nuclear infrastructure is intertwined, identification of purely civil facilities and programs that have no strategic implications proved a significant challenge. As its plan developed, the Indian government decided that the nature of the facility concerned, the activities undertaken in it, the national security significance of materials, and the location of the facilities were critical factors in determining what to declare as civilian. (In this context, India did not define or distinguish "military" from "strategic" facilities. The latter may include those having a military role, but also those having a role in India's three stage nuclear energy program.) Similarly, issues relating to fuel resource sustainability, technical design, economic viability, and smooth reactor operation were notable Indian decision criteria. The final plan released by the Indian Government notes that India's approach to the separation of its facilities would be guided by the following principles:

- Credible, feasible, and implementable in a transparent manner;

- Consistent with the understandings of the July 18, 2005 Joint Statement;
- Consistent with India's national security and research and development requirements, as well as not prejudicial to India's three-stage nuclear program;
- Must be cost-effective in its implementation; and
- Must be acceptable to India's Parliament and public opinion.

Derived from these principles, India's plan:

- Includes in the civilian list "only those facilities to be offered for safeguards that, after separation, will no longer be engaged in activities of strategic significance";
- Requires a judgment on the overarching criterion of whether subjecting a facility to IAEA safeguards would impact adversely India's national security;
- Excludes a facility from the civilian list if it is located in a larger hub of strategic significance, even if it does not engage in activities of strategic significance; and accordingly
- Identifies only those facilities that India has determined not to be relevant to its strategic program.

Specifically, India parses its existing and developmental nuclear infrastructure as follows:

- Thermal reactors: India identifies as civil 14 thermal reactors, which according to the March 2006 Separation Plan were scheduled to be offered for safeguards between 2006 and 2014. These include the four existing foreign-supplied reactors [TAPS-1 and -2 (the U.S.-supplied Tarapur reactors), RAPS-1 and -2] and the two foreign-supplied reactors under construction (KK-1 and -2). These also include eight indigenous PHWRs, each with a generating capacity of 220 MWe: RAPS-3, -4, -5 and -6, KAPS-1 and -2, and NAPS-1 and -2. India further notes that safeguards will be applied in a phased manner consistent with its agreement with the IAEA. Eight indigenous PHWRs (TAPS-3 and -4, MAPS-1 and -2, Kaiga-1, -2, -3 and -4) are to remain outside of safeguards.

- Fast breeder reactors: India opted to continue unsafeguarded operations at its operating fast breeder test reactor and also to exclude its prototype fast breeder reactor from safeguards. The fast breeder program is currently at the research and development stage and will take time to reach an advanced stage of development, according to India. India seeks to ensure that it does not face any external "encumbrances" in this process, and so chooses to exclude them from safeguards at this time. India and the United States could not engage in the type of nuclear fuel cycle cooperation authorized by the Hyde Act, the Atomic Energy Act, and the U.S.-India Agreement for Peaceful Nuclear Cooperation with regard to India's breeder reactors until India declared them "civil" and placed them under safeguards.
- Future reactors: India states that it will place under IAEA safeguards "all future civilian thermal power reactors and civilian breeder reactors," retaining for itself the right to determine such reactors as civilian. The United States and other potential suppliers to India have international, and in many cases domestic, legal and policy requirements to ensure that the types of items supplied under their agreements for peaceful nuclear cooperation serve exclusively the civil sector. All reactors, and the material that passes through them, supplied by the United States or by India's other international partners will by definition be "civil" and be subject to IAEA safeguards in perpetuity. While India retains the right to develop indigenous facilities for either civil or military purposes in the future, the separation plan notes that all future thermal and breeder reactors declared "civil" will also be placed under safeguards. Because India seeks the maximum benefit from international cooperation, as a result of

India's enduring and expanding energy requirements, and based on bilateral discussions, the United States expects the vast majority of future nuclear program growth to occur in India's civil sector.

- Research reactors: India will permanently shut down the CIRUS plutonium production reactor in 2010. It will also place the foreign-supplied fuel core from the APSARA reactor under safeguards in 2010. India has not declared as civil the Dhruva research reactor, the Advanced Heavy Water Reactor, and activities relating to naval nuclear propulsion at Kalpakkam.
- Upstream facilities: India's separation plan designates as civil the following specific facilities associated with the Nuclear Fuel Complex: the Uranium Oxide Plant (Block A); both the Palletizing and the Assembly Ceramic Fuel Fabrication Plants (Block A); the Enriched Uranium Oxide Plant; the Enriched Fuel Fabrication Plant; and the Gadolina Facility. The heavy water production plants at Thai, Tuticorin, and Hazira will also be designated as civil. While India does not consider them as "relevant for safeguards purposes," at a minimum India's Additional Protocol is expected to include them. India decided not to designate for civilian uses three additional heavy water production plants, as well as other Nuclear Fuel Complex facilities.
- Downstream facilities: India plans to continue the current policy of possible "campaign-mode" safeguards with respect to the Tarapur Power Reactor Fuel Reprocessing Plant (PREFRE). Moreover, both the Tarapur and Rajasthan "Away from Reactor" spent fuel storage pools will be made available for safeguards. India decided not to declare as civil its other spent fuel reprocessing facilities, as well as its indigenous uranium enrichment capability. Subsequent to India's March 2006 Separation Plan, the Indian Government decided to pursue development of a new civil facility dedicated to reprocessing material under safeguards. Development

of this facility (and agreement with the United States on arrangements and procedures related thereto) will be required to bring into effect the "programmatic consent" in Article 6 of the Agreement.

- Research facilities: Finally, India plans to declare as civil nine research facilities: the Tata Institute of Fundamental Research; the Variable Energy Cyclotron Centre; the Saha Institute of Nuclear Physics; the Institute for Plasma Research; the Institute of Mathematics Science; the Institute of Physics; the Tata Memorial Centre; the Board of Radiation and Isotope Technology; and the Harish Chandra Research Institute. India expects these civil facilities to play a "prominent role" in international cooperation. Other Indian nuclear and nuclear-related facilities—such as those in the Bhabha Atomic Research Center (BARC) or in the Indira Gandhi Center for Advanced Research (IGCAR)—were not declared as civil, presumably because they retain a military or strategic role.

The United States assesses India's plan to be credible, transparent, and defensible from a nonproliferation standpoint. When implemented, the total installed nuclear capacity under safeguards will rise from 19 per cent today to 65 per cent, a per centage that will increase to more than 80 per cent as India further expands its civil infrastructure through foreign supply and indigenous development. Based on India's safeguards agreement with the IAEA (discussed below), appropriate safeguards will cover India's civil nuclear fuel cycle and provide strong assurances to supplier states that material and technology provided or generated through civil nuclear cooperation will not be diverted either to the military sphere or for unauthorized purposes. In addition, the total portion of India's spent fuel and plutonium stockpiles under safeguards will rise substantially over time (although the reprocessing consent in Article 6 of the U.S.-India Agreement for Peaceful Nuclear Cooperation, if and when the consent comes into effect, could increase modestly the quantity of separated civil plutonium stored in India).

II. Nature and Scope of the Cooperation Contemplated by the Proposed Agreement

Article 2(2) of the Proposed Agreement describes in general terms the kinds of cooperative activities envisaged. These are to take place in accordance with the provisions of the Agreement and each Party's applicable treaties, national laws, regulations, and license requirements and may include, but are not limited to, the following areas:

- Advanced nuclear energy research and development in areas agreed by the Parties;
- Nuclear safety matters;
- Facilitation of exchange of scientists for visits, meetings, symposia and collaborative research;
- Full civil nuclear cooperation activities covering nuclear reactors and aspects of the associated nuclear fuel cycle including technology transfer on an industrial or commercial scale between the Parties or authorized persons;
- Development of a strategic reserve to guard against any disruption of supply over the lifetime of India's reactors;
- Advanced research and development in nuclear sciences including biological research, medicine, agriculture and industry, environment and climate change;
- Supply between the Parties, whether for use by or for the benefit of the Parties or third countries, of nuclear material;
- Alteration in form or content of nuclear material as provided for in Article 6 of the Agreement;
- Supply between the Parties of equipment, whether for use by or for the benefit of the Parties or third countries;
- Controlled thermonuclear fusion including in multilateral projects; and
- Other areas of mutual interest as may be agreed by the Parties.

In Article 2(4) of the Agreement the Parties further delimit the scope of cooperation by affirming that the purpose of the Agreement is to provide for peaceful nuclear cooperation and not to affect the unsafeguarded nuclear activities of either Party. Nothing in the Agreement is to be interpreted as affecting the rights of the Parties to use for their own purposes nuclear material, non-nuclear material, equipment, components, information or technology produced, acquired or developed by them independent of any nuclear material, non-nuclear material, equipment, components, information or technology transferred to them pursuant to the Agreement. The Agreement is to be implemented in a manner so as not to hinder or otherwise interfere with any other activities involving the use of nuclear material, non-nuclear material, equipment, components, information or technology and military nuclear facilities produced, acquired or developed by them independent of the Agreement for their own purposes.

Article 2(3) of the Agreement specifically provides that the Parties may undertake transfers between themselves or their authorized persons of nuclear material, non-nuclear material, equipment, components and information.

Article 3(1) of the Agreement again specifically provides that information may be transferred between the Parties, and that such information may cover, but need not be limited to, the following fields:

- Research, development, design, construction, operation, maintenance and use of reactors, reactor experiments, and decommissioning;
- The use of nuclear material in physical, chemical, radiological and biological research, medicine, agriculture and industry;
- Fuel cycle activities to meet future world-wide civil nuclear energy needs, including multilateral approaches to which they are parties for ensuring nuclear fuel supply and appropriate techniques for management of nuclear wastes;

- Advanced research and development in nuclear science and technology;
- Health, safety and environmental considerations related to the foregoing;
- Assessments of the role that nuclear power may play in national energy plans;
- Codes, regulations and standards for the nuclear industry;
- Research on controlled thermonuclear fusion including bilateral activities and contributions toward multilateral projects such as the International Thermonuclear Experimental Reactor (ITER); and
- Any other field mutually agreed by the Parties.

Article 3(2) provides that the above cooperation may include training, exchange of personnel, meetings, exchange of samples, materials and instruments for experimental purposes and a balanced participation in joint studies and projects.

Article 3(3) states that the Agreement does not require the transfer of any information outside the scope of the Agreement, or information that the Parties are not permitted under their respective treaties, national laws or regulations to transfer.

Article 3(4) provides that Restricted Data, as defined by each Party, shall not be transferred under the Agreement.

Article 4(1) provides *inter alia* for the Parties to facilitate nuclear trade between themselves in the mutual interests of their respective industry, utilities and consumers and also, where appropriate, trade between either Party and a third country of items obligated to the other Party.

Article 4(2) provides *inter alia* that authorizations, including export and import licenses as well as authorizations or consents to third parties relating to trade, industrial operations or nuclear material movement, should be consistent with the sound and efficient administration of the Agreement and should not be used to restrict trade.

Article 5(1) provides that nuclear material, non-nuclear material, equipment and components may be transferred for applications consistent with the Agreement. Article 5(3) provides that natural or low enriched uranium may be transferred for use as fuel in reactor experiments and in reactors, for conversion or fabrication, and for other purposes as may be agreed to by the Parties. Article 5(1) provides also that any special fissionable material transferred shall be limited to low enriched uranium, except for "small quantities," which may be transferred pursuant to Article 5(5) for use as samples, standards, detectors and targets, and the accomplishment of other purposes as agreed by the Parties.

Article 5(4) provides that the quantity of nuclear material transferred under the Agreement shall be consistent with any of the following purposes: use in reactor experiments or the loading of reactors, the efficient and continuous conduct of such reactor experiments or operation of reactors for their lifetime, use as samples, standards, detectors and targets, and other purposes as the Parties may agree.

Article 5(6) records verbatim certain political assurances relating to reliable supply of nuclear fuel given to India by the United States in March 2006. The Agreement language does not have the effect of converting these political assurances into legally binding commitments because the Agreement, like other U.S. agreements of its type, is intended as a framework agreement that does not compel specific exports.

Articles 5(2), 6-10, and 14 address the specific requirements of section 123a. of the AEA and are discussed in detail in section III below.

Article 11 provides that the Parties shall cooperate in following the best practices for minimizing the impact on the environment from any radioactive, chemical or thermal contamination arising from activities under the Agreement and in related matters of health and safety.

Article 12 contains additional provisions with regard to implementation of activities falling within the scope of the Agreement.

Article 13 provides for consultations at the request of either Party regarding implementation of the Agreement and the development of further cooperation in the field of peaceful uses of nuclear energy on a stable, reliable and predictable basis. It further provides that the Parties shall endeavor to avoid taking any action that adversely affects cooperation under Article 2, which is the general "Scope of Cooperation" Article.

Article 15 provides for dispute settlement through negotiations between the Parties.

Article 16 provides for the Agreement to have an initial duration of 40 years and to continue in force for additional periods of 10 years each, subject to a proviso that either Party may terminate the Agreement by giving written notice to the other Party six months prior to the close of a period. It also provides for continuation in effect of key nonproliferation provisions of the Agreement in the event of its termination.

Article 17 provides for the establishment of agreed-upon procedures to implement the terms of the Agreement.

The statutorily mandated nonproliferation conditions and controls contained in the Agreement are detailed and analyzed in the following section.

III. Substantive Conditions

The proposed Agreement meets the applicable requirements of the Atomic Energy Act and the NNPA. Section 123a. of the Atomic Energy Act sets forth nine specific requirements that must be met in agreements for cooperation. Sections 402 and 407 of the NNPA set forth supplementary requirements. The provisions contained in the proposed Agreement satisfy those requirements as follows:

Application of Safeguards

Section 123a.(1) requires a guaranty from the cooperating party that safeguards as set forth in the agreement for cooperation will be maintained with respect to all nuclear materials and equipment transferred pursuant thereto and with respect to all special nuclear material used in or produced through the use of such transferred nuclear materials and equipment, so long as the material or equipment remains under the jurisdiction or control of the cooperating party, irrespective of the duration of the other provisions in the agreement or whether the agreement is terminated or suspended for any reason.

This requirement is satisfied by Articles 10 and 16(3) of the Agreement. Safeguards are mandated by Article 10(1) on "all nuclear material and equipment transferred pursuant to this Agreement and with respect to special fissionable material used in or produced through the use of such nuclear material and equipment, so long as the material or equipment remains under the jurisdiction or control of the cooperating party." Article 10(2) provides that nuclear material and equipment transferred from the U.S. to India and "any nuclear material used in or produced through the use of nuclear material, non-nuclear material, equipment or components so transferred shall be subject to safeguards in perpetuity in accordance with" the India-IAEA safeguards agreement, which was recently approved by the IAEA Board of Governors.

Article 16(3) provides the assurance that, notwithstanding the termination or expiration of the Agreement or the withdrawal of a Party from the Agreement, the safeguards required under Article 10 shall "continue in effect so long as any nuclear material, non-nuclear material, by-product material, equipment or components subject to [Article 10] remains in the territory of the Party concerned or under its jurisdiction or control anywhere, or until such time as the Parties agree that such nuclear material is no longer usable for any nuclear activity relevant from the point of view of safeguards." In addition, Article 10(4) provides that both countries shall consult regarding appropriate verification measures in the event that the application of IAEA safeguards is no longer possible.

Full-Scope Safeguards

The requirement for full-scope safeguards as a condition of cooperation mandated by section 123a.(2) is to be exempted pursuant to section 104 of the Hyde Act (the Henry J. Hyde United States-India Peaceful Atomic Energy Cooperation Act of 2006, Public Law 109-401).

Peaceful Use

The requirement of section 123a.(3) of the AEA for a guaranty against explosive or military uses of nuclear materials and equipment transferred and special nuclear material produced through the use of such items is met by Article 9 of the Agreement, which provides that:

> Nuclear material, equipment and components transferred pursuant to this Agreement and nuclear material and by-product material used or produced through the use of any nuclear material, equipment, and components so transferred shall not be used by the recipient Party for any nuclear explosive device, for research on or development of any nuclear explosive device or for any military purpose.

Right of Return

Section 123a.(4) of the AEA requires a stipulation that, in the event of a nuclear detonation by a non-nuclear weapon state cooperating party or termination or abrogation of an IAEA safeguards agreement by such a party, the United States shall have a right to the return of any nuclear materials and equipment transferred pursuant to the agreement for cooperation and any special nuclear material produced through the use of such transferred items. This requirement is met by Article 14 of the Agreement, which provides a right of return regarding "any nuclear material, equipment, non-nuclear material or components transferred under this Agreement and any special fissionable material produced through their use" [Article 14(4)]. The procedure for exercising this right of return is as follows:

- Pursuant to Article 14(1), either Party has the right to terminate the Agreement on one year's written notice to the other Party;
- The Party seeking termination has the right to cease further cooperation if it determines that "a mutually acceptable resolution of outstanding issues has not been possible or cannot be achieved through consultations" [Article 14(2)];
- Either party may exercise the right of return "following the cessation of cooperation" as provided for in Article

14(2) and "on or before the date of termination" as provided for in Article 14(1).

Thus, the right of return provided for in Article 14 of the Agreement fully satisfies the requirements of section 123a.(4) in terms of the items subject to the right of return and the circumstances under which it may be exercised.

Retransfer Consent

Section 123a.(5) of the AEA requires a guaranty by the cooperating party that any material, Restricted Data, and production or utilization facility transferred pursuant to the agreement "or any special nuclear material produced through the use of any such [facility or material] will not be transferred to unauthorized persons or beyond the jurisdiction or control of the cooperating party" without prior U.S. consent. This requirement is met by Article 7(2) of the Agreement. [The transfer of Restricted Data is precluded by Article 3(4) of the Agreement.]

Physical Security

The requirement of section 123a.(6) of the AEA for a guaranty that adequate physical security will be maintained with respect to any nuclear material transferred pursuant to an agreement of cooperation and any special nuclear material used in or produced through the use of nuclear material, production facility or utilization facility transferred pursuant to the agreement is met by Article 8 of the Agreement.

Enrichment/Reprocessing/Alteration Consent Right

Section 123a.(7) of the AEA requires a guaranty that "no material transferred pursuant to the agreement for cooperation and no material used in or produced through the use of any material, production facility, or utilization facility transferred pursuant to the agreement will be reprocessed, enriched or (in the case of plutonium, uranium 233, or uranium enriched to greater than 20 per cent in the isotope 235, or other nuclear materials which have been irradiated) otherwise altered in form or content without the prior approval of the United States."

In Article 6, the Parties provide mutual consent for enrichment up to 20 per cent in the isotope 235 of uranium subject to the Agreement. The Parties also provide mutual consent to reprocessing and alteration in form or content of nuclear material subject to the Agreement, except that to bring this right into effect in the case of India, India must establish a new national reprocessing facility dedicated to reprocessing safeguarded nuclear material under IAEA safeguards and both Parties must agree on arrangements and procedures under which the reprocessing or other alteration in form or content will take place in the new facility, including provisions with respect to the application of IAEA safeguards to all facilities concerned with these activities, as well as provisions relating to physical protection, storage, environmental protection, and use of any separated special fissionable material only in national facilities under IAEA safeguards. Article 14(9) provides that the above "arrangements and procedures" are subject to suspension by either Party in exceptional circumstances, as defined by the Parties, after consultations as specified in that paragraph. [Since Article 14 is not among those continuing in effect if the Agreement as a whole were to be terminated (Article 16(3)), a Party intending to suspend the "arrangements and procedures" under Article 6 would need to do so prior to termination of the Agreement itself.]

Article 6 also satisfies section 402(a) of the NNPA, which states that, except as specifically provided in any agreement for cooperation, no source or special nuclear material exported from the United States after the date of the NNPA may be enriched after export without the prior approval of the United States for such enrichment.

Storage Consent Right

The requirement of section 123a.(8) of the AEA for a guaranty of a right of prior U.S. approval over facilities for the storage of specified nuclear materials is met by Article 7(1).

Sensitive Nuclear Technology

The requirement of section 123a.(9) pertains to situations that may result when sensitive nuclear technology is transferred pursuant to a section 123 agreement for cooperation. Article

5(2) of the Agreement provides that sensitive nuclear technology shall only be transferred under the Agreement if provided for by an amendment to the Agreement, and Article 5(2) further provides that sensitive nuclear facilities and major critical components thereof shall only be transferred under the Agreement if provided for by an amendment to the Agreement. Accordingly, the requirement in section 123a.(9) is not relevant to the proposed Agreement, and the requirement in section 402(b) of the NNPA precluding the transfer of major critical components of facilities for uranium enrichment, nuclear fuel reprocessing, or heavy water production unless an agreement for cooperation "specifically designates such components as items to be exported pursuant to [such] agreement" is also satisfied.

Environmental: Article 11 of the proposed Agreement provides that the Parties "shall follow the best practices for minimizing the impact on the environment from any radioactive, chemical or thermal contamination arising from peaceful activities under this Agreement," thereby satisfying section 407 of the NNPA.

Proportionality: For the purpose of implementing rights specified in Articles 6 and 7 of the proposed Agreement, "produced" special nuclear material is defined in terms of proportionality in the Agreed Minute to the Agreement. Thus, if U.S. nuclear material is used in a non-U.S. reactor, the special nuclear material produced will be attributed to the U.S. in the proportion of the U.S. nuclear material to the total amount of nuclear material used, and similarly for subsequent generations. It has been our consistent view that sections 123 and 127 of the AEA allow this concept of proportionality to be used in determining the reasonable application of U.S. consent rights. Indeed, all of the agreements negotiated since the enactment of the NNPA in 1978 contain a similar proportionality provision.

The proposed Agreement thus satisfies all the substantive requirements specified for agreements for cooperation by the AEA and the NNPA, with the exception of section 123a.(2), from which it is to be exempted.

IV. Other Nonproliferation Policy Issues

Safeguards

Full-Scope versus INF CIRC/66 safeguards

A non-nuclear weapons state party to the NPT is required to have in place a "full-scope" safeguards agreement, applicable to all nuclear material and activities in the state. Such an agreement, based on IAEA document INFCIRC/153, has historically been considered the gold standard of safeguards. Such full-scope safeguards, in conjunction with an assessment that a state's political situation was consistent with adherence to nonproliferation norms, was seen as meeting the safeguards standard for the NPAS. More recently, the United States and others have indicated that they consider that the new safeguards standard should be a full-scope safeguards agreement with an Additional Protocol. Whereas the 153-based safeguards agreement focuses on declared material and facilities, the Additional Protocol provides the IAEA with additional information and access, to provide increased assurance of the absence of undeclared activities.

For a non-nuclear weapon state party to the NPT, safeguards are required to be able to detect in a timely manner, and thereby deter, the diversion of one weapons-quantity (called by the IAEA a "significant quantity") of nuclear material from declared facilities. Clearly, the diversion of even one weapons-quantity of material by a NNWS NPT party would have very serious implications, both in terms of regional stability and damage to the nonproliferation regime. The IAEA has therefore adopted standards for timeliness of detection consistent with the detection of one weapons-quantity of material within a time approximately equal to that needed to convert that material into weapons-usable form; this was deemed to provide time for political action. There are no such quantitative standards for implementation of the Additional Protocol, as activities related to detecting undeclared activities do not lend themselves to quantification and are somewhat dependent on external sources of information.

Because India is not an NPT signatory, the Indian safeguards agreement is not based on INFCIRC/153, but on another document, INFCIRC/66, discussed further below. The context in which safeguards will be applied in India differs importantly from that of a NNWS NPT signatory. India has already acquired nuclear weapons, has a fully capable nuclear weapons complex, all of the technical expertise necessary to produce weapons-grade materials, and a large stockpile of nuclear material that is outside of the safeguards agreement. The facilities retained by India outside the agreement constitute the full nuclear fuel cycle, including heavy water reactors, advanced reactors, uranium and plutonium fuel fabrication plants, and reprocessing plants.

In short, India's non-civil facilities already include every capability likely to exist among the facilities declared as civil; indeed, it is unlikely that India would chose to offer a facility as civil if it were needed for military purposes. India thus would have no apparent incentive to divert material, equipment, or technology from its declared civil sector to military uses. Its non-civil sector already possesses the necessary capabilities, and a diversion would risk a strong reaction from the U.S. and other nuclear cooperation partners.

India has committed to negotiating an Additional Protocol "with respect to its civilian facilities" with the IAEA. The IAEA's standard "Model Additional Protocol" (INFCIRC/540) was designed as an enhancement of an INFCIRC/153-type safeguards agreement, and to apply to the state as a whole. Thus there are bound to be important differences between the Indian AP and the Model AP. It is not clear yet what the provisions of the Indian AP will be, but it will probably provide some additional information or access to the facilities declared as civil, enhancing somewhat the effectiveness of safeguards at civil facilities. Because India will obviously have undeclared activities that are outside the scope of the safeguards agreement, the primary function of its Additional Protocol will not in general be the same as that of the Model Additional Protocol (that of detecting undeclared nuclear activities).

The safeguards agreement between India and the IAEA is based on TNFCIRC/66, the Agency's approved safeguards system for states not party to the NPT. INFCIRC/66 predated the NPT and is entitled "the Agency's Safeguards System." It is not, like INFCIRC/153, a model safeguards agreement, but contains language that 66-based safeguards agreements draw on, either verbatim or by reference. These agreements can be seen as comprising two components.

One component includes the sections on the mechanics of safeguards such as procedures, reports, inspections, exemptions, termination, transfers, and procedures for various facility types. These are generally drawn from INFCIRC/66 itself; this is the case with the Indian agreement. The technical safeguards methods provided for under an INFCIRC/66-based agreement are based on this standard language, and will be no different than those used in other safeguards agreements. We would expect that safeguards would be applied to an Indian heavy water reactor, for example, using the same technology and techniques applied to a heavy water reactor elsewhere. Some states, including Canada and Japan, are under the regime the IAEA calls "integrated safeguards" because they have an Additional Protocol in force, and because the IAEA has drawn a formal conclusion regarding the absence of undeclared activities in those states. Integrated safeguards allow the IAEA some additional flexibility in its safeguards activities, and some reductions in the intensity of inspections. We do not anticipate that such integrated safeguards would be applicable to India, because the IAEA will not be in a position to draw the relevant conclusion regarding undeclared activities. In particular, safeguards goals for timeliness and significant quantity described above are expected to apply to India, with no reductions in the frequency or extensiveness of inspections.

Safeguards on Facilities

There are also sections in the safeguards agreement identifying the scope of application of safeguards: what items the IAEA will actually inspect. This section is necessarily unique to each INFCIRC/66-based agreement; generally it names specific facilities being offered for safeguards, and describes how safeguards obligations follow material and subsequent generations of material used in or produced by that facility. In the case of the Indian safeguards agreement, no facilities or materials are offered for safeguards initially. The agreement provides that India will place a facility under safeguards in a two-step process:

- First, after entry into force of the agreement, India must "file with the Agency a Declaration, based on its sovereign decision to place voluntarily its civilian nuclear facilities under Agency safeguards in a phased manner" (para. 13); and
- Second, "India, on the basis of its sole determination, shall notify the Agency in writing of its decision to offer for Agency safeguards a facility identified by India in the Declaration referred to in paragraph 13, or any other facility to be determined by India. Any facility so notified by India to the Agency will be included in the Annex" (para. 14).

In the first step, the facilities in the declaration are expected to be those in the Indian Separation Plan, circulated to the IAEA Board of Governors as INFCIRC/731. The Separation Plan indicates that India will identify and offer for safeguards in a phased manner a number of facilities, including 14 power reactors and other facilities listed in the document. The declaration under paragraph 13 does not allow the Agency to start inspections. This can only happen after a subsequent notification under paragraph 14.

Once such a facility is notified and placed in the Annex, safeguards cannot terminate on it without a joint determination by the IAEA and India (para. 32):

> "Safeguards shall be terminated on a facility listed in the Annex after India and the Agency have jointly determined that the facility is no longer usable for any nuclear activity relevant from the point of view of safeguards."

Although the safeguards agreement includes preambular language noting India's ability to take "corrective measures" to ensure uninterrupted operation of India reactors, both the U.S. and the IAEA have concluded that the preambular language establishes the historical context of the agreement and does not affect the obligations quoted above, which are contained in the agreement's operational provisions.

The safeguards agreement allows for the possibility that safeguards could be temporarily placed on a facility not on the Annex by virtue of the fact that safeguarded material was placed in the facility (para. 11f). This is foreseen in the Indian separation plan, which indicates that an Indian reprocessing plant could be safeguarded "in campaign mode." The proposed U.S.-India agreement for cooperation stipulates that reprocessing of U.S.-obligated material will take place only in a new reprocessing facility dedicated to processing material under IAEA safeguards, subject to "arrangements and procedures" that must be agreed upon by the United States; such a facility would have to be subject to safeguards in perpetuity. It is U.S. policy not to allow export to facilities temporarily under safeguards.

Safeguards on Material

The safeguards agreement requires safeguards on material as provided for in paragraph 11:

"11. The items subject to this Agreement shall be:

(a) Any facility listed in the Annex to this Agreement...;

(b) Any nuclear material, non-nuclear material, equipment and components supplied to India which are required to be safeguarded pursuant to a bilateral or multilateral arrangement to which India is a party;

(c) Any nuclear material, including subsequent generations of special fissionable material, produced, processed or used in or by the use of a facility listed in the Annex or in or by the use of any nuclear material, non-nuclear material, equipment and components referred to in paragraph 11 (b);...."

As in all safeguards agreements, there is standard termination and suspension language that allows for material to cease being safeguarded under certain conditions; for example, if it has been diluted in a way that makes it no longer usable. The termination provision includes standard language [paragraph 30(d)] that would allow India to remove from safeguards the Indian indigenous uranium in spent fuel that had been used to fuel a reactor that was under safeguards in the Annex. In order to do so, India would have to separate out (by reprocessing) the plutonium in the spent fuel, which would remain subject to safeguards because it was produced in a reactor listed in the Annex [11(c) above]. The uranium remaining after irradiation and reprocessing would be lower in U-235 than the fresh fuel that went into the reactor to begin with, and thus less attractive for any nuclear purpose. It is unlikely that India would go to such extraordinary lengths to remove from safeguards material less attractive than what it voluntarily placed under safeguards in the first place. India's ability to withdraw such material in the situation described is, however, in accordance with Agency standards, principles, and practices.

Other Safeguards Considerations

One difference between a full-scope safeguards agreement under INFCIRC/153 and an INFCIRC/66-based agreement is that substitution of non-subject material for subject material by India is allowed [paras. 11(d), 27, 30(d)], provided the Agency agrees, and provided the amount and quality of the substituted material is at least equivalent to that of the material being substituted for. The obligations on the original material transfer to the substituted material, so there is no net impact from a nonproliferation perspective. Substitution provisions are a standard element of INFCIRC/66 and substitution is widely used in nuclear commerce.

A second difference is that the agreement allows for, but does not require, safeguards on heavy water and pieces of equipment. Such safeguards are not part of INFCIRC/153 safeguards at all; heavy water is not a "nuclear material." They are needed in this safeguards agreement because existing safeguards agreements for facilities in India have such requirements. In addition, this agreement permits, but does not require, these existing safeguards agreements to be suspended in favor of the new agreement.

Potential for Increase in Availability of Indian Indigenous Nuclear Material for Military Use as a Result of Transfers to India for Civil Use

It has been suggested that supplying nuclear fuel to India for civil purposes could assist India's nuclear weapon program by allowing India to use more of its limited domestic supply of uranium exclusively for weapon purposes. The Executive Branch has no evidence indicating that India plans to use additional domestic uranium resources in its nuclear weapons program as a consequence of implementing the Civil Nuclear Cooperation Initiative.

Moreover, the amount of fissile material available for potential weapons use is a function not just of the amount of natural uranium available, but also of factors such as overall fuel cycle capabilities, including the capacity to produce plutonium in reactors and to separate the plutonium through reprocessing. In this regard, under the Civil Nuclear Cooperation Initiative several indigenous Indian reactors, which in theory have been available to support military programs, will be placed under safeguards and no longer be available for this purpose.

As previously noted, India has substantial, albeit limited, domestic uranium reserves, estimated by the IAEA to be about 95,000 metric tons,[1] a complete functioning fuel cycle, and demonstrated competence with nuclear technologies. Limits on India's capacity to process uranium ore currently constrain domestic uranium production, but new capacity should be on line in the next several years. In short, India is capable of maintaining and expanding its existing nuclear arsenal within the limits of its indigenous resources and capabilities. This will be the situation whether or not India is supplied externally with fuel for civil nuclear power.

Finally, India's stated policies indicate a posture of restraint rather than a Cold War-style, unconstrained build up of its nuclear stockpile and forces. India has long indicated that it seeks a so-called "credible minimum deterrent," and it has articulated a no-first-use policy for nuclear weapons. India has also committed to work with the United States to achieve a multilateral Fissile Material Cut-off Treaty that would cap material available for weapons. On March 30, 2006, then Foreign Secretary Saran publicly reiterated that India "remains committed to a credible minimum deterrent. If our posture so far has been one of restraint and responsibility—not disputed even by our critics—there is no reason why we should suddenly change now." The United States will continue to urge India to maintain a posture of strategic restraint and to further strengthen its nonproliferation commitments within the context of the U.S.-India strategic partnership.

Physical Protection and Safety

India has been a member of the International Convention on the Physical Protection of Nuclear Materials since March 12, 2002; a member of the International Convention on Nuclear Safety since March 31, 2005; and a member of the International Convention on the Suppression of Acts of Nuclear Terrorism since it entered into force on July 7, 2007. It has thus undertaken a legal obligation to adhere to the terms of all three of these conventions. There are no cases known to the Executive Branch of fissile material being lost, diverted, or stolen in India.

Previous U.S.-India Peaceful Nuclear Cooperation (Tarapur)

An earlier U.S.-India agreement for peaceful nuclear cooperation, signed at Washington August 8, 1963, entered into force October 25, 1963, and expired by its terms October 25, 1993. Under that agreement, known informally as the "Tarapur Agreement," the United States initially supplied reactor units one and two at India's Tarapur site, together with low enriched uranium (LEU) fuel to operate them. (Whereas other U.S. nuclear cooperation agreements have been "framework" agreements requiring no specific transfers, the Tarapur Agreement required the supply of these items.) U.S. cooperation under the 1963 Agreement became problematic following passage of the 1978 NNPA, which among other things established full-scope IAEA safeguards (FSS) as a requirement for continued U.S.

supply of nuclear material to non-nuclear-weapon States. The NNPA provided for certain transitional arrangements for supply to India. Under these, the President in 1980 approved two further transfers of LEU fuel after the NRC determined that it could not make the findings necessary under the AEA to license the exports. One shipment was completed. The second, by mutual agreement of the Administration and Congress, was not sent. To avoid a breach of the Agreement, the United States instead engaged France as a surrogate supplier under the Tarapur Agreement. A decade later, France adopted its own FSS export policy and ended its supply for Tarapur. After expiration of the U.S.-India Agreement for Cooperation in 1993, China (which did not then have an FSS export policy) stepped in as a supplier. Later Russia stepped in as a supplier, invoking a "safety" exception in the NSG Guidelines, despite objections by the United States and most other NSG members. Russian supply is continuing.

The United States maintains, and has formally advised the Indian Government on several occasions, that certain U.S. "vested rights" have survived expiration of the 1963 Agreement, including a U.S. right to approve reprocessing of the fuel used in Tarapur reactor units one and two. India has consistently disputed the U.S. position, although it did agree "voluntarily" to maintain IAEA safeguards on the two reactors after the 1963 Agreement expired. The proposed new Agreement with India does not apply retroactively to the U.S.-supplied Tarapur reactors or their fuel. However, the Administration regards the current nonproliferation status of the Tarapur reactors and fuel as acceptable and sustainable so long as they remain under safeguards. Moreover, the Government of India has included the Tarapur reactors among the facilities to be safeguarded as part of its "civil" nuclear program; once the reactors are subject to the new safeguards agreement, they cannot be removed from safeguards unless India and the IAEA jointly determine that they are "no longer usable for any nuclear activity relevant from the point of view of safeguards" (India-IAEA Safeguards Agreement, paragraph 31).

V. Conclusion

Entry-into-force of the proposed U.S.-India Agreement will put in place a framework for mutually beneficial civil nuclear cooperation between the two countries and provide a foundation for continued collaboration on achieving nuclear non-proliferation goals.

On the basis of the analysis in this NPAS and all pertinent information of which it is aware, the Department of State has arrived at the following assessment, conclusions, views and recommendations:

1. The safeguards and other control mechanisms and the peaceful use assurances in the proposed Agreement are adequate to ensure that any assistance furnished under it will not be used to further any military or nuclear explosive purpose.
2. The Agreement meets all the legal requirements of the AEA and the NNPA, except section 123a.(2) of the AEA, which is to be exempted pursuant to section 104 of the Hyde Act.
3. Execution of the proposed Agreement would be compatible with the non-proliferation program, policy, and objectives of the United States.

Therefore, it is recommended that the President determine that the performance of the proposed Agreement will promote, and will not constitute an unreasonable risk to, the common defense and security, that he approve the Agreement and authorize its execution, and that he submit it to Congress for its approval.

NOTE

1. IAEA-TECDOC-1463, Sept. 2005. IAEA estimate included uranium in RAR, EAR-I and EAR-II categories.

Working Towards the U.S.-India Civil Nuclear Agreement

11

Richard A. Boucher, Assistant Secretary for South and Central Asian Affairs—Remarks at the U.S. Consulate Mumbai, India (August 22, 2008)

Assistant Secretary Boucher: I'm going to say a few things in the beginning. It's good to be back in India. It's good to be back in Mumbai. It has been a little while since I've come here and I try to make myself, every time I come to India, go somewhere besides Delhi. I think there's a tendency, if you only stay in meeting rooms in the capitals, to understand less about what's really going on than if you get out at least to one other city. I've tried to do that. I am glad to be here in Mumbai. We all know this is a place of education and place of business and so I've taken some time today to meet the people in the business community, to meet people to talk about agriculture, talk about retail, talk about investment, infrastructure and these kind of issues that face India and try to understand those better. And also, I will get out to see a school and meet some students.

I will be heading up to Delhi on Monday and I guess I'd say my visit this time is part of the continuing effort of the United States and India to work towards the fulfillment of the U.S.-India civil nuclear agreement. As you all know, many of our colleagues, our diplomatic colleagues, both Indian and American, are now in Vienna working that part of it. I will be able to work with some people in Delhi to make sure we continue with the other pieces, to try to bring all the pieces together in September for our Congress to look at. We've got a lot of things to do, a lot of pieces to the package. The commitments are all there and now we're trying to fulfill them all. That's where we need to move forward and run all the pieces together. We're looking to do that, and we'll continue weekly and daily consultations and work with Indian government to try to bring all this to fruition.

Beyond the nuclear deal though, part of the reason I'm coming to India is to see all the topics in the relationship that we've got. This is an enormous and rapidly expanding relationship between the United States and India. More and more Indian students are going to the United States, 88,000 Indian students now. There are also all the investors and the Indian-American community. In addition, the business opportunities that people are finding in India are increasing; this includes our defense relationship. I am very positive and optimistic on the U.S.-India relationship in general and I am positive and optimistic on getting the nuclear deal finished. So, with that, I would be glad to take your questions.

Moderator: Please introduce yourself and your paper or your affiliation when you ask a question. Our newly arrived Consul General is here, as well. I think most of you must have met him earlier.

Question: The nuclear deal appears to have met some roadblocks at the [Nuclear Suppliers Group] meeting. Do you visualize it will go through or it will be stalled?

Assistant Secretary Boucher: I think most of the countries that I have talked to and most of the countries we are hearing from in Vienna are basically positive on the deal. They understand the, sort of, big importance of having cooperation with India. They understand the benefits of having cooperation with India on nonproliferation matters. They understand the benefits of helping the Indian economy achieve its potential with clean energy. I have talked to skeptics. I have talked to countries that are raising questions and issues, but I think they are all basically positive. So I think the question is how we answer those issues that they have raised and how we answer their legitimate questions.

This is different, you have to understand, for the Nuclear Suppliers Group, for people in the Nonproliferation Treaty.

This is different than the way we have done things before. It does raise a lot of questions. A lot of people, before they do something different, will be very careful on asking proper questions and doing a very thorough analysis. We shouldn't look at that as opposition. We should look at that as a chance to explain this deal, to explain the implications, and to explain the benefits of the arrangement. I think India has done that in its meetings with the Nuclear Suppliers. We need to listen to them, to discuss how to go forward and to answer their concerns, but also to listen to them about how we can make happen.

Question: How confident are you of seeing the guidelines of the NSG coming back in its same form, and do you envisage any changes being introduced at the NSG?

Assistant Secretary Boucher: I don't know. There are countries that would like different kinds of changes to the text. Some of those may be acceptable, some may not. I think that's where I said that we have to listen carefully. We have to answer their questions to the extent that we—we meaning U.S. and India together—can sit down with what we hear in Vienna and discuss the way forward and maybe there are some things we can consider. But I think it's got to be something that we do jointly, and not about considering things that would block the cooperation or impede the process going forward.

Question: Most of the opposition seems to be coming from smaller countries like Norway and Ireland and so on. We heard yesterday that the U.S. is individually talking to some of these countries at Vienna. Is there any update on the specifics, whether there is any progress?

Assistant Secretary Boucher: No, I don't have individual updates from our team that is out there. I think, to say "smaller countries," you know, is a fact. Frankly, this is not done on the basis of population. It's not done on the basis of [Gross Domestic Product]. It is done on the basis of consensus. The Nuclear Suppliers has been a group that, whatever the size of the countries, it brings together a lot of countries that are very committed to nonproliferation in the world. They are very committed to the safety of all of us from nuclear proliferation. It is based on consensus and cooperation. It doesn't matter how big or how small a country is. Their concerns are legitimate. Their commitment to nonproliferation is unquestionable. We need to work with them.

Question: Any possibility that the deal will go?

Assistant Secretary Boucher: Any possibility that it does go? Yes, if we get our work done. That's the goal. The goal is to get it done.

Question: What about road blocks?

Assistant Secretary Boucher: I don't know if they are road blocks but there are a lot of things to do. Let's face it: we have to finish the work with the NSG, India has to finish the work that it has committed to in terms of adherence to the national export regimes and moving forward on the additional protocol. Go back to the communiqués and see all the commitments that have been made. India's got to fulfill those things. Not more, but not less, as well. And so, there are those pieces to bring together. There's the NSG piece to bring together. In the administration we have to do various studies, reports, and papers for our Congress, as we're required under the Hyde Act. The more solid the package and the more solid the commitments, the easier it will be for us to go to Congress to say: "Now that we have got it to you, can't you find a way to move forward?" Even there we're asking for expeditious handling. We've got expeditious handling from the Atomic Energy [Agency]. We're hoping to get expeditious handling from the Nuclear Suppliers Group. If we get the package together, we look for expeditions handling from our Congress, as well.

Question: You're looking at a date from the 8th of September?

Assistant Secretary Boucher: That's the date the Congress comes back into session. We'd like to have it for them on the first day of their session. We'll see with timing, and again, it is a matter of bringing all these pieces together. We have to have the full package, solid, and all wrapped up in a bow.

Question: What's your Plan B?

Assistant Secretary Boucher: Plan B is to do Plan A. Our goal is to move this whole thing forward. It is intellectually a product of different administrations in the U.S. and in India. Certainly we would like to fulfill it. We would like to finish this under President Bush and Prime Minister Singh because both of them had so much to do getting it this far. If we don't, we will just keep doing it. It is good for India, it is good for the United States, good for the nonproliferation regime and we figured its good next year, as well as this year. But let's try to get it done this year.

Question: What will be the nature of the next parliament in India: single-party rule or multi-party rule?

Assistant Secretary Boucher: I have no idea (laughter).

Question: Is the new government bound by this agreement?

Assistant Secretary Boucher: Governments are bound by what they do. If the country signs an agreement then the future governments are bound by it.

Question: Why I am asking this question is....

Assistant Secretary Boucher: You mean if a new government comes in before we finish signing this agreement then, in theory on either side, one can try to reopen it. That's happened before in other circumstances. I think it's not something we would like to see on either side. That's why it is better to get it done this year.

Question: No, why I am asking this...it is such an important deal like this, it has to be debated in the Indian parliament and it is going to the American Congress.

Assistant Secretary Boucher: Let's be honest about this. We've got a whole lot of discussions in the Indian Parliament and in between the parties. We've said India showed a great respect for our democratic procedures as we moved through to get the Hyde Act to pass. It is understood that we have to go back to our Congress under our democratic procedures. We have had the same respect for India's democratic procedures as India has worked its way through its parliamentary issues. It is better for us not to speculate on that or interfere. The Indian government will handle its democratic procedures and we will handle ours.

Question: Ambassador, there was a stage where, you were probably aware, that there was a feeling in the U.S. that the deal was jeopardy partly because of our own political compulsions here in India. Was there an apprehension at that time among all of you in the United States? And how were you viewing those developments?

Assistant Secretary Boucher: We were watching with great fascination. We learned a lot of Indian democracy, we learned a lot about Indian politics. We are not Indian politicians and we have to respect India's democratic process. We saw it play itself out, luckily, with a good result.

Question: And also the bags of currency notes shown in the Parliament?

Assistant Secretary Boucher: I said we watched with great fascination (laughter).

Question: The Indian government took a huge risk for this agreement.

Assistant Secretary Boucher: It's a good agreement. It's a good deal for India. It's a good deal for India in terms of not just the economic growth and the energy opportunities, but in terms of India's relationship with the rest of the world. This brings forward a sort of a new opportunity for India across the board and a new position for India in the international community, as a cooperating partner in some of the most sensitive, but also some of the most important issues. Establishing India in this position in the world is very important. So, it is a big deal. It's a big deal for us, and it's a big deal for India, so it's worth it on both sides. Both sides have shown a certain amount of political work.

Question: [Inaudible].

Assistant Secretary Boucher: What?

Question: Now the ball is in the U.S. court?

Assistant Secretary Boucher: For the moment the ball is in everybody's court. It's in our court to go to the Congress. It's in India's court to fulfill its commitments from the communiqués. It is in the hands of all the governments in the Nuclear Suppliers Group to review it expeditiously. We hope to get their consent.

Question: Once the nuclear deal is cleared, do you think the next step will be towards forging a strategic alliance between America and India?

Assistant Secretary Boucher: I think it's a question I can't answer completely at this point, probably for the reasons you were hinting at before. We are likely to have a new administration as we have an election in the United States. There are going to be elections in India. It is now going to go to the next government in both countries to decide where to go from there.

On the other hand, just as we went logically from Bill Clinton's time to George Bush's, and from Prime Minister Vajpayee's time to Prime Minister Singh, and continued the progress. The next steps with the U.S. and India? There are many opportunities. The fact that India is taking more of a global role, that India is becoming a major aid donor, for example, in Afghanistan and Africa, and that India is becoming a bigger economic player both for investments and for imports, these open new opportunities, and opportunities to work with India on global scale. Opportunities to look at our involvement with each other are increasing in depth and scope for each of our economies. This includes, for example, investment back and forth, people back and forth, and technology back and forth. So, I think there is a whole new dimension of relationship that will result in the coming years between the United States and India. This is an opportunity, both to deepen our own ties but also to expand our global cooperation.

Question: Let's come back to the NSG, and you were saying that India would have to accept that there may be a need for changes in the draft. Again, from what everyone is learning from the negotiations, India seems somewhat rooted in these changes by some of these countries. Do you anticipate a problem in any ways because you're sort of seen as shepherding India through the NSG?

Assistant Secretary Boucher: That's because we are. That's because we are members of (the Nuclear Suppliers Group). As I said before, none of us want to see anything that impedes cooperation or blocks cooperation. I do think that countries are going to express themselves in the meeting and maybe the terms of what they would like to see in the document. To a great extent we are just going to have to work this through. We in India and the United States have to sit down and decide what we can accommodate, and what we can't. We have to talk to the other governments involved. Part of that process is going on right now in Vienna. I think, therefore, it's important that the Indian government sat down with members of the group and talked about how they see it from their perspective so people get a clear understanding of the Indian point of view.

We are pushing for what we call "a clean exception." We are pushing for the text that we submitted. We are trying to push for, trying to get people to understand, that their questions have answers and that they don't need to try to write everything into the text they might have ever thought about this. We will see if we can come out with that clean text we would like to.

Question: And there are concerns by countries that would raise the NPT question again and again and making the exception for India.

Assistant Secretary Boucher: This is an exception. There has to be a certain logic to it. If you are making an exception, you can't say that they have to meet the rules if they are making the exceptions. Some of these things people understand we can't do in this. We can't change everything about India's history by having a resolution in the Nuclear Suppliers Group. There are some things that probably everybody knows will not fly. We will listen to the questions and hopefully answer the questions, and will be able to move forward.

Question: One of your citizens, Kenneth Haywood, has caused enormous embarrassment to the Indian police by fleeing even as he was in the investigations regarding the Ahmadabad serial blasts are concerned. Would you care to comment on that?

Assistant Secretary Boucher: No. I don't know the details of it, so I am not going to comment on it. It's an individual personal case and a judicial matter for India. This is the way I read it in the papers but I didn't quite read it in the way you just explained.

Question: Just to come back, are there any specifics in terms of changes that you see already coming up, out of whatever has happened so far?

Assistant Secretary Boucher: No, I don't. I think it's too early to say that. As I said, we are going to push for a clean exception. Things come up that might be accommodated and then we might have to sit down with India and work through some of that stuff and see what's possible and what's not. But as I said, we are not going to allow anything that will impede or harm the cooperation; we are not going to put anything in it that's going to make it impossible to carry out the deal on either side.

We're not going to put in anything that changes the terms of the agreement as far as we're concerned. We reached an agreement with India. It's been public. It's been known through the communiqués, through the statements. That's the deal. That's what you've got to say 'yes' or 'no' to.

Question: Would you like to comment on the current developments in Kashmir. There is a lot of violence, and the former Pakistani President has raised it in an international forum. Do you want to comment on this?

Assistant Secretary Boucher: I don't want to comment on the internal matters in Kashmir. Those are questions that the Indian government and the people of the region are going to have to deal with. I think the one thing from the point of view of the United States is that over the last several years there has been significant progress in terms of understanding the situation, in terms of how understanding how it might be resolved—confidence building measures, lessening of tensions back and forth between India and Pakistan. Our hope, on both sides, is to see that process continued. We have discussed with Prime Minister Gillani, when he was in Washington, our desire to see this process and intentions continue. We heard from the Pakistani government their desire to continue. I think we've heard the same from India. Without commenting on the specific events we might see—the overall process of reducing the overall tensions between India and Pakistan and moving towards a solution to the Kashmir issue—we'd like to see this process continue.

Question: Ambassador, you are here in Mumbai and shortly after the blasts here in Mumbai two years ago, India had specifically pointed towards Pakistan and said Pakistan was behind the blasts. You were quoted, or misquoted, that there wasn't enough evidence of that. Is there a growing view now in the U.S. of a shift as far as Pakistan is concerned? It is as if Pakistan and the regime in Pakistan [inaudible] to give support to terrorism. Do you see a decrease in this or is it still very unclear?

Assistant Secretary Boucher: There have been a lot of charges—sometimes its working, sometimes its not. What I think is clear, at least on the newly-elected government side, is that there is a determination to deal with the problem of terrorism. There is a determination to use every part of the government to fight the problem of terrorism—that means not just military and law enforcement matters but also development, education, economics, opening up the Tribal Areas to more integration economically in the area. There is a determination there to deal with the problem. They are still getting organized in terms of getting control of all the apparatus, of being able to line up the policy in a very clear and succinct way. What we've heard is a determination to deal with the problem of terrorism. Exactly who's behind what probably varies from case to case. Whether certain people or organizations are involved with terrorist acts isn't something that any of us can count on. At the same time, what I hear from the new Pakistani government is that they are determined to deal with terrorism and address it much more forthrightly.

Question: What about General Musharraf? Is he headed your way?

Assistant Secretary Boucher: He's no longer president. I have no idea where he's headed. He's a free man. He's unencumbered by job and by constraints. He can go where he wants.

Question: The problem is Pakistan's total disregard for a democratically elected government. That [Inter-Services Intelligence] is calling the shots and no one has any authority to reign in the ISI, that is why it is a front organization the ISI.

Assistant Secretary Boucher: I do think that every piece of national power has to be lined up in the same direction. If any organization is not pulling its full weight in fighting terrorism then authorities need to deal with that. I do think that a lot of the terrorist attacks have a variety of different groups and organizations. There were very different people involved. We're not going to get anywhere dealing with the wrong one. We have to deal with all the parts and we have to use all the tools of government to get at it.

Question: I can go on asking questions....

Assistant Secretary Boucher: Okay, let's do one or two more. I'm happy to do one or two more and we'll call it quits.

Question: I just...sort of to wrap on the energy, just to understand, what you are saying is that India will have to accept that that there may be changes to the text, but as long as it does not violate the spirit of the text, the changes may be inevitable. Is that what you....

Assistant Secretary Boucher: I don't want to say "inevitable" at this point. I don't want to lie to you. I can't rule out that there might be some changes that we could accept. What I can tell you today is that we are pushing for a clean exception. We are trying to listen to the other countries and answer their questions, just as India is trying to answer their questions. We think these questions are good questions; we think they have good answers. We don't see any reason for any changes. We do have to listen to countries and, if there is...if it comes down to it, if we think something might be done that's acceptable and that we and India could agree to, then we'll do it. Otherwise I think we'll just have to keep answering questions and keep pushing for a clean exception.

Question: Could you tell us a little bit about your meetings in Delhi?

Assistant Secretary Boucher: Some of the key players are still traveling so I'm not going to see everybody. I'm going to see some of the people at the Ministry of External Affairs, some of the key people in the Prime Minister's office, and the virtue of going to Delhi is that I can see a lot of people throughout and see commentators, smart guys, think tankers, people like that, and just get a better feel for the atmosphere as well as the specific issues. I look forward to probably seeing some parliamentarians, business people.

Question: Largely linked to the nuclear deal?

Assistant Secretary Boucher: Largely linked to the U.S.-India relationship. The nuclear deal is on everybody's mind. I was meeting with some business people and that was the first thing they wanted to ask about—not the only thing but the first thing. I would expect whether it is business people, MEA people, or parliamentarians, that will be a big part of our discussion. Part of the reason to come to India is to have the official discussions with Indian representatives about the nuclear deal and the different pieces and what's going on around the world, including Washington. I get a better feel for this and the range of opinions and different angles and aspects by coming to India. So the goal is to talk to a lot of different kinds of people.

Question: Some persons who have been designated as terrorists by the American State Department, they are still roaming about freely in Pakistan. Why is no effort being done to tackle these guys?

Assistant Secretary Boucher: They haven't been caught.

Question: Not been caught? Like who?

Assistant Secretary Boucher: Some of the people we have on our terrorist list. We haven't caught Osama Bin Laden yet. There's continuing efforts to catch these guys. There are a lot of dangerous people in India. There are dangerous people on the Afghanistan-Pakistan border. Believe you me, we're at it; the Pakistanis are at it; the Afghan are at it. The goal has to be to stop the phenomenon of terrorism, to get all these people. Also the goal has to be to develop these areas and to bring them into the rest of the country and to make them more settled and established in government.

Question: The person who is classified as most dreaded is Daoud Khaskar and he's still available on the list. I can call him right now.

Assistant Secretary Boucher: I'd rather not, thank you. (Laughter)

Question: Here's this man, roaming the world freely.

Assistant Secretary Boucher: I don't have anything specific on this man. I don't know where he is. I don't know why he's not been caught. I think the real issue is that you have to get at the real phenomenon of terrorism. We're working with the Pakistanis to stop terrorism; we're working with the Afghans to stop terrorism; we're working with the Indian government, the Bangladeshis and all governments in the region because it affects us all and we all have to understand this and we all have to go after it, not just with police and law enforcement and military means but with education. All the pieces together can establish a more settled state and a more healthy society.

Question: India's relationship with China appears to be slowly nosediving. Would you like to comment on this?

Assistant Secretary Boucher: Not particularly. We are interested in seeing good relations between India and China, as anyone is. We have good relations with China; we have good relations with India; and we'd like to see them get along, too.

Question: Are you in town for a couple of days?

Assistant Secretary Boucher: Yes, and a couple of days in Delhi.

Question: How is the U.S. going to help contain the expanding terrorism?

Assistant Secretary Boucher: The first thing we do is talk about it. We go back and forth, we have consultations with India on terrorism. We and India are both very concerned about terrorism and are pained about the blasts, the attacks that occurred in India. Wherever there's an opportunity to cooperate, we will. A lot of that means sitting down and talking about how it is manifesting itself, how it is expanding, and what these groups are up to, sharing information.

Moderator: Any other questions?

Question: Do you agree to this expression "Islamist terrorist?"

Assistant Secretary Boucher: Terror is terror wherever it comes from, whatever its reasons are. There are some people who try to wrap themselves under the cover of Islam to commit terrorist acts. Basically, they are terrorists and most of the Muslims I know say that they are not very Islamic, and not following the principals that most of the Muslims that I know say they follow in their religion. So, no, I don't think it is a subcategory, it's not a definition.

Question: Why aren't you doing any TV interviews here in Bombay?

Assistant Secretary Boucher: I guess I'm going to do some TV in New Delhi.

Question: That's unfair.

Assistant Secretary Boucher: Yes, I know. I'm going to be here a few days, seeing friends, seeing Bombay.

Question: Who stands to win—Obama or McCain?

Assistant Secretary Boucher: Yes, I predict it is going to be Obama or McCain, but I can't narrow it down farther than that.

Question: Can we attribute this all to you?

Assistant Secretary Boucher: Yes, you can. Or you can attribute it to him [Consul General Paul Folmsbee] if it sounds smart.

Thank you very much. Good to see you.

12

The India Safeguards Agreement: Moving India Towards the Nonproliferation Mainstream

Gregory L. Schulte, Ambassador, U.S. Permanent Representative to the International Atomic Energy Agency and the United Nations, London, England

(July 24, 2008)

In eight days, on August 1, the IAEA Board of Governors is scheduled to meet in Vienna to consider a draft Safeguards Agreement for India. The agreement was carefully negotiated, by the IAEA Secretariat, which has recommended it for approval. It is a solid agreement, following an approved IAEA safeguards approach. It deserves the Board's full endorsement.

The Safeguards Agreement is a key step in implementing the U.S.-India Civil Nuclear Cooperation Initiative. This historic initiative was welcomed by IAEA Director General Mohamed ElBaradei as: "a milestone, timely for ongoing efforts to consolidate the nonproliferation regime, combat nuclear terrorism, and strengthen nuclear safety."

Implementing the U.S.-India Civil Nuclear Cooperation Initiative and allowing civil nuclear cooperation between India and interested countries in Europe and elsewhere has three main benefits:

bringing India into the nuclear nonproliferation mainstream;

helping India meet its growing energy needs while protecting the environment; and

deepening the strategic partnership between our many countries and India.

I would like to expand on each of the three benefits of the initiative, then talk about the draft Safeguards Agreement itself. Bringing India into the Nuclear Nonproliferation Mainstream is a key benefit of the initiative. India has four operating nuclear power reactors under IAEA safeguards today. Under the U.S.-India Civil Nuclear Cooperation Initiative, India has committed to separate its military and civil activities and submit its entire civil program to international inspection. Under this plan, India will place under voluntarily safeguards a majority of its existing and planned nuclear power reactors (14 of 22) and all its future civil reactors.

Within a generation, it is estimated that nearly 90 per cent of India's reactors will be under IAEA safeguards. This means they will be dedicated to peaceful uses and prohibited from contributing to nuclear weapons. In addition to putting additional facilities under IAEA safeguards, India has committed to:

> sign and adhere to an Additional Protocol with respect to its civil nuclear facilities;
>
> create a robust national export control system that includes harmonization and adherence to the Missile Technology Control Regime and Nuclear Suppliers Group guidelines;
>
> refrain from transfers of enrichment and reprocessing technologies to states that do not already possess them and support efforts to limit their spread;
>
> work with the U.S. to conclude a multilateral Fissile Material Cutoff Treaty; and
>
> continue its unilateral moratorium on nuclear testing.

By themselves, each of India's commitments is significant. Collectively, they will constitute a significant gain for non-proliferation. Helping India meets its growing energy needs, while protecting the environment is the second benefit of the initiative.

As a country with one-sixth of the world's population and a rapidly growing economy, India has an enormous appetite for energy. Because it has been constrained by sanctions, India's civil nuclear sector accounts today for less than 3 per cent of electricity generation. India's government aims to increase India's nuclear power capacity to reach up to 25 per cent of electricity supply by mid-century. Nuclear energy is clean energy. It does not produce carbon dioxide or other "greenhouse" gases. Today the vast majority of India's electricity is produced with coal. This is a major reason why India is emerging as one of the world's largest producers of greenhouse gases. According to one expert, India's nuclear energy plans, by displacing coal, would avoid an estimated 130 million tons of carbon dioxide per year. Everyone worried about global warming should be an ardent supporter of helping India meet its energy requirements with clean, safeguarded, civil nuclear power.

Deepening the strategic partnership between many countries and India is the third benefit of the initiative. The rise of a democratic and increasingly prosperous India represents a singularly positive development in world affairs. The United States, the European Union, and other like-minded countries aim to develop an entirely new relationship with India, a relationship founded on cooperation rather than denial. India is a stabilizing force in the world. We share an abundance of political, economic, and security interests. Our open societies face similar threats from terrorism and organized crime. Our market-based economies embrace trade and commerce as engines of prosperity. We share an attachment to democracy and individual rights. And trade, education and travel are bringing our societies together as never before.

Listen to India's Prime Minister Singh: "Nowhere else will you find a country of India's diversity, of India's complexity, one billion people trying to seek their social and economic salvation in the framework of a democracy, in the framework of an open economy." Helping India generate electricity for growth and development, while acknowledging its commitments on safeguards and nonproliferation, is part of transforming global relations with this large and vibrant democracy. Dr. ElBaradei has observed that India is: "treated as a valued partner, a trusted contributor to international peace and security. It is difficult to understand the logic that could continue to carve out civil nuclear energy as the single area of non-cooperation."

We agree.

A Solid Safeguards Agreement

The draft Safeguards Agreement presented to the IAEA Board on July 9 was carefully negotiated by IAEA safeguards and legal experts following the safeguards approach in INFCIRC/66.

This is the approved IAEA safeguards system appropriate for states like India not under NPT full-scope safeguards. Under the draft agreement, we would expect that safeguards on civil nuclear facilities in India would resemble very closely those applied to other such facilities around the world. The Secretariat recommends that the Board authorize the Director General to sign the agreement. We hope that the Board will do so on August 1. The Board's approval is important but in many ways also routine. The draft follows standard safeguards practice, and the Board has approved over 170 other safeguards agreements. According to the IAEA Secretariat, all were approved routinely, and all were approved by consensus. After the Board's approval, the United States will work with the Nuclear Suppliers Group to reach consensus on an India-specific exception that would allow members to engage in civil nuclear cooperation with India. Cooperation between the United States and India will then require a final approval by the U.S. Congress.

Serving the Interests of India and the International Community

In conclusion, the course we are taking offers important benefits to India and the world. It will bring India into the nuclear nonproliferation mainstream. It will help India meet its growing energy needs while protecting the environment. It will deepen the strategic partnerships between many countries and India. Dr. ElBaradei said this well in welcoming the U.S.-India Civil Nuclear Cooperation Initiative: "This agreement is an important step towards satisfying India's growing need for energy, including nuclear technology and fuel, as an engine for development. It would also bring India closer as an important partner in the non-proliferation regime. It would be a milestone, timely for ongoing efforts to consolidate the non-proliferation regime, combat nuclear terrorism and strengthen nuclear safety.... This agreement would serve the interest of both India and the international community."

Once again, we agree.

13

Agreement Between the Government of India and the International Atomic Energy Agency for the Application of Safeguards to Civilian Nuclear Facilities

(July 7, 2008)

Recognizing the significance India attaches to civilian nuclear energy as an efficient, clean and sustainable energy source for meeting global energy demand, in particular for meeting India's growing energy needs;

Whereas India is committed to the full development of its national three-stage nuclear program to meet the twin challenges of energy security and protection of the environment;

Whereas India has a sovereign and inalienable right to carry out nuclear research and development activities for the welfare of its people and other peaceful purposes;

Whereas India, a State with advanced nuclear technology, wishes to expand civil nuclear cooperation for its national development;

Whereas India is desirous of further expanding cooperation with the International Atomic Energy Agency (hereinafter referred to as "the Agency") and its Member States with the objective of the full development and use of nuclear energy for peaceful purposes, on a stable, reliable and predictable basis;

Whereas India supports the role of the Agency in the promotion of the safe and peaceful uses of nuclear energy as set forth in the Statute of the Agency (hereinafter referred to as the "Statute");

Whereas India and the Agency have long-standing cooperation in various aspects of the Agency's activities;

Recognizing that such cooperation between India and the Agency must be carried out with full respect for the objectives of the Statute and with due observance of the sovereign rights of India;

Whereas the Statute authorizes the Agency to apply safeguards, at the request of the parties, to any bilateral or multilateral arrangement, or at the request of a State to any of the State's activities in the field of atomic energy and, in this context:

Noting the relevance for this Agreement of the understandings between India and the United States of America expressed in the India-U.S. Joint Statement of 18 July 2005, in which India, *inter alia*, has stated its willingness:

- to identify and separate its civilian and military nuclear facilities and programs in a phased manner;
- to file with the Agency a declaration regarding its civilian nuclear facilities (hereinafter referred to as "the Declaration");
- to take a decision to place voluntarily its civilian nuclear facilities under Agency safeguards;

Noting also for the purposes of this Agreement that:

- India will place its civilian nuclear facilities under Agency safeguards so as to facilitate full civil nuclear cooperation between India and Member States of the Agency and to provide assurance against withdrawal of safeguarded nuclear material from civilian use at any time;
- An essential basis of India's concurrence to accept Agency safeguards under an India-specific safeguards agreement (hereinafter referred to as "this Agreement") is the conclusion of international cooperation arrangements creating the necessary conditions for India to obtain access to the international fuel market,

including reliable, uninterrupted and continuous access to fuel supplies from companies in several nations, as well as support for an Indian effort to develop a strategic reserve of nuclear fuel to guard against any disruption of supply over the lifetime of India's reactors; and

- India may take corrective measures to ensure uninterrupted operation of its civilian nuclear reactors in the event of disruption of foreign fuel supplies;

Whereas India is desirous of expanding civil nuclear cooperation with other Member States of the Agency;

Whereas the conclusion of this Agreement is intended to facilitate the broadest possible cooperation between India and Member States of the Agency in the peaceful uses of nuclear energy and ensure international participation in the further development of India's civilian nuclear programme on a sustained and long-term basis;

Recalling that the Agency in accordance with its Statute and safeguards system must take into account, in the implementation of safeguards in India, the need to avoid hampering the peaceful uses of nuclear energy, economic and technological development or international cooperation in the field of peaceful uses of nuclear energy; respect health, safety and physical protection and related security provisions in force in India; and take every precaution to protect commercial, technological and industrial secrets as well as other confidential information coming to its knowledge;

Whereas the frequency and intensity of activities described in this Agreement shall be kept to the minimum consistent with the objective of effective and efficient Agency safeguards;

Whereas India has requested the Agency to apply safeguards with respect to items subject to this Agreement;

Whereas the Board of Governors of the Agency (hereinafter referred to as the "Board") acceded to that request on....;

Now therefore, taking into account the above, India and the Agency have agreed as follows:

I. GENERAL CONSIDERATIONS

A. Basic Undertakings

1. India undertakes that none of the items subject to this Agreement, as defined in paragraph 11, shall be used for the manufacture of any nuclear weapon or to further any other military purpose and that such items shall be used exclusively for peaceful purposes and shall not be used for the manufacture of any nuclear explosive device.

2. The Agency undertakes to apply safeguards, in accordance with the terms of this Agreement, to the items subject to this Agreement, as defined in paragraph 11, so as to ensure, as far as it is able, that no such item is used for the manufacture of any nuclear weapon or to further any other military purpose and that such items are used exclusively for peaceful purposes and not for the manufacture of any nuclear explosive device.

B. General Principles

3. The purpose of safeguards under this Agreement is to guard against withdrawal of safeguarded nuclear material from civilian use at any time.

4. The application of safeguards under this Agreement is intended to facilitate implementation of relevant bilateral or multilateral arrangements to which India is a party, which are essential to the accomplishment of the objective of this Agreement.

5. Bearing in mind Article II of the Statute, the Agency shall implement safeguards in a manner designed to avoid hampering India's economic or technological development, and not to hinder or otherwise interfere with any activities involving the use by India of nuclear material, non-nuclear material, equipment, components, information or technology produced, acquired or developed by India independent of this Agreement for its own purposes.

6. The safeguards procedures set forth in this document shall be implemented in a manner designed to be consistent with prudent management practices required for the economic and safe conduct of nuclear activities.

7. In implementing safeguards, the Agency shall take every precaution to protect commercial and industrial secrets. No member of the Agency's staff shall disclose, except to the Director General and to such other members of the staff as the Director General may authorize to have such information by reason of their official duties in connection with safeguards, any commercial or industrial secret or any other confidential information coming to his knowledge by reason of the implementation of safeguards by the Agency.

8. The Agency shall not publish or communicate to any State, organization or person any information obtained by it in connection with the implementation of safeguards in India, except that:

(a) Specific information relating to such implementation in India may be given to the Board and to such Agency staff members as require such knowledge by reason of their official duties in connection with safeguards, but only to the extent necessary for the Agency to fulfil its safeguards responsibilities;

(b) Summarized lists of items being safeguarded by the Agency may be published upon decision of the Board; and

(c) Additional information may be published upon decision of the Board and if all States directly concerned agree.

9. In the light of Article XII.A.5 of the Statute, safeguards shall continue with respect to produced special fissionable material and to any materials substituted therefor.

10. Nothing in this Agreement shall affect other rights and obligations of India under international law.

II. CIRCUMSTANCES REQUIRING SAFEGUARDS

A. Items Subject to this Agreement

11. The items subject to this Agreement shall be:

(a) Any facility listed in the Annex to this Agreement, as notified by India pursuant to paragraph 14(a) of this Agreement;

(b) Any nuclear material, non-nuclear material, equipment and components supplied to India which are required to be safeguarded pursuant to a bilateral or multilateral arrangement to which India is a party;

(c) Any nuclear material, including subsequent generations of special fissionable material, produced, processed or used in or by the use of a facility listed in the Annex or in or by the use of any nuclear material, non-nuclear material, equipment and components referred to in paragraph 11(b);

(d) Any nuclear material substituted in accordance with paragraph 27 or 30(d) of this Agreement for nuclear material referred to in paragraph 11(b) or 11(c) of this Agreement;

(e) Any heavy water substituted in accordance with paragraph 32 of this Agreement for heavy water subject to this Agreement;

(f) Any facility other than a facility identified in paragraph 11(a) above, or any other location in India, while producing, processing, using, fabricating or storing any nuclear material, non-nuclear material, equipment or components referred to in paragraph 11(b), (c), (d) or (e) of this Agreement, as notified by India pursuant to paragraph 14(b) of this Agreement.

12. The scope of this Agreement is limited to the items subject to this Agreement as defined in paragraph 11 above.

Declaration

13. Upon entry into force of this Agreement, and a determination by India that all conditions conducive to the accomplishment of the objective of this Agreement are in place, India shall file with the Agency a Declaration, based on its sovereign decision to place voluntarily its civilian nuclear facilities under Agency safeguards in a phased manner.

Notifications

14. (a) India, on the basis of its sole determination, shall notify the Agency in writing of its decision to offer for Agency

safeguards a facility identified by India in the Declaration referred to in paragraph 13, or any other facility to be determined by India. Any facility so notified by India to the Agency will be included in the Annex, and become subject to this Agreement, as of the date of receipt by the Agency of such written notification from India.

(b) Should India, on the basis of its sole determination, decide to import or transfer any nuclear material, non-nuclear material, equipment or components subject to this Agreement to any facility or other location in India provided for in paragraph 11(f) of this Agreement, it shall so notify the Agency. Any such facility or location so notified by India pursuant to this sub-paragraph shall become subject to this Agreement as of the date of receipt by the Agency of such written notification from India.

15. India shall notify the Agency of the receipt of any nuclear material, non-nuclear material, equipment and components referred to in paragraph 11(b) of this Agreement within four weeks of the arrival in India of such nuclear material, non-nuclear material, equipment and components.

Provision of Information to the Agency

16. In the event that India's notification pursuant to paragraph 14(a) of this Agreement relates to a facility subject to Agency safeguards under another Safeguards Agreement or Agreements in India at the time of entry into force of this Agreement, India shall provide the Agency, along with the relevant notification, such information as is required pursuant to the other Safeguards Agreement or Agreements as relates to any nuclear material, non-nuclear material, equipment and components subject to safeguards thereunder.

17. With respect to any other facility listed in the Annex pursuant to paragraph 14(a) of this Agreement, India shall provide the Agency, within four weeks of the relevant notification, with:

(a) a list of all nuclear material at each such facility; and

(b) where relevant, and if required pursuant to a bilateral or multilateral arrangement to which India is party, information relating to:

   (i) Any nuclear material, non-nuclear material, equipment and components supplied to India for production, processing, storage or use in such facility;

   (ii) Any nuclear material, including subsequent generations of special fissionable material, produced, processed or used in or by the use of such facility or in or by the use of any nuclear material, non-nuclear material, equipment and components supplied to India for production, processing or use in such facility.

18. Each notification pursuant to paragraph 15 of the Agreement shall include all information relevant to the nuclear material, non-nuclear material, equipment and components so notified, including the facility or location where the nuclear material, non-nuclear material, equipment and components so notified will be received.

19. The information provided by India pursuant to paragraphs 16, 17 and 18 of this Agreement shall specify, *inter alia*, to the extent relevant, the nuclear and chemical composition, physical form and quantity of the nuclear material; the date of shipment; the date of receipt; the identity of the consigner and the consignee; and any other relevant information, such as the type and capacity of any facility (or parts thereof), components or equipment; and the type and quantity of non-nuclear material. In the case of a facility or other location subject to this Agreement, the information to be provided shall include the type and capacity of that facility or location, and any other relevant information.

20. India shall thereafter notify the Agency by means of reports, in accordance with this Agreement, of any nuclear material, non-nuclear material, equipment and components referred to in paragraph 11(b), (c), (d) or (e) of this Agreement. The Agency may verify the calculations of the amounts and/or

quantities of such nuclear material, non-nuclear material, equipment and components, and appropriate adjustments shall be made by agreement between India and the Agency.

21. The Agency shall maintain an inventory of items subject to this Agreement. The Agency shall send a copy of the inventory it maintains with respect to such information to India every twelve months and also at any other times specified by India in a request communicated to the Agency at least two weeks in advance.

B. Safeguards Under Other Agreements

22. The application of Agency safeguards under other Safeguards Agreements concluded by India with the Agency and in force at the time of entry into force of this Agreement may, subject to agreement by the Parties to such other Safeguards Agreements and following notification by India of the relevant facilities pursuant to paragraph 14(a), be suspended while this Agreement is in force. The application of safeguards under this Agreement to nuclear material, non-nuclear material, equipment or components subject to safeguards under such other Agreements shall commence as of the date of receipt by the Agency of India's notification. India's undertaking not to use items subject thereto in such a way as to further any military purpose, and its undertaking that such items shall be used exclusively for peaceful purposes and shall not be used for the manufacture of any nuclear explosive device, shall continue to apply.

C. Exemptions from Safeguards

General Exemptions

23. Nuclear material that would otherwise be subject to safeguards shall be exempted from safeguards at the request of India, provided that the material so exempted in India may not at any time exceed:

(a) One kilogram in total of special fissionable material, which may consist of one or more of the following:

(i) Plutonium;

(ii) Uranium with an enrichment of 0.2 (20 per cent) and above, taken account of by multiplying its weight by its enrichment;

(iii) Uranium with an enrichment below 0.2 (20 per cent) and above that of natural uranium, taken account of by multiplying its weight by five times the square of its enrichment;

(b) Ten metric tons in total of natural uranium and depleted uranium with an enrichment above 0.005 (0.5 per cent);

(c) Twenty metric tons of depleted uranium with an enrichment of 0.005 (0.5 per cent) or below; and

(d) Twenty metric tons of thorium.

Exemptions Related to Reactors

24. Produced or used nuclear material that would otherwise be subject to safeguards because it is being or has been produced, processed or used in a reactor which has been supplied wholly or substantially under a project agreement, submitted to safeguards under a safeguards agreement by the parties to a bilateral or multilateral arrangement or unilaterally submitted to safeguards under a safeguards agreement; or because it is being or has been produced in or by the use of safeguarded nuclear material, shall be exempted from safeguards if:

(a) It is plutonium produced in the fuel of a reactor whose rate of production does not exceed 100 grams of plutonium per year; or

(b) It is produced in a reactor determined by the Agency to have a maximum calculated power for continuous operation of less than 3 thermal megawatts, or is used in such a reactor and would not be subject to safeguards except for such use, provided that the total power of the reactors with respect to which these exemptions apply in any State may not exceed 6 thermal megawatts.

25. Produced special fissionable material that would otherwise be subject to safeguards only because it has been produced in or by the use of safeguarded nuclear material shall in part be exempted from safeguards if it is produced in a reactor in which the ratio of fissionable isotopes within

safeguarded nuclear material to all fissionable isotopes is less than 0.3 (calculated each time any change is made in the loading of the reactor and assumed to be maintained until the next such change). Such fraction of the produced material as corresponds to the calculated ratio shall be subject to safeguards.

D. Suspension of Safeguards

26. Safeguards with respect to nuclear material may be suspended while the material is transferred, under an arrangement or agreement approved by the Agency, for the purpose of processing, reprocessing, testing, research or development, within India or to any other Member State or to an international organization, provided that the quantities of nuclear material with respect to which safeguards are thus suspended in India may not at any time exceed:

(a) One effective kilogram of special fissionable material;

(b) Ten metric tons in total of natural uranium and depleted uranium with an enrichment 0.005 (0.5 per cent);

(c) Twenty metric tons of depleted uranium with an enrichment of 0.005 (0.5 per cent) or below; and

(d) 20 metric tons of thorium.

27. Safeguards with respect to nuclear material in irradiated fuel which is transferred for the purpose of reprocessing may also be suspended if the State or States concerned have, with the agreement of the Agency, placed under safeguards substitute nuclear material in accordance with paragraph 30(d) of this Agreement for the period of suspension. In addition, safeguards with respect to plutonium contained in irradiated fuel which is transferred for the purpose of reprocessing may be suspended for a period not to exceed six months if the State or States concerned have, with the agreement of the Agency, placed under safeguards a quantity of uranium whose enrichment in the isotope uranium-235 is not less than 0.9 (90 per cent) and the uranium-235 content of which is equal in weight to such plutonium. Upon expiration of the said six months or the completion of reprocessing, whichever is earlier, safeguards

shall, with the agreement of the Agency, be applied to such plutonium and shall cease to apply to the uranium substituted therefor.

28. Under conditions specified in the Subsidiary Arrangements, the Agency shall suspend safeguards with respect to any parts of the facilities listed in the Annex which are removed for maintenance or repair.

E. Termination of Safeguards

29. The termination of safeguards on items subject to this Agreement shall be implemented taking into account the provisions of GOV/1621 (20 August 1973).

30. Nuclear material shall no longer be subject to safeguards under this Agreement after:

(a) It has been returned to the State that originally supplied it (whether directly or through the Agency), if it was subject to safeguards only by reason of such supply and if:

  (i) It was not improved while under safeguards; or

  (ii) Any special fissionable material that was produced in it under safeguards has been separated out, or safeguards with respect to such produced material have been terminated; or

(b) The Agency has determined that:

  (i) It was subject to safeguards only by reason of its use in a principal nuclear facility which has been supplied wholly or substantially under a project agreement, submitted to safeguards under a safeguards agreement by the parties to a bilateral or multilateral arrangement or unilaterally submitted to safeguards under a safeguards agreement;

  (ii) It has been removed from such a facility; and

  (iii) Any special fissionable material that was produced in it under safeguards has been separated out, or safeguards with respect to such produced material have been terminated; or

(c) The Agency has determined that it has been consumed, or has been diluted in such a way that it is no longer usable for any nuclear activity relevant from the point of view of safeguards, or has become practicably irrecoverable; or

(d) India has, with the agreement of the Agency, placed under safeguards, as a substitute, such amount of the same element, not otherwise subject to safeguards, as the Agency has determined contains fissionable isotopes:

(i) Whose weight (with due allowance for processing losses) is equal to or greater than the weight of the fissionable isotopes of the material with respect to which safeguards are to terminate; and

(ii) Whose ratio by weight to the total substituted element is similar to or greater than the ratio by weight of the fissionable isotopes of the material with respect to which safeguards are to terminate to the total weight of such material; provided that the Agency may agree to the substitution of plutonium for uranium-235 contained in uranium whose enrichment is not greater than 0.05 (5.0 per cent); or

(e) It has been transferred out of India under paragraph 33(d) of this Agreement, provided that such material shall again be subject to safeguards if it is returned to India; or

(f) The terms of this Agreement, pursuant to which it was subject to safeguards under this Agreement, no longer apply, by expiration of this Agreement or otherwise.

31. If India wishes to use safeguarded source material for non-nuclear purposes, such as the production of alloys or ceramics, it shall agree with the Agency on the circumstances under which the safeguards on such material may be terminated.

32. Safeguards shall be terminated on a facility listed in the Annex after India and the Agency have jointly determined that the facility is no longer usable for any nuclear activity relevant from the point of view of safeguards. Safeguards on non-

nuclear material, equipment and components subject to this Agreement may be terminated as and when the non-nuclear material, equipment or components have been returned to the supplier or arrangements have been made by the Agency to safeguard the non-nuclear material, equipment or components in the State to which it is being transferred, or when India and the Agency have jointly determined that the non-nuclear material, equipment or component in question has been consumed, is no longer usable for any nuclear activity relevant from the point of view of safeguards or has become practicably irrecoverable. Safeguards may be terminated on heavy water upon India's placing under safeguards as substitute the same amount of heavy water of equivalent or better heavy water concentration.

F. Transfers

33. No safeguarded nuclear material shall be transferred outside the jurisdiction of India until the Agency has satisfied itself that one or more of the following conditions apply:

(a) The material is being returned, under the conditions specified in paragraph 30(a) of this Agreement, to the State that originally supplied it; or

(b) The material is being transferred subject to the provisions of paragraph 26 or 27 of this Agreement; or

(c) Arrangements have been made by the Agency to safeguard the material in the State to which it is being transferred; or

(d) The material was not subject to safeguards pursuant to a project agreement and will be subject, in the State to which it is being transferred, to safeguards other than those of the Agency but generally consistent with such safeguards and accepted by the Agency.

34. India shall notify the Agency of its intention to transfer within its jurisdiction any nuclear material, non-nuclear material, equipment or component subject to this Agreement to any facility or location in India to which paragraph 11(f) applies and shall provide to the Agency, before such transfer is effected, the necessary information to enable the Agency to make

arrangements for the application of safeguards to such nuclear material, non-nuclear material, equipment or component after its transfer. The Agency shall also be given the opportunity as early as possible in advance of such a transfer to review the design of the facility for the sole purpose of determining that the arrangements provided for in this Agreement can be effectively applied. India may transfer the nuclear material, non-nuclear material, equipment or component only after the Agency has confirmed that it has made such arrangements.

35. India shall notify the Agency of its intention to transfer any nuclear material, non-nuclear material, equipment or component subject to this Agreement to a recipient which is not under the jurisdiction of India. Except as provided for in paragraph 30(a) of this Agreement, such nuclear material, non-nuclear material, equipment or component shall be so transferred only after the Agency has informed India that it has satisfied itself that Agency safeguards will apply with respect to the nuclear material, non-nuclear material, equipment or component in the recipient country. Upon receipt by the Agency of the notification of transfer from India and the confirmation of receipt by the recipient country, safeguards on such nuclear material, non-nuclear material, equipment or component shall be terminated under this Agreement.

36. The notifications referred to in paragraphs 34 and 35 of this Agreement shall be made to the Agency sufficiently in advance to enable it to make the arrangements required before the transfer is effected. The Agency shall promptly take any necessary action. The time limits for and the contents of these notifications shall be set out in the Subsidiary Arrangements.

III. SAFEGUARDS PROCEDURES

A. General Procedures

Introduction

37. The safeguards procedures to be applied by the Agency are those specified in this Agreement, as well as such additional procedures as result from technological developments, and other procedures as may be agreed to between the Agency and

India. The safeguards procedures set forth below shall be followed, as far as relevant, with respect to any item subject to this Agreement.

38. The Agency shall conclude with India Subsidiary Arrangements concerning the implementation of the safeguards procedures referred to above. The Subsidiary Arrangements shall also include any necessary arrangements for the application of safeguards to any item subject to this Agreement, including such containment and surveillance measures as are required for the effective implementation of safeguards. The Subsidiary Arrangements shall enter into force no later than six months after entry into force of this Agreement.

Design Review

39. The Agency shall review the design of principal nuclear facilities, for the sole purpose of satisfying itself that a facility will permit the effective application of safeguards.

40. The design review of a principal nuclear facility shall take place at as early a stage as possible. In particular, such review shall be carried out in the case of:

(a) An Agency project, before the project is approved;

(b) A bilateral or multilateral arrangement under which the responsibility for administering safeguards is to be transferred to the Agency, or an activity or facility unilaterally submitted by India, before the Agency assumes safeguards responsibilities with respect to the facility;

(c) A transfer of safeguarded nuclear material to a principal nuclear facility whose design has not previously been reviewed, before such transfer takes place; and

(d) A significant modification of a principal nuclear facility whose design has previously been reviewed, before such modification is undertaken.

41. To enable the Agency to perform the required design review, India shall submit to it relevant design information sufficient for the purpose, including information on such basic characteristics of the principal nuclear facility as may bear on

the Agency's safeguards procedures. The Agency shall require only the minimum amount of information and data consistent with carrying out its responsibility under this section. It shall complete the review promptly after the submission of this information by India and shall notify the latter of its conclusions without delay.

42. If the Agency wishes to examine design information which India regards as sensitive, the Agency shall, if India so requests, conduct the examination on premises in India. Such information should not be physically transmitted to the Agency provided that it remains readily available for examination by the Agency in India.

Records

43. India shall arrange for the keeping of records with respect to principal nuclear facilities and also with respect to all safeguarded nuclear material outside such facilities. For this purpose India and the Agency shall agree on a system of records with respect to each facility and also with respect to such material, on the basis of proposals to be submitted by India in sufficient time to allow the Agency to review them before the records need to be kept.

44. All records shall be kept in English.

45. The records shall consist, as appropriate, of:

(a) Accounting records of all safeguarded nuclear material; and

(b) Operating records for principal nuclear facilities.

46. All records shall be retained for at least two years.

Reports

General Requirements

47. India shall submit to the Agency reports with respect to the production, processing and use of safeguarded nuclear material in or outside principal nuclear facilities. For this purpose, India and the Agency shall agree on a system of reports with respect to each facility and also with respect to safeguarded nuclear material outside such facilities, on the basis

of proposals to be submitted by India in sufficient time to allow the Agency to review them before the reports need to be submitted. The reports need include only such information as is relevant for the purpose of safeguards.

48. All reports shall be submitted in English.

Routine Reports

49. Routine reports shall be based on the records compiled in accordance with paragraphs 43 to 46 of this Agreement and shall consist, as appropriate, of:

(a) Accounting reports showing the receipt, transfer out, inventory and use of all safeguarded nuclear material. The inventory shall indicate the nuclear and chemical composition and physical form of all material and its location on the date of the report; and

(b) Operating reports showing the use that has been made of each principal nuclear facility since the last report and, as far as possible, the programme of future work in the period until the next routine report is expected to reach the Agency.

50. The first routine report shall be submitted as soon as:

(a) There is any safeguarded nuclear material to be accounted for; or

(b) The principal nuclear facility to which it relates is in a condition to operate.

Progress in Construction

51. The Agency may request information as to when particular stages in the construction of a principal nuclear facility have been or are to be reached.

Special Reports

52. India shall report to the Agency without delay:

(a) If any unusual incident occurs involving actual or potential loss or destruction of, or damage to, any safeguarded nuclear material or principal nuclear facility;

(b) If there is good reason to believe that safeguarded nuclear material is lost or unaccounted for in quantities that exceed the normal operating and handling losses that have been accepted by the Agency as characteristic of the facility; or

(c) Disruption of operation of facilities listed in the Annex on account of material violation or breach of bilateral or multilateral arrangements to which India is a party.

53. India shall report to the Agency, as soon as possible, and in any case within two weeks, any transfer not requiring advance notification that will result in a significant change (to be defined by the Agency in agreement with India) in the quantity of safeguarded nuclear material in a principal nuclear facility. Such report shall indicate the amount and nature of the material and its intended use.

Amplification of Reports

54. At the Agency's request, India shall submit amplifications or clarifications of any report, in so far as relevant for the purpose of safeguards.

Inspections

General Procedures

55. The Agency may inspect any items subject to this Agreement.

56. The purpose of safeguards inspections under this Agreement shall be to verify compliance by India with this Agreement and to assist India in complying with this Agreement and in resolving any questions arising out of the implementation of safeguards.

57. The number, duration and intensity of inspections actually carried out shall be kept to the minimum consistent with the effective implementation of safeguards, and if the Agency considers that the authorized inspections are not all required, fewer shall be carried out.

58. Inspectors shall neither operate any facility themselves nor direct the staff of a facility to carry out any particular operation.

Routine Inspections

59. Routine inspections may include, as appropriate:

(a) Audit of records and reports;

(b) Verification of the amount of safeguarded nuclear material by physical inspection, measurement and sampling;

(c) Examination of principal nuclear facilities, including a check of their measuring instruments and operating characteristics; and

(d) Check of the operations carried out at principal nuclear facilities.

60. Whenever the Agency has the right of access to a principal nuclear facility at all times, it may perform inspections of which notice as required by paragraph 4 of the Inspectors Document need not be given, in so far as this is necessary for the effective application of safeguards. The actual procedures to implement these provisions shall be agreed upon between India and the Agency.

Initial Inspections of a Principal Nuclear Facility

61. To verify that the construction of a principal nuclear facility is in accordance with the design reviewed by the Agency, an initial inspection or inspections of the facility may be carried out:

(a) As soon as possible after the facility has come under Agency safeguards, in the case of a facility already in operation; and

(b) Before the facility starts to operate, in other cases.

62. The measuring instruments and operating characteristics of the facility shall be reviewed to the extent necessary for the purpose of implementing safeguards. Instruments that will be used to obtain data on the nuclear materials in the facility may be tested to determine their satisfactory functioning. Such testing may include the observation by inspectors of commissioning or routine tests by the staff of the facility, but shall not hamper or delay the construction, commissioning or normal operation of the facility.

Special Inspections

63. The Agency may carry out special inspections if:

(a) The study of a report indicates that such inspection is desirable; or

(b) Any unforeseen circumstance requires immediate action. The Board shall subsequently be informed of the reasons for and the results of each such inspection.

64. The Agency may also carry out special inspections of substantial amounts of safeguarded nuclear material that are to be transferred outside the jurisdiction of India, for which purpose India shall give the Agency sufficient advance notice of any such proposed transfer.

B. Special Procedures for Reactors

Reports

65. The frequency of submission of routine reports shall be agreed between the Agency and India, taking into account the frequency established for routine inspections. However, at least two such reports shall be submitted each year and in no case shall more than 12 such reports be required in any year.

Inspections

66. One of the initial inspections of a reactor shall if possible be made just before the reactor first reaches criticality.

67. The maximum frequency of routine inspections of a reactor and of the safeguarded nuclear material in it shall be determined from the following table:

Whichever is the largest of: (a) Facility inventory (including loading); (b) Annual throughput; (c) Maximum potential annual production of special fissionable material (Effective kilograms of nuclear material)	Maximum number of routine inspections annually
Up to 1 More than 1 and up to 5 More than 5 and up to 10 More than 10 and up to 15 More than 15 and up to 20 More than 20 and up to 25 More than 25 and up to 30 More than 30 and up to 35 More than 35 and up to 40 More than 40 and up to 45 More than 45 and up to 50 More than 50 and up to 55 More than 55 and up to 60 More than 60	0 1 2 3 4 5 6 7 8 9 10 11 12 Right of access at all times

68. The actual frequency of inspection of a reactor shall take account of:

(a) The fact that India possesses irradiated fuel reprocessing facilities;

(b) The nature of the reactor; and

(c) The nature and amount of the nuclear material produced or used in the reactor.

C. Special Procedures Relating to Safeguarded Nuclear Material Outside Principal Nuclear Facilities

Nuclear Material in Research and Development Facilities

Routine Reports

69. Only accounting reports need be submitted in respect of nuclear material in research and development facilities. The frequency of submission of such routine reports shall be agreed between the Agency and India, taking into account the frequency established for routine inspections; however, at least one such report shall be submitted each year and in no case shall more than 12 such reports be required in any year.

Routine Inspections

70. The maximum frequency of routine inspections of safeguarded nuclear material in a research and development facility shall be that specified in the table in paragraph 67 of this Agreement for the total amount of material in the facility.

Source Material in Sealed Storage

71. The following simplified procedures for safeguarding stockpiled source material shall be applied if India undertakes to store such material in a sealed storage facility and not to remove it therefrom without previously informing the Agency.

Design of Storage Facilities

72. India shall submit to the Agency information on the design of each sealed storage facility and agree with the Agency on the method and procedure for sealing it.

Routine Reports

73. Two routine accounting reports in respect of source material in sealed storage shall be submitted each year.

Routine Inspections

74. The Agency may perform one routine inspection of each sealed storage facility annually.

Removal of Material

75. India may remove safeguarded source material from a sealed storage facility after informing the Agency of the amount, type and intended use of the material to be removed, and providing sufficient other data in time to enable the Agency to continue safeguarding the material after it has been removed.

Nuclear Material in Other Locations

76. Except to the extent that safeguarded nuclear material outside of principal nuclear facilities is covered by any of the provisions set forth in paragraphs 69 to 75 of this Agreement, the following procedures shall be applied with respect to such material (for example, source material stored elsewhere than in a sealed storage facility, or special fissionable material used in a sealed neutron source in the field).

Routine Reports

77. Routine accounting reports in respect of all safeguarded nuclear material in this category shall be submitted periodically. The frequency of submission of such reports shall be agreed between the Agency and India, taking into account the frequency established for routine inspections; however, at least one such report shall be submitted each year and in no case shall more than 12 such reports be required in any year.

Routine Inspections

78. The maximum frequency of routine inspections of safeguarded nuclear material in this category shall be one inspection annually if the total amount of such material does not exceed five effective kilograms, and shall be determined from the table in paragraph 67 of this Agreement if the amount is greater.

D. Provisions for Reprocessing Plants

Introduction

79. Additional procedures applicable to the safeguarding of reprocessing plants are set out below.

Special Procedures

Reports

80. The frequency of submission of routine reports shall be once each calendar month.

Inspections

81. A reprocessing plant having an annual throughput not exceeding 5 effective kilograms of nuclear material, and the safeguarded nuclear material in it, may be routinely inspected twice a year. The reprocessing plant, having an annual throughput exceeding 5 effective kilograms of nuclear material, and the safeguarded nuclear material in it, may be inspected at all times. The arrangements for inspections set forth in paragraph 60 of this Agreement shall apply to all inspections to be made under this paragraph. It is understood that for plants having an annual throughput of more than 60 effective kilograms, the right of access at all times would be normally be implemented by means of continuous inspection.

82. When a reprocessing plant is under Agency safeguards only because it contains safeguarded nuclear material, the inspection frequency shall be based on the rate of delivery of safeguarded nuclear material.

83. India and the Agency shall cooperate in making all the necessary arrangements to facilitate the taking, shipping or analysis of samples, due account being taken of the limitations imposed by the characteristics of a plant already in operation when placed under Agency safeguards.

Mixtures of Safeguarded and Unsafeguarded Nuclear Material

84. India and the Agency may agree on the following special arrangements in the case of a reprocessing plant which has not been supplied wholly or substantially under a project agreement, submitted to safeguards under a safeguards agreement

by the parties to a bilateral or multilateral arrangement or unilaterally submitted to safeguards under a safeguards agreement, and in which safeguarded and unsafeguarded nuclear materials are present:

(a) Subject to the provisions of sub-paragraph (b) below, the Agency shall restrict its safeguards procedures to the area in which irradiated fuel is stored, until such time as all or any part of such fuel is transferred out of the storage area into other parts of the plant. Safeguards procedures shall cease to apply to the storage area or plant when either contains no safeguarded nuclear material; and

(b) Where possible, safeguarded nuclear material shall be measured and sampled separately from unsafeguarded material, and at as early a stage as possible. Where separate measurement, sampling or processing are not possible, the whole of the material being processed in that campaign shall be subject to the safeguards procedures set out in Part III.D of this Agreement. At the conclusion of the processing the nuclear material that is thereafter to be safeguarded shall be selected by agreement between India and the Agency from the whole output of the plant resulting from that campaign, due account being taken of any processing losses accepted by the Agency.

E. Provisions for Conversion Plants, Enrichment Plants and Fabrication Plants

Introduction

85. Additional procedures applicable to conversion plants and fabrication plants are set out below. This terminology is synonymous with the term "a plant for processing or fabricating nuclear material (excepting a mine or ore-processing plant)" which is used in paragraph 117 of this Agreement.

86. In the event that India decides to offer an enrichment plant in the future as a facility subject to this Agreement, the Agency and India shall consult and agree on the application of

the Agency's safeguards procedures for enrichment plants before any such facility is added to the Annex.

Special Procedures

Reports

87. The frequency of submission of routine reports shall be once each calendar month.

Inspections

88. A conversion plant or a fabrication plant which has been supplied wholly or substantially under a project agreement, submitted to safeguards under a safeguards agreement by the parties to a bilateral or multilateral arrangement, or unilaterally submitted to safeguards under a safeguards agreement, and the nuclear material in it, may be inspected at all times if the plant inventory at any time, or the annual input, of nuclear material exceeds five effective kilograms. Where neither the inventory at any time, nor the annual input, exceeds five effective kilograms of nuclear material, the routine inspections shall not exceed two a year. The arrangements for inspections set forth in paragraph 57 of this Agreement shall apply to all inspections to be made under this paragraph. It is understood that, for plants having an inventory at any time, or an annual input, of more than 60 effective kilograms, the right of access at all times would normally be implemented by means of continuous inspection. Where neither the inventory at any time nor the annual input exceeds one effective kilogram of nuclear material, the plant would not normally be subject to routine inspection.

89. When a conversion plant or a fabrication plant which has not been supplied wholly or substantially under a project agreement, submitted to safeguards under a safeguards agreement by the parties to a bilateral or multilateral arrangement or unilaterally submitted to safeguards under a safeguards agreement contains safeguarded nuclear material, the frequency of routine inspections shall be based on the inventory at any time and the annual input of safeguarded nuclear material. Where the inventory at any time, or the annual input, of safeguarded nuclear material exceeds five effective kilograms the plant may be inspected at all times. Where neither the

inventory at any time, nor the annual input, exceeds five effective kilograms of safeguarded nuclear material, the routine inspections shall not exceed two a year. The arrangements for inspection set forth in paragraph 60 shall apply to all inspections to be made under this paragraph. It is understood that, for plants having an inventory at any time, or an annual input, of more than 60 effective kilograms, the right of access at all times would normally be implemented by means of continuous inspection. Where neither the inventory at any time nor the annual input exceeds one effective kilogram of nuclear material, the plant would not normally be subject to routine inspection.

90. The intensity of inspection of safeguarded nuclear material at various steps in a conversion plant or a fabrication plant shall take account of the nature, isotopic composition and amount of safeguarded nuclear material in the plant. Safeguards shall be applied in accordance with the general principles set forth in paragraphs 4 to 8 of this Agreement. Emphasis shall be placed on inspection to control uranium of high enrichments and plutonium.

91. Where a plant may handle safeguarded and unsafeguarded nuclear material, India shall notify the Agency in advance of the programme for handling safeguarded batches to enable the Agency to make inspections during these periods, due account being also taken of the arrangements under paragraph 92 of this Agreement.

92. India and the Agency shall cooperate in making all the necessary arrangements to facilitate the preparation of inventories of safeguarded nuclear material and the taking, shipping and/or analysis of samples, due account being taken of the limitations imposed by the characteristics of a plant already in operation when placed under Agency safeguards.

Residues, Scrap and Waste

93. India shall ensure that safeguarded nuclear material contained in residues, scrap or waste created during conversion or fabrication is recovered, as far as is practicable, in its facilities and within a reasonable period of time. If such recovery is not considered practicable by India, India and the

Agency shall cooperate in making arrangements to account for and dispose of the material.

Safeguarded and Unsafeguarded Nuclear Material

94. India and the Agency may agree on the following special arrangements in the case of a conversion plant or a fabrication plant which has not been supplied wholly or substantially under a project agreement, submitted to safeguards under a safeguards agreement by the parties to a bilateral or multilateral arrangement or unilaterally submitted to safeguards under a safeguards agreement, and in which safeguarded and unsafeguarded nuclear material are both present:

(a) Subject to the provisions of sub-paragraph (b) below, the Agency shall restrict its safeguards procedures to the area in which safeguarded nuclear material is stored, until such time as all or any part of such nuclear material is transferred out of the storage area into other parts of the plant. Safeguards procedures shall cease to be applied to the storage area or plant when it contains no safeguarded nuclear material; and

(b) Where possible, safeguarded nuclear material shall be measured and sampled separately from unsafeguarded nuclear material, and at as early a stage as possible. Where separate measurement, sampling or processing is not possible, any nuclear material containing safeguarded nuclear material shall be subject to the safeguards procedures set out in Part III.E of this Agreement. At the conclusion of processing, the nuclear material that is thereafter to be safeguarded shall be selected, in accordance with paragraph 96 of this Agreement when applicable, by agreement between India and the Agency, due account being taken of any processing losses accepted by the Agency.

Blending of Nuclear Material

95. When safeguarded nuclear material is to be blended with either safeguarded or unsafeguarded nuclear material, the State shall notify the Agency sufficiently in advance of the programme of blending to enable the Agency to exercise its

right to obtain evidence, through inspection of the blending operation or otherwise, that the blending is performed according to the programme.

96. When safeguarded and unsafeguarded nuclear material are blended, if the ratio of fissionable isotopes in the safeguarded component going into the blend to all the fissionable isotopes in the blend is 0.3 or greater, and if the concentration of fissionable isotopes in the unsafeguarded nuclear material is increased by such blending, then the whole blend shall remain subject to safeguards. In other cases, the following procedures shall apply:

(a) Plutonium/plutonium blending: The quantity of the blend that shall continue to be safeguarded shall be such that its weight, when multiplied by the square of the weight fraction of contained fissionable isotopes, is not less than the weight of originally safeguarded plutonium multiplied by the square of the weight fraction of fissionable isotopes therein, provided however that:

(i) In cases where the weight of the whole blend, when multiplied by the square of the weight fraction of contained fissionable isotopes, is less than the weight of originally safeguarded plutonium multiplied by the square of the weight fraction of fissionable isotopes therein, the whole of the blend shall be safeguarded; and

(ii) The number of fissionable atoms in the portion of the blend that shall continue to be under safeguards shall in no case be less than the number of fissionable atoms in the originally safeguarded plutonium;

(b) Uranium/uranium blending: The quantity of the blend that shall continue to be safeguarded shall be such that the number of effective kilograms is not less than the number of effective kilograms in the originally safeguarded uranium, provided however that:

(i) In cases where the number of effective kilograms in the whole blend is less than in the safeguarded uranium, the whole of the blend shall be safeguarded; and

(ii) The number of fissionable atoms in the portion of the blend that shall continue to be under safeguards shall in no case be less than the number of fissionable atoms in the originally safeguarded uranium;

(c) Uranium/plutonium blending: The whole of the resultant blend shall be safeguarded until the uranium and the plutonium constituents are separated. After separation of the uranium and plutonium, safeguards shall apply to the originally safeguarded component; and

(d) Due account shall be taken of any processing losses agreed upon between the State and the Agency.

IV. AGENCY INSPECTORS

97. The provisions of paragraphs 1 to 10 and 12 to 14, inclusive, of the Inspectors Document shall apply to Agency inspectors performing functions pursuant to this Agreement. However, paragraph 4 of the Inspectors Document shall not apply with regard to any facility or to nuclear material to which the Agency has access at all times. The actual procedures to implement paragraph 60 of this Agreement shall be agreed to between the Agency and India.

98. The relevant provisions of the Agreement on the Privileges and Immunities of the Agency (INFCIRC/9/Rev.2) shall apply to the Agency, its inspectors performing functions under this Agreement and to any property of the Agency used by them in the performance of their functions under this Agreement.

V. PHYSICAL PROTECTION

99. India shall take all suitable measures necessary for the physical protection of the facilities and nuclear material subject to this Agreement, taking into account the recommendations made in Agency's document INFCIRC/225/Rev.4, as may be amended from time to time.

VI. SYSTEM OF ACCOUNTING AND CONTROL

100. India shall establish and maintain a system of accounting for and control of all items subject to safeguards under this Agreement, in accordance with provisions to be set out in the Subsidiary Arrangements.

VII. FINANCE

101. India and the Agency shall each bear any expense incurred in the implementation of their responsibilities under this Agreement. The Agency shall reimburse India for any special expenses, including those referred to in paragraph 6 of the Inspectors Document, incurred by India or persons under its jurisdiction at the written request of the Agency, if India notified the Agency before the expense was incurred that reimbursement would be required. These provisions shall not prejudice the allocation of expenses attributable to a failure by either India or the Agency to comply with this Agreement.

102. India shall ensure that any protection against third party liability, including any insurance or other financial security, in respect of a nuclear incident occurring in a facility under its jurisdiction shall apply to the Agency and its inspectors when carrying out their functions under this Agreement as that protection applies to nationals of India.

VIII. NON-COMPLIANCE

103. If the Board determines in accordance with Article XII.C of the Statute of the Agency that there has been any non-compliance by India with this Agreement, the Board shall call upon India to remedy such non-compliance forthwith, and shall make such reports as it deems appropriate. In the event of failure by India to take full remedial action within a reasonable time, the Board may take any other measures provided for in Article XII.C of the Statute. The Agency shall promptly notify India in the event of any determination by the Board pursuant in this regard.

IX. COOPERATION, INTERPRETATION AND APPLICATION OF THE AGREEMENT AND SETTLEMENT OF DISPUTES

104. The Agency and India shall cooperate to facilitate the implementation of this Agreement.

105. At the request of either India or the Agency, there shall be consultations about any question arising out of the interpretation or application of this Agreement. India and the Agency shall endeavour to settle by negotiation any dispute arising from the interpretation or application of this Agreement. India shall have the right to request that any question arising out of the interpretation or application of the Agreement be considered by the Board. The Board shall invite India to participate in the discussion of any such question by the Board.

106. In the event of any question or questions arising from the implementation of this Agreement, the Agency shall provide India with an opportunity to clarify and facilitate the resolution of such questions. The Agency shall not draw any conclusions in connection with the question or questions until India has had an opportunity to provide clarifications.

X. FINAL CLAUSES

107. India and the Agency shall, at the request of either of them, consult about amending this Agreement.

108. This Agreement shall enter into force on the date on which the Agency receives from India written notification that India's statutory and/or constitutional requirements for entry into force have been met.

109. This Agreement shall remain in force until, in accordance with its provisions, safeguards have been terminated on all items subject to this Agreement, or until terminated by mutual agreement of the parties to this Agreement.

XI. DEFINITIONS

110. "Agency" means the International Atomic Energy Agency.

111. "Board" means the Board of Governors of the Agency.

112. "Campaign" means the period during which the chemical processing equipment in a reprocessing plant is operated

between two successive wash-outs of the nuclear material present in the equipment.

113. "Conversion plant" means a facility (excepting a mine or ore-processing plant) to improve unirradiated nuclear material, or irradiated nuclear material that has been separated from fission products, by changing its chemical or physical form so as to facilitate further use or processing. The term conversion plant includes the facility's storage and analytical sections. The term does not include a plant intended for separating the isotopes of nuclear material.

114. "Director General" means the Director General of the Agency.

115. "Effective kilograms" means:

(i) In the case of plutonium, its weight in kilograms;

(ii) In the case of uranium with an enrichment of 0.01 (1%) and above, its weight in kilograms multiplied by the square of its enrichment;

(iii) In the case of uranium with an enrichment below 0.01 (1%) and above 0.005 (0.5%), its weight in kilograms multiplied by 0.0001; and

(iv) In the case of depleted uranium with an enrichment of 0.005 (0.5%) or below, and in the case of thorium, its weight in kilograms multiplied by 0.00005.

116. "Enrichment plant" means a plant for separating the isotopes of nuclear material.

117. "Facility" means, for the purposes of this Agreement:

(i) A "principal nuclear facility", which means a reactor, a plant for processing nuclear material irradiated in a reactor, a plant for separating the isotopes of a nuclear material, a plant for processing or fabricating nuclear material (excepting a mine or ore-processing plant) or a facility or plant of such other type as may be designated by the Board from time to time, including associated storage facilities, as well as a critical facility or a separate storage installation;

(ii) A research and development facility as defined in paragraph 127 of this Agreement;

(iii) Any location where nuclear material in amounts greater than one effective kilogram is customarily used;

(iv) A plant for the upgrading of heavy water or a separate storage installation for heavy water.

118. "Fuel fabrication plant" means a plant to manufacture fuel elements or other components containing nuclear material and includes the plant's storage and analytical sections.

119. "Improved" means, with respect to nuclear material, that either:

(i) The concentration of fissionable isotopes in it has been increased; or

(ii) The amount of chemically separable fissionable isotopes in it has been increased; or

(iii) Its chemical or physical form has been changed so as to facilitate further use or processing.

120. "Inspector" means an Agency official designated in accordance with the Inspectors Document.

121. "Inspectors Document" means the Annex to the Agency's document GC(V)/INF/39.

122. "Nuclear material" means any source or special fissionable material as defined in Article XX of the Statute.

123. "Produced, processed or used" means any utilization or any alteration of the physical or chemical form or composition, including any change of the isotopic composition, of nuclear material;

124. "Project agreement" means a safeguards agreement relating to an Agency project and containing provisions as foreseen in Article XI.FA(b) of the Statute.

125. "Reactor" means any device in which a controlled, self-sustaining fission chain-reaction can be maintained.

126. "Reprocessing plant" means a facility to separate irradiated nuclear materials and fission products, and includes the facility's head-end treatment section and its associated

storage and analytical sections. This term is synonymous with the term "a plant for processing nuclear material irradiated in a reactor" which is used in paragraph 117 of this Agreement.

127. "Research and development facility" means a facility, other than a principal nuclear facility, used for research or development in the field of nuclear energy.

128. "Statute" means the Statute of the Agency.

129. "Throughput" means the rate at which nuclear material is introduced into a facility operating at full capacity.

130. "Unilaterally submitted" means submitted by India to Agency safeguards.

Done at Vienna, on the day of 2008, in duplicate, in the English language.

For the *Government of India*:

For the *International Atomic Energy Agency*:

U.S.-India Relations

14

Richard A. Boucher, Assistant Secretary for South and Central Asian Affairs—Remarks at the Annual Convention of the American Association of Physicians of Indian Origin, Las Vegas, Nevada

(June 27, 2008)

Since India's independence, our interaction has been marked by cooperation, estrangement, and occasionally indifference. The potential of the relationship never seemed to become reality. Although that complicated history informs where we are today, our relationship has come very far from the Cold War differences that once defined us.

If you're reading editorials about the fate of the U.S.-India civilian nuclear deal or progress in the Doha Round, you might wonder about how far we've actually come. What is the state of cooperation between the United States and India? Let me give you the bottom line here at the very top: this is the most exciting moment in U.S.-India relations in two generations.

Years from now, when people discuss our relationship, they will talk about the across the board transformation of U.S.-India relations that took place in the first decade of the 21st century.

We've long been friends and we've always shared a commitment to democracy and peace. But for the first time since India's independence in 1947, our two governments are working *jointly* to craft solutions to the defining challenges of our age: sustaining global growth; ending poverty; fighting terror; defeating disease; and strengthening democracy around the world.

Here at home, India's cultures and traditions have become a vital part of the American melting pot. More than 80,000 Indian students now study in American universities—more than from any nation in the world. They will graduate. Many will return to India. They will play a vital role in the life of their nation while keeping ties to ours.

So, too, with all of you: the more than two million Indian-American doctors, scientists, businesspeople, and even a sitting U.S. governor. Together, you comprise a "living bridge," spanning two cultures and two countries. And the bridge is growing. Last year we issued more than 725,000 non-immigrant visas in India and the number will likely be even higher this year—a clear indication that U.S.-India relations are not simply about relations among governments.

Because of you, Indians and Americans are looking to each other to create opportunities that spur both governments to work together. Because of you—the Indian diaspora—our relations are not just deeper but broader. No longer just a South Asian power, India has become an Asian power, even a global power. It has a capacity and vision for growth and leadership that it did not possess even ten or fifteen years ago.

The trends are visible now: India participates in regional forums with Southeast Asian and East Asian countries. India's "Look East" policy has given it a bigger economic role in Southeast Asia. Its relationships in the Middle East, its deepening relations with Africa, and its role in regional maritime security are areas where the U.S. is just beginning to engage in substantive talks with India.

Given the breadth of our relationship, I could talk all afternoon, But, let me focus on three areas:

our expanding economic partnership;

our collaboration on global issues; and

the strategic relationship that has emerged between our governments.

Economic Partnership

India's remarkable growth of eight to nine per cent continues to fuel this relationship in many ways. The private sector is dynamic. Investment between the two countries has taken off, and it is not just in one direction. Indian companies are investing in the U.S. in many areas, including steel, software, health care, and textiles. U.S. exports to India were up 72 per cent last year, and two-way trade was up 30 per cent.

We in government are helping to support this—first through policy instruments, such as a Bilateral Investment Treaty, but also through high-level dialogue.

In February, we began talks on a Bilateral Investment Treaty that we believe will help to spur business in both directions. We completed another round two weeks ago in Washington, and are on an ambitious timetable to complete negotiations.

We conduct dialogues at or near the Cabinet level and nearly every area of our economic relationship.

> The U.S.-India Economic Dialogue chaired by the Economic Advisor to the President and India's Deputy Chairman of the Planning Commission.
>
> The U.S.-India Trade Policy Forum chaired by the U.S. Trade Representative and India's Minister of Commerce and Industry.
>
> The U.S.-India Commercial Dialogue, the U.S.-India Energy Dialogue, and the U.S.-India Financial and Economic Forum, involving, respectively, our Commerce, Energy and Treasury Secretaries and their Indian counterparts.

And we involve the private sector through the U.S.-India CEO Forum, the Agriculture Knowledge Initiative, the U.S.-India High-Technology Cooperation Group, and the Private Sector Advisory Group to the U.S.-India Trade Policy Forum.

Our government efforts are designed to provide a context and open up opportunities. But the work that is being done, the creative ideas, and the energy has all come from the private sector. They'll go ahead with us or without us.

Collaboration on Global Issues

Our economic partnerships are matched by collaborative initiatives to find solutions to global problems important to both societies.

Investment in science and technology innovation has yielded promising results in tackling issues related to poverty and health. The United States and Indian governments are working in conjunction with private businesses and organizations to expand the agricultural and energy sectors in India in order to make farming more sustainable and productive and to develop cleaner forms of energy. For example, we have a joint agricultural knowledge initiative working to improve farm-to-market links. U.S. experts in clean coal technology are working with Indian counterparts to ensure India's energy future and promote a cleaner environment. There is no international energy security initiative the United States has promoted that India has not been a part of.

Educational exchanges, a historic and important component of our cooperation, have broadened our understanding of our cultures and societies. Indian and American universities are working towards even greater cooperation and cross-fertilization, with an emphasis on knowledge-sharing through student and faculty exchanges and expanded access to higher education in India. We recently concluded a new agreement with the Government of India to double the number of Fulbright scholars.

Educational cooperation extends into the medical field as many of you may know well. Harvard Medical School, for example, has created a partnership with Wockhardt Hospital and Heart Institute to improve health care quality in India. In addition, well-respected specialized American hospitals, such as Mayo Clinic, are increasing their ties with medical professionals in India. High tech media make possible conferences between doctors in both countries on cutting edge procedures or involving particularly difficult treatment.

Your organization and its 42,000 members have also made many significant contributions to the development of the medical field in India. The work of Dr. Navin Shah, a co-founder and president of the American Association of Physicians of Indian Origin, demonstrates what progress can be made by bringing knowledge gained in the United States to India. Many of you may be familiar with Dr. Shah's efforts in Mumbai to implement an emergency response system similar to that of 911. After working with government officials for four years, the system was finally inaugurated in January this year.

Collaborative efforts between Indian and American medical professionals ensure that more breakthroughs like the emergency response system in Mumbai can happen in the future. There is an enthusiasm within our two medical communities to work together to fight diseases, share knowledge and provide better medical services.

In recent years India has leapt forward in the areas of disease control and access to health care. Polio, for example, is near eradication. While the efforts and achievements are commendable, more is left to be done. Investments by the private sector and the two governments, partnering with medical professionals and health institutes, are improving the quality of drugs and medical treatment. The United States is also one of the largest donors to fighting HIV/AIDS in India, providing nearly $30 million last year. These are but a few illustrative developments of the benefits reaped from U.S.-India cooperation in the field of medicine.

These public and private partnerships are but a few of the benefits arising from our relationship that holds much promise and potential. And they show no sign of slowing down.

Our Strategic Partnership

Finally, our strategic relationship has evolved over the last decade, transcending ideology. Strategic talks that began in 2000 between the then Clinton administration and the BJP government have deepened through the joint strategic partnership envisioned by President Bush and Prime Minister Singh. Our landmark nuclear deal, our expanding defense ties, and our consultations on developments in South Asia all testify to this.

You're all reading a lot these days about the status of the nuclear deal. We're currently waiting for political developments in India. We need to be patient and understand democratic consensus building in our partner country. As India moves, we will, too. As the Indian government does what it can, we will do what we can, each with an understanding of the other's democratic calendar. We'll have to talk to our Congress about what they can and cannot accomplish during the remainder of this year. But, overall, I am confident that this deal will come through sooner or later. I'm confident because it has widespread support in both countries and because it's good for India, good for the U.S., good for non-proliferation, good for the environment and good, indeed necessary, for India's long-term economic growth.

In our defense relationship, every military service now conducts joint exercises—from small unit Army counter-insurgency training to naval exercises involving aircraft carriers and submarines. Our defense trade has at last begun to flourish. Only this year, India completed the largest acquisition yet of American defense equipment in purchasing approximately $1 billion worth of Lockheed Martin's C-130 transport aircraft. And two American companies are bidding to build India's next-generation fighter with the F-16 and F-18.

We also aim to expand our cooperation through dialogue on East Asia, the Persian Gulf, and Africa. And we are cooperating on Afghanistan, where India is playing a very positive role as one of the major donors to the civilian efforts.

Of course, our shared democratic heritage remains a solid bond and enduring foundation for this relationship.

I am just enormously excited about what's happening in this relationship. And I am confident that it will be sustained into our next Administrations, just as it was sustained over the last transitions in American and Indian politics.

Those of you who studied history, or who are not as young and naïve as I am, are thinking that we've had such periods of excitement between the U.S. and India before. The bubbles burst, the enthusiasm turned to disappointment. What's to make this different? And, for those of us in government, how do we make it different this time? My answer to the first question is: YOU. You're the ones who make it different: the students, the trans-oceanic families, the academics, the doctors, the business people. You are the foundation and the dynamic between the United States and India. And, what can governments do to help you? Listen to you. Please, tell us how to open doors and remove obstacles. We'll work to help you find even more and more exciting opportunities.

At the end of the day, the key is people: individuals, like you, whose passion, dedication, and commitment has done so much to build the Indo-American relationship and will carry us forward.

So many things bind us together. It's not just the bonds of industry, and not just ties of heritage and diaspora, and not just our imperfect but wonderful democratic systems. Fundamentally, the U.S. and India share a perspective and a vision for the future that I think will grow and endure for generations to come.

15 Strategic Context of U.S.-India Relations

Evan Feigenbaum, Deputy Assistant Secretary for South and Central Asian Affairs
Briefing to Harvard University Weatherhead Fellows, Washington, DC

(April 7, 2008)

...I want to have a discussion, so I'll just do two things: I thought I'd take two minutes—well, three to five minutes—and just talk a little bit, first, about the conceptual architecture of U.S.-India relations a little bit, so you get a feel for how I think we're thinking about the place, why it's becoming important. And second, I'll just say something quickly about operationally what's going on in this relationship.

On the conceptual: It's the most interesting moment in the history of U.S.-India relations. It's fair to say, I think, that as recently as maybe seven, eight, nine, ten years ago, very few people in the United States foreign policy elite—the establishment, at least—thought about India much at all. And when they did, they thought about it usually in a very narrow South Asian context: Indo-Pak nuclear issues, issues of war and peace in Kashmir. But the notion of India on a larger strategic level really was absent from our thought on foreign policy. So there's really been a sea-change, I think, in the role that thinking about India plays.

It's reflective not just of the things happening in India, but I think of some interesting things that have happened in the US foreign policy debate writ large. I tend to divide these into three levels: One is global. The second is regional. And by "regional," I don't just mean South Asia. I mean Asia more broadly: an Asia—East, Central and South—that I think is becoming a much more integrated strategic and economic space, and I'll talk a little bit about that because it will certainly be the case as you look out prospectively over ten years. And then third, there is the bilateral level.

At a global level, I think the interesting thing, first and foremost, is that we've realized we don't live in 1948, much less 1958 or '68. And the world of 2008 is not the world of 1948. So if you think about the architecture of the international system, it's largely outdated. It's a global architecture, but it was established by the victorious powers after the Second World War, so in some sense, it's a Euro-Atlantic architecture. And so there's a mismatch, first at a formal level, between the architecture, on the one hand, and the realities of power and capacity in the world of 2008.

So first, at a very formal level, that's why you have a UN Security Council that doesn't include Japan. It's why you have an International Energy Agency that purports to coordinate among major consuming countries but doesn't include the two fastest-growing energy consumers in the world—China and India. Granted, they're not OECD members and OECD membership is a requirement. But what is it to have an IEA when you don't have China and India as part of it, just conceptually?

It's why you have—I'm not advocating this, I'm just noting—a G-8 that doesn't include China or India. If you think of the G-8 as a league of industrial democracies, okay. But if you think about it as a club of leading economies, conceptually again there's this mismatch between architecture and the realities of the world we live in today.

Likewise on something like the Bank and the Fund, the Bretton Woods institutions, where governance of the Bank and Fund is based on voting rights, weighted voting shares. And China has something like a 3.5 or 4 per cent voting share in the Bank, about the same in the Fund. So with the rapid growth of the Chinese economy, you have [people] thinking a lot about whether we need to re-weight some of the voting shares because

Asian voting rights are underweighted and the Euro-Atlantic voting shares overweighted relative to the realities of power.

So at a global level, I think there's been a recognition in this country that there's this mismatch between architecture and capacity. We look at countries like China, like India, and we see increasingly the capacity to work with the United States on an array of challenges: to sustain growth, fighting poverty, dealing with climate, dealing with HIV/AIDS, countering terrorism.

Now, whether countries like India self-define their own interest that way is a different question entirely. Part of what we're facing in India is a serious foreign policy debate among serious people, who have different views about what India's interests are in the world and the extent to which they're aligned with the United States and other Western powers.

But at least in this country, we begin with the recognition that countries like India now have capacity that wasn't there ten, fifteen years ago. And so we need to take more seriously that capacity as we think about American foreign policy interests globally. So I think at a global level, that explains, in the first instance, the growth of our interest [in India].

Second, at a regional level, as I said, we used to think about India—if we thought about it at all—I think largely in a South Asian context: which was India and Pakistan. What was happening in the nuclear balance? What was going on in the neighborhood?

But there's something interesting happening in Asia more broadly. I can't prove it to you with data; I just have to show it to you anecdotally. In fact if you look at the data, it doesn't support this, but there's something happening. And as a guy who's...covered all three regions of Asia in the Department and on the Policy Planning Staff, there's just something interesting happening anecdotally.

China is very active in the East Asian supply chain. China is becoming much, much more active, especially economically, in Central Asia. We in the Department are interested in links between Central Asia and South Asia, which are tenuous right now but we see some interesting things happening, especially in the southern Central Asian countries with Afghanistan, and to a lesser degree with Pakistan.

Then of course India is part of this—not so much in supply chain data but much more strategically: You see India in Southeast Asia working in regional organizations: things like the ASEAN Regional Forum, or the prospect of becoming a member of APEC [the Asia Pacific Economic Cooperation forum] after the membership moratorium is lifted in 2010. [India is in] the East Asia Summit. There is the quadilateral that existed for awhile between the US, India, Japan, and Australia. So just anecdotally, something's happening.

If you think out about what the world is going to look like in 15 or 20 years, I think we can make an argument that the trend is that Asia will be a more integrated space—at least strategically, maybe to some degree economically. The Chinese economy has largely been what's driving that, but India will be part of that too.

So those of us who try to be forward-thinking about the role of India in the world are starting to think about India not just as a South Asian power but as an Asian power—and about the role of India, China and Japan, these three large Asian powers, and their relations with each other in this larger... Asian space. So we spend a lot of time thinking about India *vis-à-vis* China, China *vis-à-vis* India. That doesn't mean China is the rationale for the interest in U.S.-India relations. Despite what some people say, I can think of 63 good reasons why we should have improved our relations with India a long time ago. But I won't deny that it's in the background, it's a factor. And particularly it's an economic factor.

.... Third, there's just this bilateral issue. Everybody talks a lot about what's happened between the two governments. It goes back a couple of administrations: it began under the Clinton administration; you remember Clinton's visit to India. And it's really accelerated, I think, in this administration.

But it's also been in two Indian administrations now: the former BJP government and now the United Progressive Alliance. So it's not something that you can chalk up to ideology. There's a bipartisan view in this country and a multi-party view in that country, although it's by no means uncontroversial in that country and much less controversial here.

And I think that has to do with the most interesting thing about the bilateral relationship to me, which is that it's sort of moving forward in spite of government. And in fact the most interesting and exciting things are happening outside of government: It's this very dynamic private sector. It's happening in terms of investment both ways: Indian investment into the United States, not just American investment into India, in fact now branded Indian investment in the United States. It's students, business people, citizens. There are 80,000 Indian students in the United States, more than from any country in the world. There are about three million Indian-Americans who are kind of a "human bridge" between the two countries. There's a lot of investment. The...U.S.-India Business Council tells me that, ten years ago, they were lucky if they could get three companies to show up for a meeting. Now, you go to a USIBC meeting, there will be 150 companies. That's not just big guys. It's increasingly smaller and medium-sized business, but principally big guys.

So what's most exciting, and most dynamic, is that it's happening despite government. This doesn't mean that what's happening at a government-to-government level isn't important. It's just, I think, our most mature relationships are the ones that happen despite what happens between two governments.

I guess that leads me from the conceptual to the operational. You may have noticed that this is a time when, if you read the paper, a lot of the official U.S.-India agenda has "stalled out."

.... But the good news is, again, there's a lot of excitement in the U.S.-India relationship quite apart from what's happening officially. There's a lot happening officially, but some of the bigger-ticket items have slowed down a little bit. These are things like the Civil Nuclear Initiative which we're still hopeful about but a lot of that is going to depend on political decisions that India has to make; we've done about as much as we can do from our end. The same thing on a couple of other areas. When you think about trade, whether the Doha round moves forward or doesn't move forward depends a lot on what countries like India do on agriculture and services and industrial goods; that's why it's unclear at this point.

So we're in a period in Indian politics where I think we're looking at coalition governments about as far as the eye can see. So there's going to be a lot of—ironically, despite the fact that the two major parties, the BJP on the right, and the Congress kind of on the center left—largely share consensus on moving forward on relations with the United States, we're in a period of coalition government where regional parties and other parties are really becoming much stronger. And they now have a voice on foreign policy in ways that they didn't before. So the process of forging these coalitions requires a lot of tradeoffs. And sometimes some of the initiatives that we have been interested in moving forward are sometimes caught in the midst.

.... But it's kind of an exciting moment I think in the relationship...so we're kind of aggressively working this relationship forward. But I think what really accounts for the most dramatic growth is the private sector: it's citizens, more than anything else. And that's not going to change.

The last thing I'd say is something I said in Delhi the other day to a couple of prominent "greybeard" people. We were talking about diplomatic relationships and somebody said. "if the U.S. and India stopped talking tomorrow"—which of course isn't going to happen, but if it did—they "wouldn't worry about the U.S.-India relationship because there's so much that's dynamic and active." That's not true of all of India's relationships: if you think about the India-Russia relationship, for instance, it's an important relationship but it's principally a diplomatic, defense and governmental relationship; there's virtually nothing happening in the private sector and there's not a lot happening with people to people contact.

So the United States plays an interesting role now in India's diplomacy and strategy as well. It's not something you'll find written down. But I think the trajectory is irreversible, and it's largely independent of politics. Being an election year here, and maybe an election year in India, I don't think it matters that much [to the U.S.-India relationship] who is elected president here. There may be shades of opinion, particularly on the nuclear deal. But there's a broad consensus in this country on this relationship and it's a bipartisan consensus. It extends across a couple of administrations now of both parties. A lot of people are invested on a very human level.

So we couldn't be more excited about what's happening. But I think you have to think in terms of five, ten, fifteen year increments, and not what's happening.... So that's a little bit on the conceptual and operational. I'm happy to answer your questions.

16

Remarks with Indian Minister of External Affairs Pranab Kumar Mukherjee

Secretary Condoleezza Rice—Remarks following meeting, Washington, DC

(March 24, 2008)

View Video

Secretary Rice: Good morning. I'm very pleased to welcome External Affairs Minister Mukherjee. We have had a very brief discussion this morning of some elements of the U.S.-India relationship, a relationship that has broadened and deepened during the time that President Bush and Prime Minister Singh have been in office and have been working to fully express the nature of a relationship that should exist between two of the world's great, multi-ethnic democracies.

We have had an opportunity to talk about the deepening of our economic ties, of our defense cooperation, and the deepening of our dialogue about regional issues. We had, for instance, a discussion this morning concerning Tibet and the troubling circumstances there, as well as on Burma. We have a lot more to talk about, and the Minister and I will meet for dinner tonight in order to do that. And so, thank you very much for coming and welcome. It's good to have you here.

Minister Mukherjee: Thank you, Madame Secretary. As you have stated that we have covered some areas of our cooperation and shared some parts of the issues arising in our region, shared our individual position. We had quite a satisfactory discussion this morning, but we are waiting till I meet you at night on dinner. We deeply appreciate and recognize your personal contribution, Secretary Rice, for the transformation of India-U.S. relations and giving them a strong foundation for the future. The record number of landmark developments in India-U.S. ties over the last few years would not have been possible without a broad-based convergence of interests and concerns between our two countries.

India is the fastest-growing democracy in the world. It is also, perhaps, the fastest-growing export market for U.S. business and industry. Two-way trade and investment between our two countries is growing along with our cooperation in agriculture, clean energy, environment, science and technology, health and education. A similar momentum can also be seen in our different (inaudible) for peaceful use of outer space and other high-technology areas. We believe that the India-U.S. partnership is based on a bedrock of long-term commitments and a shared vision. During my discussion with Secretary Rice we agreed to maintain the positive momentum generated particularly by the visits of Prime Minister Manmohan Singh to United States in July 2005 and that of President Bush to India in March 2006. Several critical decisions were taken during that visit on a wide spectrum of issues important to both countries. It will be our common endeavor to register progress on all of them. In this context, I discussed with Secretary Rice the recent developments related to our bilateral cooperation. Secretary Rice and I shared our views and concerns about regional and international developments. There is a broad overlap in our interests and objectives, and we intend to supplement our dialogue with a closer working-level interaction on a regular basis within the Ministry of External Affairs in India and the U.S. State Department.

Secretary Rice and I will continue, as I mentioned, our discussion this evening. I also look forward to the opportunity of meeting the National Security Advisor Stephen Hadley and calling on President George W. Bush later this afternoon. Thank you (inaudible).

Question: Secretary Rice, if the U.S.-India Civil Nuclear Cooperation deal is not completed and sent to Congress by July, do you think you will simply have to give up on it for this Administration, given the electoral calendar?

And Mr. Minister, have you made any progress in your talks with your—the government's Communist allies, members, to obtain their approval for the deal? And how close are you now to completing the IAEA safeguards agreement?

Secretary Rice, if you could just quickly address Tibet? I don't think we've had a chance to hear you talk—squarely address the question of whether the Chinese authorities have used excessive force there. And have there been any more unauthorized passport inquiries?

Secretary Rice: Well, Arshad, you managed three questions rather than one. (Laughter.) Let me try and take care of them. First of all, we have had a brief discussion of what we consider to be a landmark agreement, the Civil Nuclear Cooperation agreement with India, which I believe would be good for both sides and good for the future of nonproliferation, as many experts, including Mohamed ElBaradei, have said. And so we will continue to work on that agreement. The Indians are now in a process of working with the IAEA and we'll follow that progress, but we will have further discussions on that matter later. We spoke principally this morning about various regional issues of concern to both sides.

In that regard, on Tibet, let me just say that we believe that the answer for Tibet is to have a more sustainable policy for the Chinese Government concerning Tibet. I've spoken to my counterpart about the current situation in which there needs to be restraint, in which violence is not acceptable, but there also needs to be a day after the current events.

And that really requires a sustainable process of dealing with the problems of Tibet, and the grievances of Tibetans. And we believe that the Dalai Lama could play a very favorable role, given his belief in nonviolence, given his stated position that he does not seek political independence for Tibet, and given his unassailable, authoritative moral stature not just with the people of Tibet, but with people from around the world. And we're going to continue to encourage that dialogue because, ultimately, that is going to be the only policy that is sustainable in Tibet.

And as to passports, I know of nothing further from the beginning of the weekend.

Minister Mukherjee: Thank you. In (inaudible), as Secretary Rice has pointed out, we are interested in implementing the landmark agreement, which we finalized during the visit of Prime Minister Manmohan Singh and followed by subsequent visit of President Bush in India. But we have some political problems in our country. Currently, we are engaged in resolving those problems. Out of four stages, 123 Agreement between India and the U.S.A. has been signed. The second stage, to have the approval of the Board of Governors of IAEA in respect of India's specific safeguard agreement, we are currently engaged with IAEA. The discussions are over, but the agreements are yet to be initialed and approved by the Board of Governors. In that stage, we are currently engaged with various political parties who are supporters of our coalition government in India. And the discussion is still going on.

In the aspect of Tibet, we shared our perceptions. You are aware of the fact that 49 years ago, Dalai Lama entered into India in the month of March 1959. Since then, we are providing shelter to His Holiness Dalai Lama. He is highly respected. He is fully free to carry on his spiritual and religious activities. We have also provided shelter to his followers. I understand currently the number may be about 180,000 Tibetans who are provided shelter in India. They can carry on their religious, cultural and spiritual activities. But as part of our law, they are not entitled to carry on any political activities, as Indian citizens also cannot carry on any political activities which are inimical to any friendly countries or which can disturb the relationship between India and any other country. And all of them are to accept the law of the land, including the efforts to cross the international borders. And Tibetan refugees are also subjected to the law of the land. We have expressed our concern in Parliament about the latest development. We do hope it will be possible to resolve the issue through peaceful dialogue between the parties concerned. Thank you.

Question: Dr. Rice, what is your take on the latest challenge in Indo-U.S. relations? I mean, Speaker Pelosi's indiscretion in criticizing China on Indian soil, which many Indians have disapproved of.

And to you, Mr. Mukherjee, why are you allowing the Dalai Lama to let the Americans fire on China from Indian shoulders in violation of the Dalai Lama's long-standing commitment not to engage in political activity?

Secretary Rice: Well, let me first set aside the premise that there is some problem in Indo-U.S. relations. I don't believe that there is. Speaker Pelosi spoke with the Dalai Lama, as the President has spoken with the Dalai Lama, most recently in October when he was here to receive a Congressional Medal of Honor, our highest civilian medal. He is somebody who is respected. The Speaker respects him. The President respects him. And at this particular point in time, to have contact with him, I think, is a good thing, not a bad thing because he is a moderate voice on these issues and he is a voice that, frankly, I hope the Chinese will listen to more.

Minister Mukherjee: I think in respect of Tibet, I have already expressed my views.

Secretary Rice: Thank you very much.

Minister Mukherjee: Thank you.

Indian and U.S. Relations

17

Richard A. Boucher, Assistant Secretary for Central Asia Affairs—Remarks to the Press
New Delhi, India
(March 5, 2008)

....

Assistant Secretary Boucher: In some ways my visit is just part of our regular consultations with the Indian government about the entire breadth and depth of what is a very strong relationship. We have continuous back and forth at a high level. You saw Secretary Gates was just here. We've seen our Indian colleagues in Washington and New York in the last year or so a couple of times. I'll be out periodically as well.

On the other hand, we come at a moment of great promise and opportunity in the U.S.-India relationship and I think we're all looking in 2008 to make this a year where we take a lot of the trends and the things that have been done and finish them up, solidify them, build on them, for new administrations next year in the United States and potentially in India as well.

I think every time I come here I'm struck by the real depth and the solid momentum, the underlying flow of U.S.-Indian relations: the dramatic expansion in ties between people, between academics, between businesses. So I've spent some time during this visit with people in the business community, I'll see some more this evening. I'll spend time with folks in the education community because of the explosion in U.S.-Indian educational ties, but also a real opportunity there, I think, for collaboration by universities and scholars.

I spent time with our consular section at the embassy, the young people who work very very hard to make sure that the Indians going back and forth get their visas. They've again this year broken a new record in terms of the number of visas they've been able to issue and Indian travelers they've been able to take care of.

I've also spent time with the Indian government talking about things going on outside of India: places in the region that we're both concerned about, opportunities in Central Asia, or areas of cooperation in other parts of the world where I think the United States and India have an increasing interest in our cooperation, at least in knowing what each other's doing and having the advantage of each other's insights. So I found those discussions very productive as well.

So in all these areas we have, I think, a very strong momentum in the relationship and we'll continue to move that forward as well as to kind of put the pieces in place that give it a foundation for the future. That's what this visit is about and I think that's what my future visits will be as well.

Now we did spend a fair amount of time looking at the U.S.-India civil nuclear agreement, civil nuclear relationship. India has just had a team in Vienna negotiating for the Safeguards Agreement for the International Atomic Energy Agency. That's a very important piece of the puzzle that needs to be put in place. We still have several other pieces of the puzzle to be put in place before the actual trade can begin. I think both sides are very committed to doing that. We do understand that time is short, that we are under various time pressures, and we do understand that we both have political processes and democratic processes to go through. I think it's the goal of all of us to work within our democratic systems so that we can go forward in a way that allows this deal to come to fruition, and that show we're going to work it, that's how the Indians are going to work it.

At this particular moment India is looking to conclude its Safeguards Agreement with the International Atomic Energy Agency. After that we go forward with other pieces, and we're ready to go as soon as the Indians are. So we compared notes about how to proceed, how to get the job done in the future.

With that I'd like to stop and be glad to take your questions.

Question: Matt Rosenberg, Associated Press. We've heard the last few weeks various deadlines of the nuke deal. Under Secretary Burns said it had to be ready for Congress by May, then somebody else suggested September. Realistically, when does India have to have the IAEA, the NSG agreement set and the final bill to Congress to get passed this year?

Assistant Secretary Boucher: Realistically I think the authoritative voice on this is Senator Biden. He's chairman of the committee in the Congress that handles foreign affairs and he probably knows better than any what we have to do. What he said is, realistically, in the United States political system you need to get it through Congress by July. In order to do that we need to get it to Congress by June, which means we need to get some of the other steps completed by the end of May. You start walking backwards and you see that it is still possible to do all these things, but they're each going to require an accelerated timetable and a lot of effort. We're prepared to make that effort. But I think realistically in the U.S. system what Senator Biden says is probably the best and most authoritative.

Question: Are you optimistic that it can be done?

Assistant Secretary Boucher: I'm optimistic because I think it's a good deal. It's a good deal for India. It's a good deal for the United States. I think both sides understand that and both sides are committed to making it work. But having said that, it ain't over until it's over. There's a lot of work to do. We're really going to have to apply ourselves to make it all happen.

Question: Ranjit Kumar from *Navbharat Times*, India and IAEA have both reported to have finalized the Safeguards Agreement. Have you seen, have you gone through that draft and are you satisfied with the draft?

Assistant Secretary Boucher: No on the first part. I haven't gone through the draft, so I can't answer the second part. That's an agreement between India and the International Atomic Energy Agency. It has to meet certain standards of the agency.

We'll see when it's finalized what it looks like, but I'm assuming it will be a good agreement for both India and the Agency and that it will meet the international standard requirements.

Question: Manish Chand from IANS. How much time do you think it will take in the NSG? And do you visualize any problem countries there [inaudible]?

Assistant Secretary Boucher: It's hard to say exactly how long it takes. I think we need to allow a month or two to work carefully with the countries, at least that much. The Nuclear Suppliers Group is a consensus organization and it's an organization of people who are very committed to non-proliferation goals, to making sure that we keep the world safe from the dangers of nuclear proliferation. There are people who believe very strongly in this. They're going to have a lot of questions to raise because we do recognize that while this deal is important to bring India into the nonproliferation mainstream, it doesn't do it in, you might say, the traditional way. And therefore there are going to be questions about how it applies and how it works.

I think those questions all have good answers, because as I said, I think it's a good deal. It's a good deal for India, it's a good deal for the U.S., it's a good deal for nonproliferation generally in the world. But I do think because it's a consensus organization we have to work with the countries involved and help them understand what the implications are and why this is good for everybody. So it will take a little patience and firmness as well.

Question: My name is Sheila Mart, I'm from Rediff.com. I have two questions. One is I just want to double check that is America not concerned that in India, even if this deal is through, in the sense that this government's commitment is there to operationalize the deal very soon so that it can go to Congress by June/July. But are you overlooking the fact which is that the majority of parliamentarians, it is said that they are against the deal? But technically this government can do it so they may do it. But are you overlooking that fact, and you are not concerned what happens after this government?

And second, my question is that recently Mr. Gates said that the Prime Minister told him that India is happy with what it is doing in Afghanistan. Since you are also handling Afghanistan I would like to know, do you have any more expectations from India to join in any other manner than what they are doing now?

Assistant Secretary Boucher: Do I get to pick which one of those questions to answer? Let me try to remember both.

On the question of the government, we deal with the government that's in place. That's true of all of us in democracies. Governments handle their own politics domestically, without us being involved. That's the way it should be. That's the way it is for India, that's the way it is for the United States. We're in charge of getting U.S. congressional approval. They're in charge of completing their own domestic procedures. So we deal with the government that is in power, that is duly elected and represents India. Whatever political considerations they have, they'll take care of. That is the way international relations work between democracies. I don't find anything unusual about the current situation. If they feel they're in a position to go forward, then we go forward. It's pretty simple as far as we're concerned.

On the issue of India and Afghanistan, I do think we're good partners there. India is one of the major donors. India has done some very important things, continues to do some important things. And I did have a chance to compare notes with some of the people at the Ministry of External Affairs on Afghanistan, the projects that India is undertaking, the areas of cooperation, the areas of emphasis.

One of the things we're all emphasizing, I think, is training of officials for Afghanistan. They need people who can go out and undertake projects and provide good governance on behalf of the government. India has ramped up a fairly extensive training program in that regard, and that's, I think, one of the most welcome things that India has been doing is helping to train public servants in Afghanistan. So we talked about how that could be done more efficiently or expanded. We talked about some of the other projects India has underway in Afghanistan.

We welcome it. We welcome India's commitment. We look forward to working with India in the future.

Question: [Inaudible]?

Assistant Secretary Boucher: There are always new things to do. We're going to look at, in Afghanistan there's a national development strategy that's going through the World Bank this spring and we'll all look at it again in June at a donor's conference where we expect to be in Paris. I'm sure India will participate, and I hope they show up with some new ideas.

Question: [Inaudible].

Assistant Secretary Boucher: NATO has asked for India's help? I'm not aware of anything specific. Certainly NATO has a big role to play in Afghanistan and so does India, so there's plenty of cooperation. I'm not aware that NATO has asked India for anything particular at this point.

Question: Nick Schifrin, ABC News. I apologize, I do have two questions. The first is about the nuclear agreement. To what extent is the agreement just part of the bilateral relationship and to what extent is it kind of the touchstone of the relationship that speaks to whether the U.S. and the Indian government can work closely?

My other question is about Pakistan. The U.S. has been severely, severely criticized for what a lot of Pakistanis believe is propping up Musharraf, as I'm sure you know. So my question is: do you believe that criticism, and do you think that there is a point at which the U.S. will have to come up with a plan to have a Pakistani government without Musharraf?

Assistant Secretary Boucher: The nuclear deal is very important. It's big progress. It's a great new area of cooperation, but it's frankly one of several areas of big progress and new opportunities for cooperation.

I would say the touchstone of the U.S.-Indian relationship is students and scholars, because those are the people who go back and forth. Those are the people who get educated, who start businesses, who create business opportunities through new technology and across the Pacific, who have led to this explosion of ties between the United States and India. And whatever we do as governments, as long as we keep the students and scholars and business people flowing back and forth I think we'll have a very strong and almost familial relationship between the United States and India.

Now there [are] things the governments are doing that really do help expand that: I think cooperation in the field of education is one of them—the Fulbright program that we have and that we are looking to revitalize and expand, I think that's another area where we're looking at that kind of dramatic expansion; Defense cooperation, not just in terms of technology sales but just in terms of understanding each other's security needs and working together. You saw that in the visit of Secretary Gates; an expanded, you might say, foreign policy sort of cooperation is another area that's really going quickly with India, as well as the nuclear deal. So, you have probably five or six different centers of expansion right now, of real strong flowering in the U.S.-India relationship. I don't see it as a stem with one flower, it's sort of a tree with a lot of different fruit. And some of those are ripening faster than others, but we're really doing a lot of big things in the relationship right now. I think we want to make sure they all succeed, including the nuclear one.

As far as Pakistan, I agree with you that we've been severely and I would say unfairly criticized for the relationship we have. We have a very fundamental relationship with Pakistan as a nation, as a society, and trying to help Pakistan achieve success as a stable democracy, as a democracy that's able to protect itself against extremism. And that's something we share with the people of Pakistan. We have a lot of our programs and money focused on opening the economy, giving them education, helping them with their governance and social organization, things like that are fundamentally what we're going to continue to do with the new government. We look forward to working with an elected government with a new Prime Minister, work with whoever emerges from that democratic process. But we'll also work with all the leaders of Pakistan, all the people in different parts of society and different offices of government because Pakistan needs that kind of stable center in order to succeed. That's essentially where we are right now with policy.

Question: [Inaudible] Musharraf [inaudible]?

Assistant Secretary Boucher: He's President of Pakistan. He's one of those leaders.

Question: Sandeep with the Hindu. You spoke about cooperation in Central Asia. Could you amplify on that? And what are the other major issues that you discussed here?

Assistant Secretary Boucher: I mentioned Central Asia just because it's probably not something most people associate with the U.S.-India relationship. It's, shall we say, just at the beginning of starting to look at what we might be able to do together. I think just comparing notes on interests, interests in education and cultural developments in the area, interest in energy developments in the area. Right now we're just sort of going back and forth and trying to examine what we're doing and what we're interested in. Whether we end up working directly together or just having a better understanding of our own interests, each other's interests, I don't know yet.

Question: My name is Dinesh, I'm from Star News. I wanted to ask you, going back to Pakistan, the two parties, the People's party and Nawaz Sharif, should they both work with President Musharraf?

Assistant Secretary Boucher: We're interested in working with everybody. That's where I'm going to stop. What the parties decide to do in terms of governments, coalitions, that's democracy. That's what we wanted. They're going to figure it out and decide.

Question: Nidhi Razdan from NDTV. What's the Indian government tell you about the status of the negotiations with the IAEA?

Assistant Secretary Boucher: That they've been having negotiations with the IAEA and that they'll tell us when they're ready to move on to the next stage. I can't speak on their behalf, they'll have to talk about it themselves.

Question: Just to add to what Nidhi asked. I'm Suhasini from CNN-IBN. You call it an important piece of the puzzle, the negotiations with the IAEA. Later this month we're expecting to see the Foreign Minister come to Washington. Would you expect that by then we will have a draft agreement with the IAEA agreed to? What else are you expecting in that visit?

Assistant Secretary Boucher: That again, is a question for the India government, where they want to be when the Foreign Minister visits. All I'll say is we're looking forward to a visit by the Foreign Minister. We'd like to welcome him to Washington. But again, I'll leave it to the Indian government to announce when he might be able to come visit.

But we have an ongoing pattern of high level consultations. We've got a lot of ongoing work to do together. At every stage we need to compare notes, decide how to go to the next stage, decide how to go to the nuclear suppliers, to the IAEA, and things like that. So we're constantly working these issues and we'll work them at every opportunity we have to visit with each other.

Question: Manish Chand, IANS. Do you sincerely believe that if the deal were not to go through, this entire spectrum of blossoming U.S.-India ties would not be affected? How would it affect [Indo-U.S. ties], would it marginally affect, would it substantially affect?

Assistant Secretary Boucher: I'm always asked: what are you going to do when everything falls apart? I guess that's part of the nature of your business and my business, but I certainly am aware that things fall apart. But on the other hand I think my job is to make them work. What I'm focused on right now is how to make this work and how to make it succeed. I think that's what the Indian government is focused on right now because we both want this to happen.

Time is tight. Time is very tight. But we have to figure out ways to get the work done. We have to understand each other's needs and political situations. But I think we can make this happen and we're going to work hard to make it happen.

If for some reason it doesn't, we still have a relationship. The United States and India still have fundamental interests together. We still have fundamental involvement with each other. We have the people, the scholars, the businesses, the government agreements, the potential for cooperation in many many areas. Economics, education, anything you can name.

So I don't want to miss the opportunity. I don't think any of us should miss the opportunity. On the other hand, we have many opportunities, many things going on right now.

Question: So the fundamental interest is common to both India and Pakistan as you have said. I want to ask about your views on Pakistan when it comes to non-proliferation and the nuclear technologies?

Assistant Secretary Boucher: My views on Pakistan and nonproliferation? Everybody needs to uphold the standards of nonproliferation. That's about all there is to say.

Interview with *The Times of India* 18

R. Nicholas Burns, Under Secretary for Political Affairs, Washington, DC

(February 29, 2008)

Question: Secretary Burns, I was just reading that I believe you were at the FPC, Foreign Press Center, yesterday and you asked for bold decision to be taken by the Indian government about the nuclear deal. And I was wondering what you meant. Are you asking the government to defy the sort of limited political mandate it has, knowing that it might precipitate an early election?

Under Secretary Burns: Well, first of all let me say that the last thing I would wish to do is to interfere in the internal politics of India and with the coalition in India. So I will not do that and I will steer clear of that. But I will say this: this agreement between the United States and India is really an agreement between India and the world community. Because what it does is it brings India out of the isolation in which it's been for well over 35 years. It allows India to be treated in a more egalitarian way. It allows India access to nuclear fuel and civil nuclear technology which will be critical for its economic development, for electricity production, and for the international goal of reducing carbon emissions. And it does all that, and it has its champions Russia, China, France, Britain and the United States. So I think it's a deal that makes—if I could say this as an outsider—it really makes sense for India.

There is a calendar and there is a clock ticking. And there's no escaping that. For the process to be completed, the IAEA

Board of Governors, the Nuclear Suppliers Group and the U.S. Congress, this agreement would have to get to the U.S. Congress by May or June, as Senator Biden said last week, for the Congress to act before its summer recess in July. If you back up from there, that means that the IAEA safeguards agreement will need to be completed and approved by the Board of Governors in a very short period of time from now. Because we assume that the Nuclear Suppliers Group is going to be a lengthy, quite involved and complicated process involving 45 countries. Any time you have 45 countries, you know, involve themselves in anything like this it's going to be very, very complicated and complex. And so that's why I think it's very important for the Indian government now to act quickly and decisively. And our view is that this agreement is worth defending and worth supporting.

Question: Okay. Just walk me through the timeline again, Secretary Burns. You mentioned May or June?

Under Secretary Burns: Yes. Senator Biden when he gave his press conference in Delhi last week said that in order for the Congress to be able to vote by no later than July, then he thought that this had to get to the Congress by May or June. Meaning the IAEA and NSG processes would have concluded by then. And that's a very tall order, and it means that things have to happen rather quickly.

Question: Right. I also heard you mention China as one of the champions. That sounds like a new development. Are you saying the Chinese are on board on this one?

Under Secretary Burns: I don't think that China would block the deal. I think that China understands that this deal is going to go forward with a great deal of support. And so therefore I think the Indian public should look at this as an international show of interest in India, and that India in achieving this agreement would I think strengthen its international position across the board.

Question: Right. I mean, saying China won't block the deal is a little different from touting China as a champion of the deal, which is I believe the word you used. I'm a little mystified as to, is there such a strong support for the deal from China? Is it something you sense from Beijing? Or is this a new development?

Under Secretary Burns: Well, you have to ask the Chinese; I can't speak for them. But I can say this: it's our firm impression that China will support this deal at the NSG.

Question: What do you think is holding up the deal right now? Is it just the political situation in India? Or do you think the negotiation with IAEA is genuinely complex as some Indian officials have claimed?

Under Secretary Burns: Well, my view has been that the IAEA process is a relatively simple and straightforward process. And in our view it could be concluded quite rapidly should the Indian government wish to do that and should the IAEA be fully engaged, and I think it is. And so I don't think there's a problem there and I think that—it's fairly clear to us that this process will move as fast as the Indian government wishes it to move.

Question: So does it mean the primary hurdle is actually political?

Under Secretary Burns: Well I think that's obvious. I think that this is a question—and again, I don't want to get into the politics of this, it's not for me to do that. But I think, you know, we've reached a point where it is clearly time for a decision. And we hope that decision, obviously, will be positive.

Question: Nick, is it frustrating for you—and I want to take you back to something that you said earlier, in fact I had asked a question when we had a briefing at the State Department about how many hours and days it had taken you. And my—I don't have my notes in front of me in Bangalore, but my recollection is that something like 300 hours. And I think you mentioned several cities, a number of cities in which you had negotiated.

Under Secretary Burns: This has been one of the most complex negotiations that I've ever been involved in. It's really been a marathon. It's—yes, we've negotiated over three years. I've made eight trips to New Delhi during that time. And we've met, of course, in the United States, in Washington, in New

York. We have negotiated this in Vienna, in Madrid, in Paris. It's been quite an odyssey, very much worthwhile. And I must say I had the great good fortune to have two Indian counterparts who are supremely effective professional diplomats—Shankar Menon, the current Foreign Secretary, and Shyam Saran, his predecessor. And it's been a privilege to work with both of them. Both are friends, I count them among my friends, of course, and I've been very impressed by the way that India has negotiated in such an effective fashion, but also one that has brought a lot of trust between our two governments.

Question: So what I'm asking is that, on a day when you're actually leaving the service, I believe you would have liked to have sort of wrapped this up as a sort of crowning glory. And it looks as of now, although Secretary Rice has just mentioned that you will be sort of seconded to the State Department for some more months, it looks as if at least in the official scenario you're not going to go home with this all wrapped up.

Under Secretary Burns: I think it's quite clear as I'm leaving my position as Under Secretary today, obviously it's going to take some more time. But we'll be wishing India well.

I think this is an important moment for India. India is clearly a rising power in the world. This agreement signifies and symbolizes that rise. It symbolizes the fact that the international community I think fully embraces the fact that India must be treated with greater respect and equality. And as an American diplomat let me say that I think our government recognized this earlier than most others did. We made a strategic decision to improve our relations with India. We were willing on our own to overcome and defy 30 years of conventional orthodox wisdom in the United States about India and its nuclear program. We've completely overturned the way we work with India. And we've achieved a historic vote in the United States Congress 15 months ago, the Hyde Act's passage. We still have strong bipartisan majority support for India and the India civil nuclear deal in the United States Congress. And I am proud as an American that my country has led the way to embrace India's growing role in the world and to see it as a positive development. And I think this does mirror—it also mirrors the rapid growth of the relationship in agriculture, in science, in space technology, in business, in military cooperation, in counterterrorism—there's been a huge expansion in this relationship, which I do think is in the interest of both countries. And it would be my strong wish that this trend continue and that India and the United States continue to improve our relationship.

Question: Nick, there were things also in India, during my several trips here, and I'm sure you would have read it through your reports, your own, you know, political reports from the embassy. This deal has public support in India. This deal has largely, you know, editorial support in India. So why isn't the Indian government using that, you know? The momentum it has from people and from the media, do you think?

Under Secretary Burns: I don't want to second guess—I would never want to second guess the Indian government. We have too much respect and trust in the government to want to give it public advice like that. So I would leave that to the Indian government to characterize.

I think the Indian government is a very serious, competent, professional government that is trying to do its best, and obviously there are—it's a very delicate time and sensitive one for domestic politics and we understand that. All democratic countries, of course, have a balance of competing interests inside their government. We certainly do in the United States in our separation of powers between the Congress and the Executive Branch. So I don't want to second guess—

Question: And what happens to you after you leave the administration? You've been part of the Foreign Service, part of the State Department for so long, and counted as one of the most brilliant diplomats, so I'm wondering—

Under Secretary Burns: Well, I'm retiring from the Foreign Service and the diplomatic corps and I'll be entering private life. I have not yet announced what I'm going to be doing, but I will do that shortly. And I'm going to miss diplomacy very much, at least miss working for my government very much. I've been very fortunate to have had just an interesting career. And I must say that this issue of the U.S. and India has been a great passion of mine for many years. And I believe strongly in the potential for a strong friendship between the U.S. and India. I think we can see it on the horizon. We can see how it will be structured. I think that Prime Minister Singh and President Bush have given this a major boost forward.

But the key thing is, remember when President Clinton was in office he was working with BJP governments and they worked well together too. So I think in essence you have bipartisan support on both sides of this relationship.

Question: And it's not unusual for, you know, career Foreign Service officers to actually serve beyond the professional period, right? Tom Pickering comes to mind, who came back to the department I think after he retired. So, can we expect to see you back?

Under Secretary Burns: I don't know. That's a question—it's hard to see into the future and to predict the future, isn't it? I will go into private life. And I'm looking forward to the many challenges there. It's been a privilege to serve in the government and I would never turn that opportunity down, of course, should it arise in the future. But I'm expecting this to be a move into the private sector for several years.

Question: Okay. I hate to ask this, but I can't let go because my one last question—what happens if the deal doesn't go through?

Under Secretary Burns: If the civ-nuke deal doesn't go through?

Question: Yes.

Under Secretary Burns: Well you know, I think it will be a great missed opportunity. Here we have probably the single most important opportunity to advance U.S.-India relations in 35 years. We have substantial public support in both countries. We have the leaders of both countries wishing it to happen. And so if it doesn't go through I think it will be a great loss for both countries. And so we must try everything we can to avoid that. We must preserve this deal and put it forward.

I would also say, however, that the relationship is quite strong and quite broadly gauged. If you think about all the different areas in which our two governments are working and also think about the private sector connections between the two countries, this is a relationship that can withstand a lot, and that's positive. But certainly the civil nuclear deal has become, symbolically, in many ways the centerpiece of this relationship. So there will be great disappointment in both countries if it doesn't materialize. I know that's the case in the U.S. Congress where it has very strong support.

So I do think it's time for us to redouble our efforts to put this agreement forward and to work as hard as we can to finish it this year.

Question: Right. The reason I'm asking—the reason I ask this is, I've been in India for a week now and I'm sure by now you know how India works. You know, for every little thing we hark back to 5,000 years of civilization. And for many Indians, too, it's very frustrating to face what I call a very karmic approach, you know, the sense of karma and the attitude here is, oh well, if we miss this, so what? It's not the end of the world kind of attitude.

Under Secretary Burns: Well, I frankly disagree with that.

Question: And Indians find it frustrating too.

Under Secretary Burns: Yeah, I frankly very much disagree with that. I think that this would be a major missed opportunity. The timing is important here. It is—you know, we don't have all the time in the world to carry this forward.

Question: Alright. Thanks, I really appreciate you opening up and talking to me.

Under Secretary Burns: It's a pleasure.

Question: And when I come back to D.C. I hope I can come by and meet you and say hello and—

Under Secretary Burns: Please do.

Question: Is there a timeline to which you continue to be associated with the State Department and this deal?

Under Secretary Burns: Yes, until April 30th.

Question: Okay. Is that also a good indication of when the U.S. expects to have this wrapped up?

Under Secretary Burns: Well, we'd like to get it wrapped up yesterday. Right?

Question: [Laughter] Right.

Under Secretary Burns: Anyway, I think we're seeing the emergence of a very positive relationship between the countries and we should continue to work hard to fulfill that promise.

19

Implementation of the India-United States Joint Statement of July 18, 2005: India's Separation Plan

The resumption of full civilian nuclear energy cooperation between India and the United States arose in the context of India's requirement for adequate and affordable energy supplies to sustain its accelerating economic growth rate and as recognition of its growing technological prowess. It was preceded by discussions between the two governments, particularly between President Bush and Prime Minister Manmohan Singh, of the global energy scenario and the long-term implications of increasing pressure on hydrocarbon resources and rising oil prices. These developments led to the announcement in April 2005 of an Indo-U.S. Energy Dialogue that encompassed the entire spectrum of energy options ranging from oil and gas to coal, alternative fuels and civilian nuclear energy. Through the initiation of a sustained dialogue to address energy security concerns, the two countries sought to promote stable, efficient, predictable and cost effective solutions for India's growing requirements. At the same time, they also agreed on the need to develop and deploy cleaner, more efficient, affordable and diversified energy technologies to deal with the environmental implications of energy consumption. India had developed proven and wide ranging capabilities in the nuclear sector, including over the entire nuclear fuel cycle. It is internationally recognized that India has unique contributions to make to international efforts towards meeting these objectives. India has become a full partner in ITER, with the full support of the U.S. and other partners. India also accepted the U.S. invitation to join the initiative on Clean Development Partnership.

2. Noting the centrality of civilian nuclear energy to the twin challenges of energy security and safeguarding the environment, the two Governments agreed on 18 July 2005 to undertake reciprocal commitments and responsibilities that would create a framework for the resumption of full cooperation in this field. On its part, the United States undertook to:

- Seek agreement from the Congress to adjust U.S. laws and policies to achieve full civil nuclear energy cooperation.
- Work with friends and allies to adjust international regimes to enable full civil nuclear energy cooperation and trade with India, including but not limited to expeditious consideration of fuel supplies for safeguarded nuclear reactors at Tarapur.
- In the meantime, encourage its partners to consider fuel supply to Tarapur expeditiously.
- To consult with its partners to consider India's participation in ITER.
- To consult with other participants in the Generation IV International Forum with a view towards India's inclusion.

3. India had conveyed its readiness to assume the same responsibilities and practices and acquire the same benefits and advantages as other leading countries with advanced nuclear technology, such as the United States. Accordingly, India for its part undertook the following commitments:

- Identifying and separating civilian and military nuclear facilities and programmes in a phased manner.
- Filing a declaration regarding its civilian facilities with the IAEA.

- Taking a decision to place voluntarily its civilian nuclear facilities under IAEA safeguards, and
- Signing and adhering to an Additional Protocol with respect to civilian nuclear facilities.

4. Other commitments undertaken by India have already been fulfilled in the last year. Among them are:

- India's responsible non-proliferation record, recognized by the U.S., continues and is reflected in its policies and actions.
- The harmonization of India's export controls with NSG and MTCR Guidelines even though India is not a member of either group. These guidelines and control lists have been notified and are being implemented.
- A significant upgrading of India's non-proliferation regulations and export controls has taken place as a result of Weapons of Mass Destruction Act of May 2005. Inter-Ministerial consultations are ongoing to examine and amend other relevant Acts as well as framing appropriate rules and regulations.
- Refrain from transfer of enrichment and reprocessing technologies to states that do not have them and supporting international efforts to limit their spread. This has guided our policy on non-proliferation.
- Continued unilateral moratorium on nuclear testing, and
- Willingness to work with the United States for the conclusion of a multilateral Fissile Material Cut-off Treaty.

5. The Joint Statement of 18 July 2005, recognized that India is ready to assume the same responsibilities and practices as other leading countries with advanced nuclear technology, such as the United States. India has an impeccable record in nonproliferation. The Joint Statement acknowledges that India's nuclear programme has both a military and a civilian component. Both sides had agreed that the purpose was not to constrain

India's strategic programme but to enable resumption of full civil nuclear energy cooperation in order to enhance global energy and environmental security. Such cooperation was predicated on the assumption that any international civil nuclear energy cooperation (including by the U.S.) offered to India in the civilian sector should, firstly, not be diverted away from civilian purposes, and secondly, should not be transferred from India to third countries without safeguards. These concepts will be reflected in the Safeguards Agreement to be negotiated by India with IAEA.

6. India's nuclear programme is unique as it is the only state with nuclear weapons not to have begun with a dedicated military programme. It must be appreciated that the strategic programme is an offshoot of research on nuclear power programme and consequently, it is embedded in a larger undifferentiated programme. Identification of purely civilian facilities and programmes that have no strategic implications poses a particular challenge. Therefore, facilities identified as civilian in the Separation Plan will be offered for safeguards in phases to be decided by India. The nature of the facility concerned, the activities undertaken in it, the national security significance of materials and the location of the facilities are factors taken into account in undertaking the separation process. This is solely an Indian determination.

7. The nuclear establishment in India not only built nuclear reactors but promoted the growth of a national industrial infrastructure. Nuclear power generation was envisaged as a three-stage programme with PHWRs chosen for deployment in the first stage. As indigenous reactors were set up, several innovative design improvements were carried out based on Indian R&D and a standardized design was evolved. The research and technology development spanned the entire spectrum of the nuclear fuel cycle including the front end and the back end. Success in the technologies for the back end of the fuel cycle allowed us to launch the second stage of the programme by constructing a Fast Breeder Test Reactor. This reactor has operated for 20 years based on a unique carbide fuel

and has achieved all technology objectives. We have now proceeded further and are constructing a 500 MWe Prototype Fast Breeder Reactor. Simultaneously, we have launched design and development of reactors aimed at thorium utilization and incorporating inherent safety features.

8. Concepts such as grid connectivity are not relevant to the separation exercise. Issues related to fuel resource sustainability, technical design and economic viability, as well as smooth operation of reactors are relevant factors. This would necessitate grid connectivity irrespective of whether the reactor concerned is civilian or not civilian.

9. It must be recognized that the Indian nuclear programme still has a relatively narrow base and cannot be expected to adopt solutions that might be deemed viable by much larger programmes. A comparison of the number of reactors and the total installed capacity between India and the P-5 brings this out graphically:

Country	Number of Reactors	Total Installed Capacity	
India	15	3.04	GWe (2.8% of the total production)
U.S.A.	104 (103 operational)	99.21	GWe (19.9% of the total production)
France	59	63.36	GWe (78.1% of the total production)
UK	23	11.85	GWe (19.4% of the total production)
Russia	31	21.74	GWe (15.6% of the total production)
China	9	6.602	GWe (2.2% of the total production)

Source: Nuclear Energy Institute, Washington, DC

10. Another factor to be taken into account is the small capacity of the reactors produced indigenously by India, some of which would remain outside safeguards. Therefore, in assessing the extent of safeguards coverage, it would be important to look at both the number of reactors and the percentage of installed capacity covered. An average Indian reactor is of 220 MW and its output is significantly smaller than the standard reactor in a P-5 economy. The chart below illustrates this aspect:

Country	Most Common Reactor	Number of Such Reactors
India	PHWRs 220 MWe	12
USA	69 PWRs and 34 BWRs.	Most plants are in the range of 1000-1250 MWe 51 Reactors in the range of 1000 MWe to 1250 MWe
France	PWRs of 900 MWe and 1300 MWe size	34 PWRs of 900 MWe and 20 PWRs of 1300 MWe
UK	No standard size. AGR is the most common in the range of 600-700 MWe	14 AGRs
Russia	3rd Generation VVER-1000 PWRs and RBMK 1000 Light Water Graphite Reactors	9 third Generation VVER1000 PWRs and 11 RBMK 1000 Light Water Graphite Reactors
China	PWRs 984 MWe	Four

Source: Uranium Information Centre, Melbourne

11. The complexity of the separation process is further enhanced by the limited resources that India has devoted to its nuclear programme as compared to P-5 nations. Moreover, as India expands international cooperation, the percentage of its thermal power reactor installed capacity under safeguards would rise significantly as fresh capacity is added through such cooperation.

12. India's approach to the separation of its civilian nuclear facilities is guided by the following principles:

- Credible, feasible, and implementable in a transparent manner;
- Consistent with the understandings of the 18 July Statement;
- Consistent with India's national security and R&D requirements as well as not prejudicial to the three-stage nuclear programme in India;
- Must be cost effective in its implementation; and
- Must be acceptable to Parliament and public opinion.

13. Based on these principles, India will:

- Include in the civilian list only those facilities offered for safeguards that, after separation, will no longer be engaged in activities of strategic significance.

- The overarching criterion would be a judgment whether subjecting a facility to IAEA safeguards would impact adversely on India's national security.
- However, a facility will be excluded from the civilian list if it is located in a larger hub of strategic significance, notwithstanding the fact that it may not be normally engaged in activities of strategic significance.
- A civilian facility would therefore, be one that India has determined not to be relevant to its strategic programme.

14. Taking the above into account, India, on the basis of reciprocal actions by the U.S., will adopt the following approach:

(i) **Thermal Power Reactors:** India will identify and offer for safeguards 14 thermal power reactors between 2006 and 2014. This will include the 4 presently safeguarded reactors (TAPS 1 & 2, RAPS 1 & 2) and in addition KK 1 & 2 that are under construction. 8 other PHWRs, each of a capacity of 220MWe, will be offered. The overall plan will be as follows:

Sl. No.	Facility	Year offered for safeguards
1.	TAPS 1	2006
2.	TAPS 2	2006
3.	RAPS 1	2006
4.	RAPS 2	2006
5.	KK 1	2006
6.	KK 2	2006
7.	RAPS 5	2007
8.	RAPS 6	2008
9.	RAPS 3	2010
10.	RAPS 4	2010
11.	KAPS 1	2012
12.	KAPS 2	2012
13.	NAPS 1	2014
14.	NAPS 2	2014

The above offer would, in effect, cover 14 out of the 22 thermal power reactors in operation or currently under construction to be placed under safeguards, and would raise the total installed Thermal Power capacity by MWe under safeguards from the present 19 per cent to 65 per cent by 2014.

(ii) **Fast Breeder Reactors:** India is not in a position to accept safeguards on the Prototype Fast Breeder Reactors (PFBR) and the Fast Breeder Test Reactor (FBTR), both located at Kalpakkam. The Fast Breeder Programme is at the R&D stage and its technology will take time to mature and reach an advanced stage of development.

(iii) **Future Reactors:** India has decided to place under safeguards all future civilian thermal power reactors and civilian breeder reactors, and the Government of India retains the sole right to determine such reactors as civilian.

(iv) **Research Reactors:** India will permanently shut down the CIRUS reactor, in 2010. It will also be prepared to shift the fuel core of the APSARA reactor that was purchased from France outside BARC and make the fuel core available to be placed under safeguards in 2010.

(v) **Upstream Facilities:** The following upstream facilities would be identified and separated as civilian:

List of specific facilities in the Nuclear Fuel Complex, Hyderabad which will be offered for safeguards by 2008 is given below:

- Uranium Oxide Plant (Block A)
- Ceramic Fuel Fabrication Plant (Palletizing) (Block A)
- Ceramic Fuel Fabrication Plant (Assembly) (Block A)
- Enriched Uranium Oxide Plant
- Enriched Fuel Fabrication Plant
- Gadolinia Facility

The Heavy Water Production plants at Thal, Tuticorin and Hazira are proposed to be designated for civilian use between 2006-2009. We do not consider these plants as relevant for safeguards purposes.

(vi) **Downstream Facilities:** The following downstream facilities would be identified and separated as civilian:

- India is willing to accept safeguards in the 'campaign' mode after 2010 in respect of the Tarapur Power Reactor Fuel Reprocessing Plant.
- The Tarapur and Rajasthan 'Away From Reactors' spent fuel storage pools would be made available for safeguards with appropriate phasing between 2006-2009.

(vii) **Research Facilities:** India will declare the following facilities as civilian:

(a) Tata Institute of Fundamental Research

(b) Variable Energy Cyclotron Centre

(c) Saha Institute of Nuclear Physics

(d) Institute for Plasma Research

(e) Institute of Mathematics Science

(f) Institute of Physics

(g) Tata Memorial Centre

(h) Board of Radiation and Isotope Technology

(i) Harish Chandra Research Institute

These facilities are safeguards-irrelevant. It is our expectation that they will play a prominent role in international cooperation.

15. Safeguards

(a) The United States has conveyed its commitment to the reliable supply of fuel to India. Consistent with the July 18, 2005, Joint Statement, the United States has also reaffirmed its assurance to create the necessary conditions for India to have assured and full access to fuel for its reactors. As part of its implementation of the July 18, 2005, Joint Statement the United States is committed to seeking agreement from the U.S. Congress to amend its domestic laws and to work with friends and allies to adjust the practices of the Nuclear Suppliers Group to create the necessary conditions for India to obtain full access to the international fuel market, including reliable, uninterrupted and continual access to fuel supplies from firms in several nations.

(b) To further guard against any disruption of fuel supplies, the United States is prepared to take the following additional steps:

(i) The United States is willing to incorporate assurances regarding fuel supply in the bilateral U.S.-India agreement on peaceful uses of nuclear energy under Section 123 of the U.S. Atomic Energy Act, which would be submitted to the U.S. Congress.

(ii) The United States will join India in seeking to negotiate with the IAEA an India-specific fuel supply agreement.

(iii) The United States will support an Indian effort to develop a strategic reserve of nuclear fuel to guard against any disruption of supply over the lifetime of India's reactors.

(iv) If despite these arrangements, a disruption of fuel supplies to India occurs, the United States and India would jointly convene a group of friendly supplier countries to include countries such as Russia, France and the United Kingdom to pursue such measures as would restore fuel supply to India.

(c) In light of the above understandings with the United States, an India-specific safeguards agreement will be negotiated between India and the IAEA providing for safeguards to guard against withdrawal of safeguarded nuclear material from civilian use at any time as well as providing for corrective measures that India may take to ensure uninterrupted operation of its civilian nuclear reactors in the event of disruption of foreign fuel supplies. Taking this into account, India will place its civilian nuclear facilities under India-specific safeguards in perpetuity and negotiate an appropriate safeguards agreement to this end with the IAEA.

16. This plan is in conformity with the commitments made to Parliament by the Government.

{Tabled in Parliament on May 11, 2006}

Interview with *Hindustan Times* 20

R. Nicholas Burns, Under Secretary for Political Affairs, Washington, DC

(February 29, 2008)

Question: Let's start off with the Indo-U.S. civilian nuclear deal. What are your expectations right now?

Under Secretary Burns: I think we're at a critical time in the—on this deal because we've had three years of negotiations, we've had multiple agreements between the governments, and now it is time to internationalize the deal, to gain the international approval through the IAEA Board of Governors, the Nuclear Suppliers Group as well as the U.S. Congress to make this a reality, to bring the deal to operation.

And there is a timeline at work here. There isn't all the time in the world left. That timeline dictates that India needs to move more quickly in order to secure the Board of Governors' approval at the IAEA so that we can try to get this to the U.S. Congress by the spring and summer. As Senator Biden said publicly...there is a timeline and that means that things have to start happening now.

So we hope very much that the Indian government will be able to move this forward as quickly as possible.

Question: One thing that struck me is that you've—you know, what I remember when I was in Washington, everybody said January was going to be the last, it had to be done by January. Then it moved to April. Now the Senator's come and is saying well, maybe it's open all the way to June. This deadline seems to be a little stretchable.

Under Secretary Burns: Well actually I think if you listen closely to Senator Biden he said, you know, it has to get to the Congress by then. If you back up from there it really means that the Indian government needs to move in the month of March on the IAEA Board of Governors because that will take some time. And then I think there will be a fairly complicated and complex process in the Nuclear Suppliers Group. And so I actually think there is not all the time in the world and things now need to proceed quite rapidly.

Question: And how optimistic are you about getting this through the Board of Governors and the NSG in the first place?

Under Secretary Burns: Well, I think that with the United States as the backer of India that there's a very good chance that we'll gain approval of the Nuclear Suppliers Group, but it's going to be—it's a complicated process that will require many meetings. It's not going to happen overnight, which is another reason why we need to move this very quickly.

Question: And you are similarly of the view about the IAEA Board of Governors?

Under Secretary Burns: Yes, I think that once India achieves a safeguards agreement with Dr. ElBaradei, I do believe this will receive the approval of the IAEA Board of Governors. Yes, I do.

Question: You recently said that you wanted—the Indian government had to make a courageous decision regarding this—the deal. And I presume you're talking about regarding the internal politics of the Manmohan Singh coalition.

Under Secretary Burns: Well, I certainly do not want to interfere in the internal politics of India. I won't do that. But I think it's just a—it just makes common sense right now that the Indian government is going to have to act because the time will run out. None of us want to see that happen, because the stakes are very high.

This agreement is indisputably in India's national interest from our perspective. It will deliver India from over 30 years of international isolation. It will allow the country to be treated in a fair and egalitarian way. It will allow the country to be—to take its place among the leaders of the civil nuclear community and the world today as a responsible state. It will improve, I think, India's relations with France and Britain and Russia, all of whom will be part of the group of countries that want to work with India. So I actually think there's a lot riding on this.

And it also mirrors the growth in the U.S.-India relationship, which is very positive. The relationship between our two countries has improved considerably over the last several years, and we expect that to continue in the future.

Question: The Senators argued that a Democratic administration would almost certainly renegotiate the nuclear deal. What in your judgment would they be renegotiating if that were to happen? What would they add to the table?

Under Secretary Burns: Well, it's very hard to predict what's going to happen in our own political system, but I think that Senator Biden's comments were quite—should be listened to very carefully. He's a very distinguished member of our Senate. He's a leader. And I think that this is a very controversial agreement in the United States. I argued for it and testified before Congress quite strongly in support of it, but there were many people in our country who did not favor this agreement.

And so it's going to be important for Indians to realize that, and to realize that this is an agreement that cannot be duplicated, I think, by another administration. I don't think it will be duplicated by another administration. So the only opportunity to realize the potential of this deal is with the administration of President Bush.

Question: Would you say that a future Democratic administration would add something like the FMC, fissile material cutoff, or the CTBP to the table?

Under Secretary Burns: It's very difficult for me to predict that. Very difficult to predict it. But I do know that this deal was put together in such a careful way that I think it will never be able to be duplicated or replicated. If it is not passed, voted upon in President Bush's term of office I think it's very likely that we will not see it continued by a new administration. I think there would be a—most likely a reconsideration of it. And therefore the time to act is now.

Question: You may have seen Shyam Saran's recent speech saying the international environment will be more hostile to the deal to the coming years—in the coming years. Do you agree with that?

Under Secretary Burns: Do I agree with—excuse me?

Question: Shyam Saran gave a speech saying that he felt that the international environment regarding the deal would be more hostile in the coming years.

Under Secretary Burns: I think the time is—I think that Shyam is correct in saying that this is a propitious time for this agreement. We ought to try to get it done in the next few months. That there's a great risk in waiting longer. To have consensus break down in the international community as well as in the United States.

Question: I remember when you began acting as a negotiator for this deal two and a half years ago, three years ago. I met members of your staff and I met Indian diplomats who were negotiating with you and they said oh, Burns is doing this because you've got orders to do so. And then after about a year or so they all used to say well, Burns actually now believes very strongly in the India-U.S. relationship. How do you explain your shift over the years? How did you actually become a true believer in the Indo-U.S....

Under Secretary Burns: Well, I guess I don't agree with the conventional wisdom. Secretary Rice and I talked about this strategic opportunity at length in the spring of 2005 to form a closer U.S.-India relationship. I always believed in it. And that new relationship encompasses the civil nuclear agreement, much closer India-U.S. cooperation in South Asia on issues like Nepal and Sri Lanka and Afghanistan. It certainly encompasses the newfound cooperation we've had in defense and counter-terrorism. It extends to our very ambitious joint undertaking to try to produce a second Green Revolution in India and to further the gains that we've made in education.

And so, I think—I wrote an article in one of our leading foreign policy journals, *Foreign Affairs*, just in the autumn of—just a few months ago, in the autumn, making the case that Americans should look at India in a very friendly way, that we should see a strategic opportunity to improve our relations, and so I have been one of the, you know, a leading advocate for this in our country as well as in our government.

Question: Where do you see the relationship going in the next five to ten years?

Under Secretary Burns: Well, I think there's enormous promise in this relationship. In fact I think it's certainly on the—there's an upward trajectory in the relationship. And I—one of the great strengths is that we have a bipartisan consensus in the United States among Democrats and Republicans that India is important and that it deserves full and fair treatment from the United States. I think that's also true in India. As an outsider, you know, we have worked well with the current government. We—our country has worked well with the previous BJP governments. And so I see a consensus in both countries that we need to grab this opportunity to make progress in all these areas.

Question: And how badly would this be affected, in your view, by the nuclear deal not coming to fruition?

Under Secretary Burns: Oh, I think it would be a great disappointment and frankly a great loss if the U.S.-India nuclear deal did not go forward. Because it's so important for the future of both of our countries.

Now the relationship would survive, surely, because it's a broad relationship and very deeply rooted. But still, it's been a generation, more than a generation since India has been living in isolation, and surely it's in the interest of India and Indians to see that change.

I'm afraid I'm going to have to run in about two minutes. I apologize.

Question: What's going on in your mind, now that you're actually leaving after 26 years...in the service?

Under Secretary Burns: Yes. Well, I'm obviously very grateful for the opportunity to have served here at the State Department in the diplomatic corps. I will leave office believing that this major opportunity with India should be realized. I will be an advocate for India and the U.S.-India relationship outside of government. I look forward, you know, to working in India, to being in India in the future.

But mostly I think that our two countries, because of the size and importance and power of our countries, we do bear responsibility, we're among the leading powers in the world to make the world more peaceful and more stable. And that's a responsibility we take here in the United States very seriously.

Question: In your record of diplomacy, how does the Indo-U.S. civilian nuclear deal fit in terms of its complexity and toughness? Has it been unusually tough, or have you done stuff like this before?

Under Secretary Burns: Well, I'm a veteran of many different negotiations in all parts of the world. This is one of the most complex negotiations in which I've ever been involved, given the technical complexity of the issues, but it's certainly a negotiation that was built on trust between the two countries and governments. And I developed a very close working relationship with both Foreign Secretary Shankar Menon as well as his predecessor, former Foreign Secretary Shyam Saran. Both men are friends of mine. I was very impressed by the professionalism of the Indian negotiators—Saran, Menon, Jaishankar who is now the Indian High Commissioner in Singapore. These are outstanding individuals. They were—I can assure you they were very capable and competent defenders of India and I expect that—I think this whole negotiation has strengthened relations between our two countries. It's brought us so close together. You know, I negotiated this agreement with them in Delhi, in the United States, in many cities of Europe, and I'm just particularly grateful for the opportunity I've had to become so enmeshed in U.S.-Indian affairs.

Question: So out of curiosity, are you still—have you still not publicly stated what you will be doing after you leave office?

Under Secretary Burns: I have not, no. I have not gone into that. I will do that at the right time, but that's ahead of us.

Question: Rice has mentioned that when you announced your departure that you would still continue to be Special Envoy to the nuclear deal, even after you leave the State Department.

Under Secretary Burns: Well, I think what she said was that I'm actually going to be still officially a diplomat until April. And so if it's necessary and if there's movement in the agreement, then, you know, I'd be happy to help out. But at this rate I'm going to leave the day-to-day involvement to Assistant Secretary of State Richard Boucher.

Question: Right. Okay well, is there anything else you'd like to add to any of this?

Under Secretary Burns: Just that I think this relationship has enormous promise and we should grab this opportunity to try to push things over the finish line. Thank you very much for the interview. I appreciate it very much.

Question: Not at all. It was good that you would spend time on your last day in office.

Under Secretary Burns: Thank you very much. You've been very kind with your time. Thank you.

Question: Thank you.

21

An Act to Exempt from Certain Requirements of the Atomic Energy Act of 1954 a Proposed Nuclear Agreement for Cooperation with India

Henry J. Hyde, United States-India Peaceful Atomic Energy Cooperation Act of 2006

TITLE I—UNITED STATES AND INDIA NUCLEAR COOPERATION

SEC. 101. Short Title

This title may be cited as the "Henry J. Hyde United States-India Peaceful Atomic Energy Cooperation Act of 2006".

SEC. 102. Sense of Congress

It is the sense of Congress that—

(1) preventing the proliferation of nuclear weapons, other weapons of mass destruction, the means to produce them, and the means to deliver them are critical objectives for United States foreign policy;

(2) sustaining the Nuclear Non-Proliferation Treaty (NPT) and strengthening its implementation, particularly its verification and compliance, is the keystone of United States nonproliferation policy;

(3) the NPT has been a significant success in preventing the acquisition of nuclear weapons capabilities and maintaining a stable international security situation;

(4) countries that have never become a party to the NPT and remain outside that treaty's legal regime pose a potential challenge to the achievement of the overall goals of global nonproliferation, because those countries have not undertaken the NPT obligation to prohibit the spread of nuclear weapons capabilities;

(5) it is in the interest of the United States to the fullest extent possible to ensure that those countries that are not States Party to the NPT are responsible in the disposition of any nuclear technology they develop;

(6) it is in the interest of the United States to enter into an agreement for nuclear cooperation arranged pursuant to section 123 of the Atomic Energy Act of 1954 (42 U.S.C. 2153) with a country that has never been a State Party to the NPT if—

(A) the country has demonstrated responsible behavior with respect to the nonproliferation of technology related to nuclear weapons and the means to deliver them;

(B) the country has a functioning and uninterrupted democratic system of government, has a foreign policy that is congruent to that of the United States, and is working with the United States on key foreign policy initiatives related to nonproliferation;

(C) such cooperation induces the country to promulgate and implement substantially improved protections against the proliferation of technology related to nuclear weapons and the means to deliver them, and to refrain from actions that would further the development of its nuclear weapons program; and

(D) such cooperation will induce the country to give greater political and material support to the achievement of United States global and regional nonproliferation objectives, especially with respect to dissuading, isolating, and, if necessary, sanctioning and containing states that sponsor terrorism and terrorist groups that are seeking to acquire a nuclear weapons capability or other weapons of mass destruction capability and the means to deliver such weapons;

(7) the United States should continue its policy of engagement, collaboration, and exchanges with and between India and Pakistan;

(8) strong bilateral relations with India are in the national interest of the United States;

(9) the United States and India share common democratic values and the potential for increasing and sustained economic engagement;

(10) commerce in civil nuclear energy with India by the United States and other countries has the potential to benefit the people of all countries;

(11) such commerce also represents a significant change in United States policy regarding commerce with countries that are not States Party to the NPT, which remains the foundation of the international nonproliferation regime;

(12) any commerce in civil nuclear energy with India by the United States and other countries must be achieved in a manner that minimizes the risk of nuclear proliferation or regional arms races and maximizes India's adherence to international nonproliferation regimes, including, in particular, the guidelines of the Nuclear Suppliers Group (NSG); and

(13) the United States should not seek to facilitate or encourage the continuation of nuclear exports to India by any other party if such exports are terminated under United States law.

SEC. 103. Statements of Policy

(a) *In General*: The following shall be the policies of the United States:

(1) Oppose the development of a capability to produce nuclear weapons by any non-nuclear weapon state, within or outside of the NPT.

(2) Encourage States Party to the NPT to interpret the right to "develop research, production and use of nuclear energy for peaceful purposes", as set forth in Article IV of the NPT, as being a right that applies only to the extent that it is consistent with the object and purpose of the NPT to prevent the spread of nuclear weapons and nuclear weapons capabilities, including by refraining

from all nuclear cooperation with any State Party that the International Atomic Energy Agency (IAEA) determines is not in full compliance with its NPT obligations, including its safeguards obligations.

(3) Act in a manner fully consistent with the Guidelines for Nuclear Transfers and the Guidelines for Transfers of Nuclear-Related Dual-Use Equipment, Materials, Software and Related Technology developed by the NSG, and decisions related to those guidelines, and the rules and practices regarding NSG decision-making.

(4) Strengthen the NSG guidelines and decisions concerning consultation by members regarding violations of supplier and recipient understandings by instituting the practice of a timely and coordinated response by NSG members to all such violations, including termination of nuclear transfers to an involved recipient, that discourages individual NSG members from continuing cooperation with such recipient until such time as a consensus regarding a coordinated response has been achieved.

(5) Given the special sensitivity of equipment and technologies related to the enrichment of uranium, the reprocessing of spent nuclear fuel, and the production of heavy water, work with members of the NSG, individually and collectively, to further restrict the transfers of such equipment and technologies, including to India.

(6) Seek to prevent the transfer to a country of nuclear equipment, materials, or technology from other participating governments in the NSG or from any other source if nuclear transfers to that country are suspended or terminated pursuant to this title, the Atomic Energy Act of 1954 (42 U.S.C. 2011 et seq.), or any other United States law.

(b) *With Respect to South Asia.*—The following shall be the policies of the United States with respect to South Asia:

(1) Achieve, at the earliest possible date, a moratorium on the production of fissile material for nuclear explosive

purposes by India, Pakistan, and the People's Republic of China.

(2) Achieve, at the earliest possible date, the conclusion and implementation of a treaty banning the production of fissile material for nuclear weapons to which both the United States and India become parties.

(3) Secure India's—

(A) full participation in the Proliferation Security Initiative;

(B) formal commitment to the Statement of Interdiction Principles of such Initiative;

(C) public announcement of its decision to conform its export control laws, regulations, and policies with the Australia Group and with the Guidelines, Procedures, Criteria, and Control Lists of the Wassenaar Arrangement;

(D) demonstration of satisfactory progress toward implementing the decision described in subparagraph (C); and

(E) ratification of or accession to the Convention on Supplementary Compensation for Nuclear Damage, done at Vienna on September 12, 1997.

(4) Secure India's full and active participation in United States efforts to dissuade, isolate, and, if necessary, sanction and contain Iran for its efforts to acquire weapons of mass destruction, including a nuclear weapons capability and the capability to enrich uranium or reprocess nuclear fuel, and the means to deliver weapons of mass destruction.

(5) Seek to halt the increase of nuclear weapon arsenals in South Asia and to promote their reduction and eventual elimination.

(6) Ensure that spent fuel generated in India's civilian nuclear power reactors is not transferred to the United States except pursuant to the Congressional review

procedures required under section 131f. of the Atomic Energy Act of 1954 [42 U.S.C. 2160(f)].

(7) Pending implementation of the multilateral moratorium described in paragraph (1) or the treaty described in paragraph (2), encourage India not to increase its production of fissile material at unsafeguarded nuclear facilities.

(8) Ensure that any safeguards agreement or Additional Protocol to which India is a party with the IAEA can reliably safeguard any export or reexport to India of any nuclear materials and equipment.

(9) Ensure that the text and implementation of any agreement for cooperation with India arranged pursuant to section 123 of the Atomic Energy Act of 1954 (42 U.S.C. 2153) meet the requirements set forth in subsections a.(1) and a.(3) through a.(9) of such section.

(10) Any nuclear power reactor fuel reserve provided to the Government of India for use in safeguarded civilian nuclear facilities should be commensurate with reasonable reactor operating requirements.

SEC. 104. Waiver Authority and Congressional Approval

(a) *In General.*—If the President makes the determination described in subsection (b), the President may—

(1) exempt a proposed agreement for cooperation with India arranged pursuant to section 123 of the Atomic Energy Act of 1954 (42 U.S.C. 2153) from the requirement of subsection a.(2) of such section;

(2) waive the application of section 128 of the Atomic Energy Act of 1954 (42 U.S.C. 2157) with respect to exports to India; and

(3) waive with respect to India the application of—

(A) section 129 a.(1)(D) of the Atomic Energy Act of 1954 (42 U.S.C. 2158(a)(1)(D)); and

(B) section 129 of such Act (42 U.S.C. 2158) regarding any actions that occurred before July 18, 2005.

(b) *Determination by the President.*—The determination referred to in subsection (a) is a determination by the President that the following actions have occurred:

(1) India has provided the United States and the IAEA with a credible plan to separate civil and military nuclear facilities, materials, and programs, and has filed a declaration regarding its civil facilities and materials with the IAEA.

(2) India and the IAEA have concluded all legal steps required prior to signature by the parties of an agreement requiring the application of IAEA safeguards in perpetuity in accordance with IAEA standards, principles, and practices [including IAEA Board of Governors Document GOV/1621 (1973)] to India's civil nuclear facilities, materials, and programs as declared in the plan described in paragraph (1), including materials used in or produced through the use of India's civil nuclear facilities.

(3) India and the IAEA are making substantial progress toward concluding an Additional Protocol consistent with IAEA principles, practices, and policies that would apply to India's civil nuclear program.

(4) India is working actively with the United States for the early conclusion of a multilateral treaty on the cessation of the production of fissile materials for use in nuclear weapons or other nuclear explosive devices.

(5) India is working with and supporting United States and international efforts to prevent the spread of enrichment and reprocessing technology to any state that does not already possess full-scale, functioning enrichment or reprocessing plants.

(6) India is taking the necessary steps to secure nuclear and other sensitive materials and technology, including through—

(A) the enactment and effective enforcement of comprehensive export control legislation and regulations;

(B) harmonization of its export control laws, regulations, policies, and practices with the guidelines and practices of the Missile Technology Control Regime (MTCR) and the NSG; and

(C) adherence to the MTCR and the NSG in accordance with the procedures of those regimes for unilateral adherence.

(7) The NSG has decided by consensus to permit supply to India of nuclear items covered by the guidelines of the NSG.

(c) *Submission to Congress*

(1) *In General.*—The President shall submit to the appropriate congressional committees the determination made pursuant to subsection (b), together with a report detailing the basis for the determination.

(2) *Information to be Included.*—To the fullest extent available to the United States, the report referred to in paragraph (1) shall include the following information:

(A) A summary of the plan provided by India to the United States and the IAEA to separate India's civil and military nuclear facilities, materials, and programs, and the declaration made by India to the IAEA identifying India's civil facilities to be placed under IAEA safeguards, including an analysis of the credibility of such plan and declaration, together with copies of the plan and declaration.

(B) A summary of the agreement that has been entered into between India and the IAEA requiring the application of safeguards in accordance with IAEA practices to India's civil nuclear facilities as declared in the plan described in subparagraph (A), together with a copy of the agreement, and a description of the progress toward its full implementation.

(C) A summary of the progress made toward conclusion and implementation of an Additional Protocol between India and the IAEA, including a description of the scope of such Additional Protocol.

(D) A description of the steps that India is taking to work with the United States for the conclusion of a multilateral treaty banning the production of fissile material for nuclear weapons, including a description of the steps that the United States has taken and will take to encourage India to identify and declare a date by which India would be willing to stop production of fissile material for nuclear weapons unilaterally or pursuant to a multilateral moratorium or treaty.

(E) A description of the steps India is taking to prevent the spread of nuclear-related technology, including enrichment and reprocessing technology or materials that can be used to acquire a nuclear weapons capability, as well as the support that India is providing to the United States to further United States objectives to restrict the spread of such technology.

(F) A description of the steps that India is taking to secure materials and technology applicable for the development, acquisition, or manufacture of weapons of mass destruction and the means to deliver such weapons through the application of comprehensive export control legislation and regulations, and through harmonization with and adherence to MTCR, NSG, Australia Group, and Wassenaar Arrangement guidelines, compliance with United Nations Security Council Resolution 1540, and participation in the Proliferation Security Initiative.

(G) A description and assessment of the specific measures that India has taken to fully and actively participate in United States and international efforts to dissuade, isolate, and, if necessary, sanction and contain Iran for its efforts to acquire weapons of mass destruction, including a nuclear weapons capability and the capability to enrich uranium or reprocess nuclear fuel and the means to deliver weapons of mass destruction.

(H) A description of the decision of the NSG relating to nuclear cooperation with India, including whether nuclear cooperation by the United States under an agreement for cooperation arranged pursuant to section 123 of the Atomic Energy Act of 1954 (42 U.S.C. 2153) is consistent with the decision, practices, and policies of the NSG.

(I) A description of the scope of peaceful cooperation envisioned by the United States and India that will be implemented under the agreement for nuclear cooperation, including whether such cooperation will include the provision of enrichment and reprocessing technology.

(J) A description of the steps taken to ensure that proposed United States civil nuclear cooperation with India will not in any way assist India's nuclear weapons program.

(d) *Restrictions on Nuclear Transfers*

(1) *In General.*—Pursuant to the obligations of the United States under Article I of the NPT, nothing in this title constitutes authority to carry out any civil nuclear cooperation between the United States and a country that is not a nuclearweapon State Party to the NPT that would in any way assist, encourage, or induce that country to manufacture or otherwise acquire nuclear weapons or nuclear explosive devices.

(2) *NSG Transfer Guidelines.*—Notwithstanding the entry into force of an agreement for cooperation with India arranged pursuant to section 123 of the Atomic Energy Act of 1954 (42 U.S.C. 2153) and pursuant to this title, no item subject to such agreement or subject to the transfer guidelines of the NSG, or to NSG decisions related thereto, may be transferred to India if such transfer would be inconsistent with the transfer guidelines of the NSG in effect on the date of the transfer.

(3) *Termination of Nuclear Transfers to India.*—

(A) *In General.*—Notwithstanding the entry into force of an agreement for cooperation with India arranged pursuant to section 123 of the Atomic Energy Act of 1954 (42 U.S.C. 2153) and pursuant to this title, and except as provided under subparagraph (B), exports of nuclear and nuclear-related material, equipment, or technology to India shall be terminated if there is any materially significant transfer by an Indian person of—

(i) nuclear or nuclear-related material, equipment, or technology that is not consistent with NSG guidelines or decisions, or

(ii) ballistic missiles or missile-related equipment or technology that is not consistent with MTCR guidelines, unless the President determines that cessation of such exports would be seriously prejudicial to the achievement of United States nonproliferation objectives or otherwise jeopardize the common defense and security.

(B) *Exception.*—The President may choose not to terminate exports of nuclear and nuclear-related material, equipment, and technology to India under subparagraph (A) if—

(i) the transfer covered under such subparagraph was made without the knowledge of the Government of India;

(ii) at the time of the transfer, either the Government of India did not own, control, or direct the Indian person that made the transfer or the Indian person that made the transfer is a natural person who acted without the knowledge of any entity described in subparagraph (B) or (C) of section 110(5); and

(iii) the President certifies to the appropriate congressional committees that the Government of India has taken or is taking appropriate judicial or other enforcement actions against the Indian person with respect to such transfer.

(4) *Exports, Reexports, Transfers, and Retransfers to India Related to Enrichment, Reprocessing, and Heavy Water Production.*—

(A) *In General.*—

(i) *Nuclear Regulatory Commission.*—The Nuclear Regulatory Commission may only issue licenses for the export or reexport to India of any equipment, components, or materials related to the enrichment of uranium, the reprocessing of spent nuclear fuel, or the production of heavy water if the requirements of subparagraph (B) are met.

(ii) *Secretary of Energy.*—The Secretary of Energy may only issue authorizations for the transfer or retransfer to India of any equipment, materials, or technology related to the enrichment of uranium, the reprocessing of spent nuclear fuel, or the production of heavy water (including under the terms of a subsequent arrangement under section 131 of the Atomic Energy Act of 1954 [42 U.S.C. 2160)] if the requirements of subparagraph (B) are met.

(B) *Requirements for Approvals.*—Exports, reexports, transfers, and retransfers referred to in subparagraph (A) may only be approved if—

(i) the end user—

(I) is a multinational facility participating in an IAEA-approved program to provide alternatives to national fuel cycle capabilities; or

(II) is a facility participating in, and the export, reexport, transfer, or retransfer is associated with, a bilateral or multinational program to develop a proliferation-resistant fuel cycle;

(ii) appropriate measures are in place at any facility referred to in clause (i) to ensure that no sensitive nuclear technology, as defined in section 4(5) of the Nuclear Nonproliferation Act of 1978 [22 U.S.C. 3203(5)], will be diverted to any person, site, facility, location, or program not under IAEA safeguards; and

(iii) the President determines that the export, reexport, transfer, or retransfer will not assist in the manufacture or acquisition of nuclear explosive devices or the production of fissile material for military purposes.

(5) *Nuclear Export Accountability Program.*—

(A) *In General.*—The President shall ensure that all appropriate measures are taken to maintain accountability with respect to nuclear materials, equipment, and technology sold, leased, exported, or reexported to India so as to ensure—

(i) full implementation of the protections required under section 123 a.(1) of the Atomic Energy Act of 1954 [42 U.S.C. 2153 (a)(1)]; and

(ii) United States compliance with Article I of the NPT.

(B) *Measures.*—The measures taken pursuant to subparagraph (A) shall include the following:

(i) Obtaining and implementing assurances and conditions pursuant to the export licensing authorities of the Nuclear Regulatory Commission and the Department of Commerce and the authorizing authorities of the Department of Energy, including, as appropriate, conditions regarding end-use monitoring.

(ii) A detailed system of reporting and accounting for technology transfers, including any retransfers in India, authorized by the Department of Energy pursuant to section 57 b. of the Atomic Energy Act of 1954 [42 U.S.C. 2077(b)]. Such system shall be capable of providing assurances that—

(I) the identified recipients of the nuclear technology are authorized to receive the nuclear technology;

(II) the nuclear technology identified for transfer will be used only for peaceful safeguarded nuclear activities and will not be used for any military or nuclear explosive purpose; and

(III) the nuclear technology identified for transfer will not be retransferred without the prior consent of the United States, and facilities, equipment, or materials derived through the use of transferred technology will not be transferred without the prior consent of the United States.

(iii) In the event the IAEA is unable to implement safeguards as required by an agreement for cooperation arranged pursuant to section 123 of the Atomic Energy Act of 1954 (42 U.S.C. 2153), appropriate assurance that arrangements will be put in place expeditiously that are consistent with the requirements of section 123 a.(1) of such Act [42 U.S.C. 2153(a)(1)] regarding the maintenance of safeguards as set forth in the agreement regardless of whether the agreement is terminated or suspended for any reason.

(C) *Implementation.*—The measures described in subparagraph (B) shall be implemented to provide reasonable assurances that the recipient is complying with the relevant requirements, terms, and conditions of any licenses issued by the United States regarding such exports, including those relating to the use, retransfer, safe handling, secure transit, and storage of such exports.

(e) *Joint Resolution of Approval Requirement.*—Section 123 d. of the Atomic Energy Act of 1954 [42 U.S.C. 2153(d)] is amended in the second proviso by inserting after "that subsection" the following: ", or an agreement exempted pursuant to section 104(a)(1) of the Henry J. Hyde United States-India Peaceful Atomic Energy Cooperation Act of 2006,".

(f) *Sunset.*—The authority provided under subsection (a)(1) to exempt an agreement shall terminate upon the enactment of a joint resolution under section 123 d. of the Atomic Energy Act of 1954 [42 U.S.C. 2153(d)] approving such an agreement.

(g) *Reporting to Congress.*—

(1) *Information on Nuclear Activities of India.*—The President shall keep the appropriate congressional committees fully and currently informed of the facts and implications of any significant nuclear activities of India, including—

(A) any material noncompliance on the part of the Government of India with—

(i) the nonproliferation commitments undertaken in the Joint Statement of July 18, 2005, between the President of the United States and the Prime Minister of India;

(ii) the separation plan presented in the national parliament of India on March 7, 2006, and in greater detail on May 11, 2006;

(iii) a safeguards agreement between the Government of India and the IAEA;

(iv) an Additional Protocol between the Government of India and the IAEA;

(v) an agreement for cooperation between the Government of India and the United States Government arranged pursuant to section 123 of the Atomic Energy Act of 1954 (42 U.S.C. 2153) or any subsequent arrangement under section 131 of such Act (42 U.S.C. 2160);

(vi) the terms and conditions of any approved licenses regarding the export or reexport of nuclear material or dual-use material, equipment, or technology; and

(vii) United States laws and regulations regarding such licenses;

(B) the construction of a nuclear facility in India after the date of the enactment of this title;

(C) significant changes in the production by India of nuclear weapons or in the types or amounts of fissile material produced; and

(D) changes in the purpose or operational status of any unsafeguarded nuclear fuel cycle activities in India.

(2) *Implementation and Compliance Report.*—Not later than 180 days after the date on which an agreement for cooperation with India arranged pursuant to section 123 of the Atomic Energy Act of 1954 (42 U.S.C. 2153) enters into force, and annually thereafter, the

President shall submit to the appropriate congressional committees a report including—

(A) a description of any additional nuclear facilities and nuclear materials that the Government of India has placed or intends to place under IAEA safeguards;

(B) a comprehensive listing of—

(i) all licenses that have been approved by the Nuclear Regulatory Commission and the Secretary of Energy for exports and reexports to India under parts 110 and 810 of title 10, Code of Federal Regulations;

(ii) any licenses approved by the Department of Commerce for the export or reexport to India of commodities, related technology, and software which are controlled for nuclear nonproliferation reasons on the Nuclear Referral List of the Commerce Control List maintained under part 774 of title 15, Code of Federal Regulation, or any successor regulation;

(iii) any other United States authorizations for the export or reexport to India of nuclear materials and equipment; and

(iv) with respect to each such license or other form of authorization described in clauses (i), (ii), and (iii)—

(I) the number or other identifying information of each license or authorization;

(II) the name or names of the authorized end user or end users;

(III) the name of the site, facility, or location in India to which the export or reexport was made;

(IV) the terms and conditions included on such licenses and authorizations;

(V) any post-shipment verification procedures that will be applied to such exports or reexports; and

(VI) the term of validity of each such license or authorization;

(C) a description of any significant nuclear commerce between India and other countries, including any such trade that—

(i) is not consistent with applicable guidelines or decisions of the NSG; or

(ii) would not meet the standards applied to exports or reexports of such material, equipment, or technology of United States origin;

(D) either—

(i) an assessment that India is in full compliance with the commitments and obligations contained in the agreements and other documents referenced in clauses (i) through (vi) of paragraph (1)(A); or

(ii) an identification and analysis of all compliance issues arising with regard to the adherence by India to its commitments and obligations, including—

(I) the measures the United States Government has taken to remedy or otherwise respond to such compliance issues;

(II) the responses of the Government of India to such measures;

(III) the measures the United States Government plans to take to this end in the coming year; and

(IV) an assessment of the implications of any continued noncompliance, including whether nuclear commerce with India remains in the national security interest of the United States;

(E) (i) an assessment of whether India is fully and actively participating in United States and international efforts to dissuade, isolate, and, if necessary, sanction and contain Iran for its efforts to acquire weapons of mass destruction, including a nuclear weapons capability (including the capability to enrich uranium or reprocess nuclear fuel), and the means to deliver weapons of mass destruction, including a description of the specific measures that India has taken in this regard; and

(ii) if India is not assessed to be fully and actively participating in such efforts, a description of—

(I) the measures the United States Government has taken to secure India's full and active participation in such efforts;

(II) the responses of the Government of India to such measures; and

(III) the measures the United States Government plans to take in the coming year to secure India's full and active participation;

(F) an analysis of whether United States civil nuclear cooperation with India is in any way assisting India's nuclear weapons program, including through—

(i) the use of any United States equipment, technology, or nuclear material by India in an unsafeguarded nuclear facility or nuclear-weapons related complex;

(ii) the replication and subsequent use of any United States technology by India in an unsafeguarded nuclear facility or unsafeguarded nuclear weaponsrelated complex, or for any activity related to the research, development, testing, or manufacture of nuclear explosive devices; and

(iii) the provision of nuclear fuel in such a manner as to facilitate the increased production by India of highly enriched uranium or plutonium in unsafeguarded nuclear facilities;

(G) a detailed description of—

(i) United States efforts to promote national or regional progress by India and Pakistan in disclosing, securing, limiting, and reducing their fissile material stockpiles, including stockpiles for military purposes, pending creation of a worldwide fissile material cutoff regime, including the institution of a Fissile Material Cut-off Treaty;

(ii) the responses of India and Pakistan to such efforts; and

(iii) assistance that the United States is providing, or would be able to provide, to India and Pakistan to promote the objectives in clause (i), consistent with its obligations under international law and existing agreements;

(H) an estimate of—

(i) the amount of uranium mined and milled in India during the previous year;

(ii) the amount of such uranium that has likely been used or allocated for the production of nuclear explosive devices; and

(iii) the rate of production in India of—

(I) fissile material for nuclear explosive devices; and

(II) nuclear explosive devices;

(I) an estimate of the amount of electricity India's nuclear reactors produced for civil purposes during the previous year and the proportion of such production that can be attributed to India's declared civil reactors;

(J) an analysis as to whether imported uranium has affected the rate of production in India of nuclear explosive devices;

(K) a detailed description of efforts and progress made toward the achievement of India's—

(i) full participation in the Proliferation Security Initiative;

(ii) formal commitment to the Statement of Interdiction Principles of such Initiative;

(iii) public announcement of its decision to conform its export control laws, regulations, and policies with the Australia Group and with the Guidelines,

Procedures, Criteria, and Controls List of the Wassenaar Arrangement; and

(iv) effective implementation of the decision described in clause (iii); and

(L) the disposal during the previous year of spent nuclear fuel from India's civilian nuclear program, and any plans or activities relating to future disposal of such spent nuclear fuel.

(3) *Submittal with other Annual Reports.—*

(A) *Report on Proliferation Prevention.*—Each annual report submitted under paragraph (2) after the initial report may be submitted together with the annual report on proliferation prevention required under section 601(a) of the Nuclear Non-Proliferation Act of 1978 [22 U.S.C. 3281(a)].

(B) *Report on Progress Toward Regional Nonproliferation.* —The information required to be submitted under paragraph (2)(F) after the initial report may be submitted together with the annual report on progress toward regional nonproliferation required under section 620F(c) of the Foreign Assistance Act of 1961 [22 U.S.C. 2376(c)].

(4) *Form.*—Each report submitted under this subsection shall be submitted in unclassified form, but may contain a classified annex.

SEC. 105. United States Compliance with its Nuclear Nonproliferation Treaty Obligations

Nothing in this title constitutes authority for any action in violation of an obligation of the United States under the NPT.

SEC. 106. Inoperability of Determination and Waivers

A determination and any waiver under section 104 shall cease to be effective if the President determines that India has detonated a nuclear explosive device after the date of the enactment of this title.

SEC. 107. MTCR Adherent Status

Congress finds that India is not an MTCR adherent for the purposes of section 73 of the Arms Export Control Act (22 U.S.C. 2797b).

SEC. 108. Technical Amendment

Section 1112(c)(4) of the Arms Control and Nonproliferation Act of 1999 [title XI of the Admiral James W. Nance and Meg Donovan Foreign Relations Authorization Act, Fiscal Years 2000 and 2001 (as enacted into law by section 1000(a)(7) of Public Law 106–113 and contained in appendix G of that Act; 113 Stat. 1501A–486)] is amended—

(1) in subparagraph (B), by striking "and" after the semicolon at the end;

(2) by redesignating subparagraph (C) as subparagraph (D); and

(3) by inserting after subparagraph (B) the following new subparagraph:

"(C) so much of the reports required under section 104 of the Henry J. Hyde United States-India Peaceful Atomic Energy Cooperation Act of 2006 as relates to verification or compliance matters; and".

SEC. 109. United States-India Scientific Cooperative Nuclear Nonproliferation Program

(a) *Establishment.*—The Secretary of Energy, acting through the Administrator of the National Nuclear Security Administration, is authorized to establish a cooperative nuclear nonproliferation program to pursue jointly with scientists from the United States and India a program to further common nuclear nonproliferation goals, including scientific research and development efforts, with an emphasis on nuclear safeguards (in this section referred to as "the program").

(b) *Consultation.*—The program shall be carried out in consultation with the Secretary of State and the Secretary of Defense.

(c) *National Academies Recommendations.—*

(1) *In General.*—The Secretary of Energy shall enter into an agreement with the National Academies to develop recommendations for the implementation of the program.

(2) *Recommendations.*—The agreement entered into under paragraph (1) shall provide for the preparation by qualified individuals with relevant expertise and knowledge and the communication to the Secretary of Energy each fiscal year of—

(A) recommendations for research and related programs designed to overcome existing technological barriers to nuclear nonproliferation; and

(B) an assessment of whether activities and programs funded under this section are achieving the goals of the activities and programs.

(3) *Public Availability.*—The recommendations and assessments prepared under this subsection shall be made publicly available.

(d) *Consistency with Nuclear Non-Proliferation Treaty.*— All United States activities related to the program shall be consistent with United States obligations under the Nuclear Non-Proliferation Treaty.

(e) *Authorization of Appropriations.*—There are authorized to be appropriated such sums as may be necessary to carry out this section for each of fiscal years 2007 through 2011.

SEC. 110. Definitions

In this title:

(1) The term "Additional Protocol" means a protocol additional to a safeguards agreement with the IAEA, as negotiated between a country and the IAEA based on a Model Additional Protocol as set forth in IAEA information circular (INFCIRC) 540.

(2) The term "appropriate congressional committees" means the Committee on Foreign Relations of the Senate and

the Committee on International Relations of the House of Representatives.

(3) The term "dual-use material, equipment, or technology" means material, equipment, or technology that may be used in nuclear or non-nuclear applications.

(4) The term "IAEA safeguards" has the meaning given the term in section 830(3) of the Nuclear Proliferation Prevention Act of 1994 [22 U.S.C. 6305(3)].

(5) The term "Indian person" means—

(A) a natural person that is a citizen of India or is subject to the jurisdiction of the Government of India;

(B) a corporation, business association, partnership, society, trust, or any other nongovernmental entity, organization, or group, that is organized under the laws of India or has its principal place of business in India; and

(C) any Indian governmental entity, including any governmental entity operating as a business enterprise.

(6) The terms "Missile Technology Control Regime", "MTCR", and "MTCR adherent" have the meanings given the terms in section 74 of the Arms Export Control Act [22 U.S.C. 2797(c)].

(7) The term "nuclear materials and equipment" means source material, special nuclear material, production and utilization facilities and any components thereof, and any other items or materials that are determined to have significance for nuclear explosive purposes pursuant to subsection 109 b. of the Atomic Energy Act of 1954 [42 U.S.C. 2139(b)].

(8) The terms "Nuclear Non-Proliferation Treaty" and "NPT" mean the Treaty on the Non-Proliferation of Nuclear Weapons, done at Washington, London, and Moscow July 1, 1968, and entered into force March 5, 1970 (21 UST 483).

(9) The terms "Nuclear Suppliers Group" and "NSG" refer to a group, which met initially in 1975 and has met at least annually since 1992, of Participating Governments that have promulgated and agreed to adhere to Guidelines for Nuclear Transfers (currently IAEA INFCIRC/254/Rev.8/Part 1) and Guidelines for Transfers of Nuclear-Related Dual-Use Equipment, Materials, Software, and Related Technology (currently IAEA INFCIRC/254/Rev.7/Part 2).

(10) The terms "nuclear weapon" and "nuclear explosive device" mean any device designed to produce an instantaneous release of an amount of nuclear energy from special nuclear material that is greater than the amount of energy that would be released from the detonation of one pound of trinitrotoluene (TNT).

(11) The term "process" includes the term "reprocess".

(12) The terms "reprocessing" and "reprocess" refer to the separation of irradiated nuclear materials and fission products from spent nuclear fuel.

(13) The term "sensitive nuclear technology" means any information, including information incorporated in a production or utilization facility or important component part thereof, that is not available to the public and which is important to the design, construction, fabrication, operation, or maintenance of a uranium enrichment or nuclear fuel reprocessing facility or a facility for the production of heavy water.

(14) The term "source material" has the meaning given the term in section 11z. of the Atomic Energy Act of 1954 [42 U.S.C. 2014(z)].

(15) The term "special nuclear material" has the meaning given the term in section 11 aa. of the Atomic Energy Act of 1954 [42 U.S.C. 2014(aa)].

(16) The term "unsafeguarded nuclear fuel-cycle activity" means research on, or development, design, manufacture, construction, operation, or maintenance of—

(A) any existing or future reactor, critical facility, conversion plant, fabrication plant, reprocessing plant, plant for the separation of isotopes of source or special fissionable material, or separate storage installation with respect to which there is no obligation to accept IAEA safeguards at the relevant reactor, facility, plant, or installation that contains source or special fissionable material; or

(B) any existing or future heavy water production plant with respect to which there is no obligation to accept IAEA safeguards on any nuclear material produced by or used in connection with any heavy water produced therefrom.

TITLE II—UNITED STATES ADDITIONAL PROTOCOL IMPLEMENTATION

SEC. 201. Short Title

This title may be cited as the "United States Additional Protocol Implementation Act".

SEC. 202. Findings

Congress makes the following findings:

(1) The proliferation of nuclear weapons and other nuclear explosive devices poses a grave threat to the national security of the United States and its vital national interests.

(2) The Nuclear Non-Proliferation Treaty has proven critical to limiting such proliferation.

(3) For the Nuclear Non-Proliferation Treaty to be effective, each of the non-nuclear-weapon State Parties must conclude a comprehensive safeguards agreement with the IAEA, and such agreements must be honored and enforced.

(4) Recent events emphasize the urgency of strengthening the effectiveness and improving the efficiency of the safeguards system. This can best be accomplished by providing IAEA inspectors with more information about,

and broader access to, nuclear activities within the territory of non-nuclear-weapon State Parties.

(5) The proposed scope of such expanded information and access has been negotiated by the member states of the IAEA in the form of a Model Additional Protocol to its existing safeguards agreements, and universal acceptance of Additional Protocols by non-nuclear weapons states is essential to enhancing the effectiveness of the Nuclear Non-Proliferation Treaty.

(6) On June 12, 1998, the United States, as a nuclear-weapon State Party, signed an Additional Protocol that is based on the Model Additional Protocol, but which also contains measures, consistent with its existing safeguards agreements with its members, that protect the right of the United States to exclude the application of IAEA safeguards to locations and activities with direct national security significance or to locations or information associated with such activities.

(7) Implementation of the Additional Protocol in the United States in a manner consistent with United States obligations under the Nuclear Non-Proliferation Treaty may encourage other parties to the Nuclear Non-Proliferation Treaty, especially non-nuclear-weapon State Parties, to conclude Additional Protocols and thereby strengthen the Nuclear Non-Proliferation Treaty safeguards system and help reduce the threat of nuclear proliferation, which is of direct and substantial benefit to the United States.

(8) Implementation of the Additional Protocol by the United States is not required and is completely voluntary given its status as a nuclear-weapon State Party, but the United States has acceded to the Additional Protocol to demonstrate its commitment to the nuclear nonproliferation regime and to make United States civil nuclear activities available to the same IAEA inspections as are applied in the case of non-nuclear-weapon State Parties.

(9) In accordance with the national security exclusion contained in Article 1.b of its Additional Protocol, the United States will not allow any inspection activities, nor make any declaration of any information with respect to, locations, information, and activities of direct national security significance to the United States.

(10) Implementation of the Additional Protocol will conform to the principles set forth in the letter of April 30, 2002, from the United States Permanent Representative to the International Atomic Energy Agency and the Vienna Office of the United Nations to the Director General of the International Atomic Energy Agency.

SEC. 203. Definitions

In this title:

(1) *Additional Protocol.*—The term "Additional Protocol", when used in the singular form, means the Protocol Additional to the Agreement between the United States of America and the International Atomic Energy Agency for the Application of Safeguards in the United States of America, with Annexes, signed at Vienna June 12, 1998 (T. Doc. 107–7).

(2) *Appropriate Congressional Committees.*—The term "appropriate congressional committees" means the Committee on Armed Services, the Committee on Foreign Relations, and the Committee on Appropriations of the Senate and the Committee on Armed Services, the Committee on International Relations, the Committee on Science, and the Committee on Appropriations of the House of Representatives.

(3) *Complementary Access.*—The term "complementary access" means the exercise of the IAEA's access rights as set forth in Articles 4 to 6 of the Additional Protocol.

(4) *Executive Agency.*—The term "executive agency" has the meaning given such term in section 105 of title 5, United States Code.

(5) *Facility.*—The term "facility" has the meaning set forth in Article 18i. of the Additional Protocol.

(6) *IAEA.*—The term "IAEA" means the International Atomic Energy Agency.

(7) *Judge of the United States.*—The term "judge of the United States" means a United States district judge, or a United States magistrate judge appointed under the authority of chapter 43 of title 28, United States Code.

(8) *Location.*—The term "location" means any geographic point or area declared or identified by the United States or specified by the International Atomic Energy Agency.

(9) *Nuclear Non-proliferation Treaty.*—The term "Nuclear Non-Proliferation Treaty" means the Treaty on the Non-Proliferation of Nuclear Weapons, done at Washington, London, and Moscow July 1, 1968, and entered into force March 5, 1970 (21 UST 483).

(10) *Nuclear-weapon State Party and Non-nuclear-weapon State Party.*—The terms "nuclear-weapon State Party" and "non-nuclear-weapon State Party" have the meanings given such terms in the Nuclear Non-Proliferation Treaty.

(11) *Person.*—The term "person", except as otherwise provided, means any individual, corporation, partnership, firm, association, trust, estate, public or private institution, any State or any political subdivision thereof, or any political entity within a State, any foreign government or nation or any agency, instrumentality, or political subdivision of any such government or nation, or other entity located in the United States.

(12) *Site.*—The term "site" has the meaning set forth in Article 18b. of the Additional Protocol.

(13) *United States.*—The term "United States", when used as a geographic reference, means the several States of the United States, the District of Columbia, and the commonwealths, territories, and possessions of the

United States and includes all places under the jurisdiction or control of the United States, including—

(A) the territorial sea and the overlying airspace;

(B) any civil aircraft of the United States or public aircraft, as such terms are defined in paragraphs (17) and (41), respectively, of section 40102(a) of title 49, United States Code; and

(C) any vessel of the United States, as such term is defined in section 3(b) of the Maritime Drug Law Enforcement Act [46 U.S.C. App. 1903(b)].

(14) *Wide-area Environmental Sampling.*—The term "wide-area environmental sampling" has the meaning set forth in Article 18g. of the Additional Protocol.

SEC. 204. Severability

If any provision of this title, or the application of such provision to any person or circumstance, is held invalid, the remainder of this title, or the application of such provision to persons or circumstances other than those as to which it is held invalid, shall not be affected thereby.

SUBTITLE A—GENERAL PROVISIONS

SEC. 211. Authority

(a) *In General.*—The President is authorized to implement and carry out the provisions of this title and the Additional Protocol and shall designate through Executive order which executive agency or agencies of the United States, which may include but are not limited to the Department of State, the Department of Defense, the Department of Justice, the Department of Commerce, the Department of Energy, and the Nuclear Regulatory Commission, shall issue or amend and enforce regulations in order to implement this title and the provisions of the Additional Protocol.

(b) *Included Authority.*—For any executive agency designated under subsection (a) that does not currently possess the authority to conduct site vulnerability assessments and related activities, the authority provided in subsection (a) includes such authority.

(c) *Exception.*—The authority described in subsection (b) does not supersede or otherwise modify any existing authority of any Federal department or agency already having such authority.

SUBTITLE B—COMPLEMENTARY ACCESS

SEC. 221. Requirement for Authority to Conduct Complementary Access

(a) *Prohibition.*—No complementary access to any location in the United States shall take place pursuant to the Additional Protocol without the authorization of the United States Government in accordance with the requirements of this title.

(b) *Authority.*—

(1) *In General.*—Complementary access to any location in the United States subject to access under the Additional Protocol is authorized in accordance with this title.

(2) *United States Representatives.*—

(A) *Restrictions.*—In the event of complementary access to a privately owned or operated location, no employee of the Environmental Protection Agency or of the Mine Safety and Health Administration or the Occupational Safety and Health Administration of the Department of Labor may participate in the access.

(B) *Number.*—The number of designated United States representatives accompanying IAEA inspectors shall be kept to the minimum necessary.

SEC. 222. Procedures for Complementary Access

(a) *In General.*—Each instance of complementary access to a location in the United States under the Additional Protocol shall be conducted in accordance with this subtitle.

(b) *Notice.*—

(1) *In General.*—Complementary access referred to in subsection (a) may occur only upon the issuance of an actual written notice by the United States Government

to the owner, operator, occupant, or agent in charge of the location to be subject to complementary access.

(2) *Time of Notification.*—The notice under paragraph (1) shall be submitted to such owner, operator, occupant, or agent as soon as possible after the United States Government has received notification that the IAEA seeks complementary access. Notices may be posted prominently at the location if the United States Government is unable to provide actual written notice to such owner, operator, occupant, or agent.

(3) *Content of Notice.*—

(A) *In General.*—The notice required by paragraph (1) shall specify—

(i) the purpose for the complementary access;

(ii) the basis for the selection of the facility, site, or other location for the complementary access sought;

(iii) the activities that will be carried out during the complementary access;

(iv) the time and date that the complementary access is expected to begin, and the anticipated period covered by the complementary access; and

(v) the names and titles of the inspectors.

(4) *Separate Notices Required.*—A separate notice shall be provided each time that complementary access is sought by the IAEA.

(c) *Credentials.*—The complementary access team of the IAEA and representatives or designees of the United States Government shall display appropriate identifying credentials to the owner, operator, occupant, or agent in charge of the location before gaining entry in connection with complementary access.

(d) *Scope.*—

(1) *In General.*—Except as provided in a warrant issued under section 223, and subject to the rights of the

United States Government under the Additional Protocol to limit complementary access, complementary access to a location pursuant to this title may extend to all activities specifically permitted for such locations under Article 6 of the Additional Protocol.

(2) *Exception.*—Unless required by the Additional Protocol, no inspection under this title shall extend to—

(A) financial data (other than production data);

(B) sales and marketing data (other than shipment data);

(C) pricing data;

(D) personnel data;

(E) patent data;

(F) data maintained for compliance with environmental or occupational health and safety regulations; or

(G) research data.

(e) *Environment, Health, Safety, and Security.*—In carrying out their activities, members of the IAEA complementary access team and representatives or designees of the United States Government shall observe applicable environmental, health, safety, and security regulations established at the location subject to complementary access, including those for protection of controlled environments within a facility and for personal safety.

SEC. 223. Consents, Warrants, and Complementary Access

(a) *In General.*—

(1) *Procedure.*—

(A) *Consent.*—Except as provided in paragraph (2), an appropriate official of the United States Government shall seek or have the consent of the owner, operator, occupant, or agent in charge of a location prior to entering that location in connection with complementary access pursuant to sections 221 and 222. The owner, operator, occupant, or agent in charge of the location may withhold consent for any reason or no reason.

(B) *Administrative Search Warrant.*—In the absence of consent, the United States Government may seek an administrative search warrant from a judge of the United States under subsection (b). Proceedings regarding the issuance of an administrative search warrant shall be conducted ex parte, unless otherwise requested by the United States Government.

(2) *Expedited Access.*—For purposes of obtaining access to a location pursuant to Article 4b.(ii) of the Additional Protocol in order to satisfy United States obligations under the Additional Protocol when notice of two hours or less is required, the United States Government may gain entry to such location in connection with complementary access, to the extent such access is consistent with the Fourth Amendment to the United States Constitution, without obtaining either a warrant or consent.

(b) *Administrative Search Warrants for Complementary Access.*—

(1) *Obtaining Administrative Search Warrants.*—For complementary access conducted in the United States pursuant to the Additional Protocol, and for which the acquisition of a warrant is required, the United States Government shall first obtain an administrative search warrant from a judge of the United States. The United States Government shall provide to such judge all appropriate information regarding the basis for the selection of the facility, site, or other location to which complementary access is sought.

(2) *Content of Affidavits for Administrative Search Warrants.*—A judge of the United States shall promptly issue an administrative search warrant authorizing the requested complementary access upon an affidavit submitted by the United States Government—

(A) stating that the Additional Protocol is in force;

(B) stating that the designated facility, site, or other location is subject to complementary access under the Additional Protocol;

(C) stating that the purpose of the complementary access is consistent with Article 4 of the Additional Protocol;

(D) stating that the requested complementary access is in accordance with Article 4 of the Additional Protocol;

(E) containing assurances that the scope of the IAEA's complementary access, as well as what it may collect, shall be limited to the access provided for in Article 6 of the Additional Protocol;

(F) listing the items, documents, and areas to be searched and seized;

(G) stating the earliest commencement and the anticipated duration of the complementary access period, as well as the expected times of day during which such complementary access will take place; and

(H) stating that the location to which entry in connection with complementary access is sought was selected either—

(i) because there is probable cause, on the basis of specific evidence, to believe that information required to be reported regarding a location pursuant to regulations promulgated under this title is incorrect or incomplete, and that the location to be accessed contains evidence regarding that violation; or

(ii) pursuant to a reasonable general administrative plan based upon specific neutral criteria.

(3) *Content of Warrants.*—A warrant issued under paragraph (2) shall specify the same matters required of an affidavit under that paragraph. In addition, each warrant shall contain the identities of the representatives

of the IAEA on the complementary access team and the identities of the representatives or designees of the United States Government required to display identifying credentials under section 222(c).

SEC. 224. Prohibited Acts Relating to Complementary Access

It shall be unlawful for any person willfully to fail or refuse to permit, or to disrupt, delay, or otherwise impede, a complementary access authorized by this subtitle or an entry in connection with such access.

SUBTITLE C—CONFIDENTIALITY OF INFORMATION

SEC. 231. Protection of Confidentiality of Information

Information reported to, or otherwise acquired by, the United States Government under this title or under the Additional Protocol shall be exempt from disclosure under section 552 of title 5, United States Code.

SUBTITLE D—ENFORCEMENT

SEC. 241. Recordkeeping Violations

It shall be unlawful for any person willfully to fail or refuse—

(1) to establish or maintain any record required by any regulation prescribed under this title;

(2) to submit any report, notice, or other information to the United States Government in accordance with any regulation prescribed under this title; or

(3) to permit access to or copying of any record by the United States Government in accordance with any regulation prescribed under this title.

SEC. 242. Penalties

(a) *Civil.*—

(1) *Penalty Amounts.*—Any person that is determined, in accordance with paragraph (2), to have violated section 224 or section 241 shall be required by order to pay a civil penalty in an amount not to exceed $25,000 for each violation. For the purposes of this paragraph, each

day during which a violation of section 224 continues shall constitute a separate violation of that section.

(2) *Notice and Hearing.—*

(A) *In General.*—Before imposing a penalty against a person under paragraph (1), the head of an executive agency designated under section 211(a) shall provide the person with notice of the order. If, within 15 days after receiving the notice, the person requests a hearing, the head of the designated executive agency shall initiate a hearing on the violation.

(B) *Conduct of Hearing.*—Any hearing so requested shall be conducted before an administrative judge. The hearing shall be conducted in accordance with the requirements of section 554 of title 5, United States Code. If no hearing is so requested, the order imposed by the head of the designated agency shall constitute a final agency action.

(C) *Issuance of Orders.*—If the administrative judge determines, upon the preponderance of the evidence received, that a person named in the complaint has violated section 224 or section 241, the administrative judge shall state the findings of fact and conclusions of law, and issue and serve on such person an order described in paragraph (1).

(D) *Factors for Determination of Penalty Amounts.*—In determining the amount of any civil penalty, the administrative judge or the head of the designated agency shall take into account the nature, circumstances, extent, and gravity of the violation or violations and, with respect to the violator, the ability to pay, effect on ability to continue to do business, any history of such violations, the degree of culpability, the existence of an internal compliance program, and such other matters as justice may require.

(E) *Content of Notice.*—For the purposes of this paragraph, notice shall be in writing and shall be verifiably served upon the person or persons subject to an order described in paragraph (1). In addition, the notice shall—

(i) set forth the time, date, and specific nature of the alleged violation or violations; and

(ii) specify the administrative and judicial remedies available to the person or persons subject to the order, including the availability of a hearing and subsequent appeal.

(3) *Administrative Appellate Review.*—The decision and order of an administrative judge shall be the recommended decision and order and shall be referred to the head of the designated executive agency for final decision and order. If, within 60 days, the head of the designated executive agency does not modify or vacate the decision and order, it shall become a final agency action under this subsection.

(4) *Judicial Review.*—A person adversely affected by a final order may, within 30 days after the date the final order is issued, file a petition in the Court of Appeals for the District of Columbia Circuit or in the Court of Appeals for the district in which the violation occurred.

(5) *Enforcement of Final Orders.*—

(A) *In General.*—If a person fails to comply with a final order issued against such person under this subsection and—

(i) the person has not filed a petition for judicial review of the order in accordance with paragraph (4), or

(ii) a court in an action brought under paragraph (4) has entered a final judgment in favor of the designated executive agency, the head of the designated executive agency shall commence a civil action to seek compliance with the final order in any appropriate district court of the United States.

(B) *No Review.*—In any such civil action, the validity and appropriateness of the final order shall not be subject to review.

(C) *Interest.*—Payment of penalties assessed in a final order under this section shall include interest at currently prevailing rates calculated from the date of expiration of the 60-day period referred to in paragraph (3) or the date of such final order, as the case may be.

(b) *Criminal.*—Any person who violates section 224 or section 241 may, in addition to or in lieu of any civil penalty which may be imposed under subsection (a) for such violation, be fined under title 18, United States Code, imprisoned for not more than five years, or both.

SEC. 243. Specific Enforcement

(a) *Jurisdiction.*—The district courts of the United States shall have jurisdiction over civil actions brought by the head of an executive agency designated under section 211(a)—

(1) to restrain any conduct in violation of section 224 or section 241; or

(2) to compel the taking of any action required by or under this title or the Additional Protocol.

(b) *Civil Actions.*—

(1) *In General.*—A civil action described in subsection (a) may be brought—

(A) in the case of a çivil action described in paragraph (1) of such subsection, in the United States district court for the judicial district in which any act, omission, or transaction constituting a violation of section 224 or section 241 occurred or in which the defendant is found or transacts business; or

(B) in the case of a civil action described in paragraph (2) of such subsection, in the United States district court for the judicial district in which the defendant is found or transacts business.

(2) *Service of Process.*—In any such civil action, process shall be served on a defendant wherever the defendant may reside or may be found.

SUBTITLE E—ENVIRONMENTAL SAMPLING

SEC. 251. Notification to Congress of IAEA Board Approval of Wide Area Environmental Sampling

(a) *In General.*—Not later than 30 days after the date on which the Board of Governors of the IAEA approves wide area environmental sampling for use as a safeguards verification tool, the President shall notify the appropriate congressional committees.

(b) *Content.*—The notification under subsection (a) shall contain—

(1) a description of the specific methods and sampling techniques approved by the Board of Governors that are to be employed for purposes of wide area sampling;

(2) a statement as to whether or not such sampling may be conducted in the United States under the Additional Protocol; and

(3) an assessment of the ability of the approved methods and sampling techniques to detect, identify, and determine the conduct, type, and nature of nuclear activities.

SEC. 252. Application of National Security Exclusion to Wide Area Environmental Sampling

In accordance with Article 1(b) of the Additional Protocol, the United States shall not permit any wide area environmental sampling proposed by the IAEA to be conducted at a specified location in the United States under Article 9 of the Additional Protocol unless the President has determined and reported to the appropriate congressional committees with respect to that proposed use of environmental sampling that—

(1) the proposed use of wide area environmental sampling is necessary to increase the capability of the IAEA to detect undeclared nuclear activities in the territory of a non-nuclear-weapon State Party;

(2) the proposed use of wide area environmental sampling will not result in access by the IAEA to locations, activities, or information of direct national security significance; and

(3) the United States—

(A) has been provided sufficient opportunity for consultation with the IAEA if the IAEA has requested complementary access involving wide-area environmental sampling; or

(B) has requested under Article 8 of the Additional Protocol that the IAEA engage in complementary access in the United States that involves the use of wide-area environmental sampling.

SEC. 253. Application of National Security Exclusion to Location-specific Environmental Sampling

In accordance with Article 1(b) of the Additional Protocol, the United States shall not permit any location-specific environmental sampling in the United States under Article 5 of the Additional Protocol unless the President has determined and reported to the appropriate congressional committees with respect to that proposed use of environmental sampling that—

(1) the proposed use of location-specific environmental sampling is necessary to increase the capability of the IAEA to detect undeclared nuclear activities in the territory of a non-nuclear-weapon State Party;

(2) the proposed use of location-specific environmental sampling will not result in access by the IAEA to locations, activities, or information of direct national security significance; and

(3) with respect to the proposed use of environmental sampling, the United States—

(A) has been provided sufficient opportunity for consultation with the IAEA if the IAEA has requested complementary access involving location-specific environmental sampling; or

(B) has requested under Article 8 of the Additional Protocol that the IAEA engage in complementary access in the United States that involves the use of location-specific environmental sampling.

SEC. 254. Rule of Construction

As used in this subtitle, the term "necessary to increase the capability of the IAEA to detect undeclared nuclear activities in the territory of a non-nuclear-weapon State Party" shall not be construed to encompass proposed uses of environmental sampling that might assist the IAEA in detecting undeclared nuclear activities in the territory of a non-nuclear-weapon State Party by—

(1) setting a good example of cooperation in the conduct of such sampling; or

(2) facilitating the formation of a political consensus or political support for such sampling in the territory of a non-nuclear-weapon State Party.

SUBTITLE F—PROTECTION OF NATIONAL SECURITY INFORMATION AND ACTIVITIES

SEC. 261. Protection of Certain Information

(a) *Locations and Facilities of Direct National Security Significance.*—No current or former Department of Defense or Department of Energy location, site, or facility of direct national security significance shall be declared or be subject to IAEA inspection under the Additional Protocol.

(b) *Information of Direct National Security Significance.*—No information of direct national security significance regarding any location, site, or facility associated with activities of the Department of Defense or the Department of Energy shall be provided under the Additional Protocol.

(c) *Restricted Data.*—Nothing in this title shall be construed to permit the communication or disclosure to the IAEA or IAEA employees of restricted data controlled by the provisions of the Atomic Energy Act of 1954 (42 U.S.C. 2011 et seq.), including in particular "Restricted Data" as defined under paragraph (1) of section 11y. of such Act [42 U.S.C. 2014(y)].

(d) *Classified Information.*—Nothing in this Act shall be construed to permit the communication or disclosure to the IAEA or IAEA employees of national security information and other classified information.

SEC. 262. IAEA Inspections and Visits

(a) *Certain Individuals Prohibited from Obtaining Access.*— No national of a country designated by the Secretary of State under section 620A of the Foreign Assistance Act of 1961 (22 U.S.C. 2371) as a government supporting acts of international terrorism shall be permitted access to the United States to carry out an inspection activity under the Additional Protocol or a related safeguards agreement.

(b) *Presence of United States Government Personnel.*— IAEA inspectors shall be accompanied at all times by United States Government personnel when inspecting sites, locations, facilities, or activities in the United States under the Additional Protocol.

(c) *Vulnerability and Related Assessments.*—The President shall conduct vulnerability, counterintelligence, and related assessments not less than every 5 years to ensure that information of direct national security significance remains protected at all sites, locations, facilities, and activities in the United States that are subject to IAEA inspection under the Additional Protocol.

SUBTITLE G—REPORTS

SEC. 271. Report on Initial United States Declaration

Not later than 60 days before submitting the initial United States declaration to the IAEA under the Additional Protocol, the President shall submit to Congress a list of the sites, locations, facilities, and activities in the United States that the President intends to declare to the IAEA, and a report thereon.

SEC. 272. Report on Revisions to Initial United States Declaration

Not later than 60 days before submitting to the IAEA any revisions to the United States declaration submitted under the Additional Protocol, the President shall submit to Congress a list of any sites, locations, facilities, or activities in the United

States that the President intends to add to or remove from the declaration, and a report thereon.

SEC. 273. Content of Reports on United States Declarations

The reports required under section 271 and section 272 shall present the reasons for each site, location, facility, and activity being declared or being removed from the declaration list and shall certify that—

(1) each site, location, facility, and activity included in the list has been examined by each agency with national security equities with respect to such site, location, facility, or activity; and

(2) appropriate measures have been taken to ensure that information of direct national security significance will not be compromised at any such site, location, facility, or activity in connection with an IAEA inspection.

SEC. 274. Report on Efforts to Promote the Implementation of Additional Protocols

Not later than 180 days after the entry into force of the Additional Protocol, the President shall submit to the appropriate congressional committees a report on—

(1) measures that have been or should be taken to achieve the adoption of additional protocols to existing safeguards agreements signed by non-nuclear-weapon State Parties; and

(2) assistance that has been or should be provided by the United States to the IAEA in order to promote the effective implementation of additional protocols to existing safeguards agreements signed by non-nuclear-weapon State Parties and the verification of the compliance of such parties with IAEA obligations, with a plan for providing any needed additional funding.

SEC. 275. Notice of IAEA Notifications

The President shall notify Congress of any notifications issued by the IAEA to the United States under Article 10 of the Additional Protocol.

SUBTITLE H—AUTHORIZATION OF APPROPRIATIONS

SEC. 281. Authorization of Appropriations

There are authorized to be appropriated such sums as may be necessary to carry out this title.

Speaker of the House of Representatives.

Vice President of the United States and President of the Senate.

Contributors

K.R. Gupta. Former Professor, University of Jammu, J&K. He is a prolific writer and a well-known economist.

Col Ved Prakash. E-12A, Sector-41, Noida, Uttar Pradesh.

Prakash Karat. General Secretary of the Communist Party of India (Marxist).

M.V. Ramana. Fellow, Centre for Interdisciplinary Studies in Environment and Development, ISEC Campus, Nagarabhavi, Bangalore 560072, India.
E-mail: ramana@princeton.edu

Antonette D'Sa.

Amulya K.N. Reddy.

Zia Mian. Research Scientist and Director of the Project on Peace and Security in South Asia, Program on Science and Global Security, Woodrow Wilson School of Public and International Affairs Princeton University, 221 Nassau Street, 2nd Floor Princeton, NJ 08542-4601 USA
Email Address: zia@princeton.edu